Lieutenant Enloe Wanted Us to See Something Else Before We Left . . .

He motioned toward the dry, unweeded grass of the next-door lot. "This is where we found the teeth. See up there?" He pointed to the second-floor window just above us. "That's her bedroom. We figure she threw the teeth out when she thought we were going to search the house on Friday. We got one body without any teeth."

"What would she do with the teeth?" Tim Frawley, from the DA's office, asked.

"Hard to ID somebody without dental work. It's going to be hard to ID these bodies anyway. They're in bad shape." Enloe grinned. He knew Dorothea Montalvo Puente's past record by that time. "Besides, some of them were gold teeth."

THE BONE GARDEN

THE SACRAMENTO BOARDINGHOUSE MURDERS

William P. Wood

ibooks
new york
www.ibooks.net

DISTRIBUTED BY SIMON & SCHUSTER, INC.

A Publication of ibooks, inc.

Copyright © 1994 by William P. Wood

An ibooks, inc. Book

Distributed by Simon & Schuster, Inc.
1230 Avenue of the Americas, New York, NY 10020

ibooks, inc.
24 West 25th Street
New York, NY 10010

The ibooks World Wide Web Site Address is:
http://www.ibooks.net

ISBN 0-7434-8693-5
First ibooks, inc. printing July 2004
10 9 8 7 6 5 4 3 2 1

Printed in the U.S.A.

Old cases sometimes come back at you.

Anyone who has been in criminal law has had it happen to them. The unexpected phone call. The fugitive arrested in a border city. The jail escapee caught during a robbery. The witness found dead.

Then the cops or the DA or a defense lawyer want to talk to you about something you did or didn't do years before.

The material contained in this book comes from police reports, evidence adduced at trial and at pretrial hearings, and conversations I had with various individuals connected to the case. Although this book is a factual account of a true story, certain events and dialogue have been reconstructed based on these sources.

When I left the Sacramento County District Attorney's Office in California after five years in 1982, I hoped I had heard the last of Dorothea Montalvo Puente. I had just sent her to prison for five years for robbing and drugging elderly people. I was appalled at the coldblooded way this sweet-looking, grandmotherly woman had deceived six victims and nearly killed another.

Then a family came forward and told me she had murdered their mother.

I thought I might hear about Dorothea Puente again.

It was November 1988 when I picked up a newspaper, read my own name, and saw that a body had been dug up in a yard downtown.

Then I saw the landlady's name. I was sick at heart. It was six years later, and eight more people had died. Nothing had been done to stop Puente. When she got out of prison on my cases, she had started killing again.

And I remembered the first victim, because I had never stopped thinking about her.

Her name was Ruth Munroe.

THE
BONE
GARDEN

Prologue

THE WOMAN LAY ON HER SIDE IN THE UPSTAIRS BEDROOM. SHE wore a pink nightgown. It was night outside and the lights were on in the room. The woman's eyes were open and she was trying to move.

Ruth Munroe had struggled to turn over, raise her hand, open her mouth to scream ever since she heard the voices downstairs. But she couldn't move at all. She could only stare at the wall.

She strained to hear who was downstairs. Sometimes her daughter Rosemary, Rosie she called her, came to visit. But for the last few nights it had been her son Bill, stopping by 1426 F Street after work to see how she was.

Ruth fought frantically to say something Bill would hear. Her mouth wouldn't open.

She had been drugged. She knew that. She had been working in a pharmacy at Gemco for ten years. She knew drugs and how they worked. This paralysis was unnatural. Someone had put something in her food.

Inwardly Munroe cringed. For the last three days she

1

hadn't eaten any solid food. All she had had were crème de menthe cocktails mixed by Dorothea. It will soothe you, Dorothea had said softly, it will make you feel better.

Ruth tried to cry out and failed again. She recognized Dorothea's voice and now she heard Bill's, too. He had come to see her, to make sure she was, as she had heard Dorothea tell him, getting better.

There's nothing wrong with me, she wanted to shout. She and Dorothea lived alone in the house. Ruth cursed herself as she lay paralyzed. She had moved in with Dorothea only a few weeks earlier. They had planned to go into business together, catering parties. It was something to fill Ruth's retirement.

She tried to talk. She had to talk, to get help from Bill.

She had her family to live for, grandchildren she loved. She didn't want to die.

The bedroom door opened. Ruth heard only one person come in. It was not Dorothea. Ruth knew those deliberate footsteps.

Bill sat down on the bed. He leaned over and spoke to her. "How are you, Mom?" he asked quietly.

Ruth tried to say something, anything.

Bill stroked her shoulder. "Everything's going to be okay. You're going to get better. Believe me."

Ruth twisted and writhed futilely inside her mind.

Bill was nearer. She could see his worried face, the dark brown hair, mustache. He said comfortingly, "Dorothea's going to look after you."

He kissed her. Ruth felt a tear roll down her cheek, from her open right eye. When he got up and left, she lay still on the bed, the tears dropping slowly.

Ruth must have slept or lost consciousness. Time passed. When she opened her eyes again, she was still on her side. The bedroom was dark, though, and the street outside utterly quiet. It felt like it was deep in the night or early morning.

Then the bedroom door opened. Ruth tried to squeeze against the wall, away from Dorothea who came resolutely to the bed, sat down, and with strong, determined hands, turned her on her back.

Dorothea was saying something. In the half-light from the hallway, her white hair was stark, her glasses dark, and Ruth realized Dorothea was swearing obscenely.

Roughly, Dorothea pulled Ruth's head up with one hand.

Ruth quavered. In her other hand, Dorothea was forcing a glass of sweet-tasting, minty liquid down Ruth's throat.

PART 1

"That corpse you planted last year in your garden,
"Has it begun to sprout? Will it bloom this year?
"Or has the sudden frost disturbed its bed?
"O keep the Dog far hence, that's friend to men,
"Or with his nails he'll dig it up again!"

T. S. Eliot,
The Waste Land

1

On Saturday morning, November 12, 1988, the crowd
started gathering early across the street from the gray-blue
gingerbread Victorian house at 1426 F Street in downtown
Sacramento, California.

The crowd was larger than the day before, when it had
first formed, drawn by the news that a body had been found
in the backyard of the house. From across the street, held
back by police barricades, the crowd could see that the
two-story house was already festively decorated for Christmas and Thanksgiving.

On the dim, wet morning, the police floodlights were
finally turned off after illuminating the house and yard all
night. The police guard remained stoically in front of the
brick and wrought-iron fence that framed the yard of 1426 F
Street. More Sacramento city police officers, more diggers,
more trucks, more coroner's deputies would be arriving
soon.

And the crowd—restless, chattering, some holding um-
brellas or pieces of plastic over their heads in the light

rain—hoped to glimpse a shrouded shape or body bag being lugged from the backyard. All of the crowd—men, women, the crying or laughing children—wanted also to see the woman who ran 1426 F Street as a board-and-care home for the sick, drunk, and crazy.

Many people in the crowd knew about Dorothea Puente. Some had lived briefly at 1426 F Street, then left or been thrown out. They moved among the crowd, spreading tales of the tyrannical woman. She alternately cared for them and terrorized them. The former tenants and people who had heard other, more terrible rumors, all shivered with loathing and anticipation. For a long time many of them had believed people were dying strangely behind the gray walls, the high windows, the wrought-iron fence at 1426 F Street.

Every so often, Puente peered down from a second-story window at the crowd and the TV news trucks wedged tightly into the street.

By 8:00 A.M. the police had returned in force. They planned to dig up the entire L-shaped yard that ran from the driveway of 1426 F Street, around the house in a narrow course to the right, and ended against the next-door neighbor's wooden fence.

The long police barricades kept the growing crowd, somewhere near three hundred, across the street. The whole block of F Street was closed off at either end. The loud rumble of TV trucks' generators, a backhoe working the yard, and the massed voices thickened the air. The rain that had started on Friday, Veterans Day, tapered into a persistent dreary drizzle, fanned by a cold wind from the gray sky.

Inside 1426 F Street only a few tenants remained. Some had left when the police began seriously asking questions the day before. But Puente stayed. She was up early, around six, and ate a simple meal of eggs and toast. She was agitated and started drinking, too. Although she hated drunks, Puente often drank heavily, mostly in private, sometimes in bars, but usually only with people she trusted, like the man who joined her for breakfast, Mervin John McCauley. He was her longtime friend and sometime victim. They had vodka and orange juice cocktails.

They ate in the second floor kitchen, separated from the tenants who had their own stove downstairs. McCauley was like Puente, in his early sixties. He had a scraggly gray beard, and his thin body trembled because he was an antique alcoholic. He waved his bandaged left hand and chain-smoked as they drank and talked.

It was an uncomfortable morning for them both. They could hear the people outside and the loud noise, the men moving around the yard and the machinery. Puente swore to McCauley. Her face was still unnaturally tight from a recent cosmetic operation so she looked like she was half-grimacing. She wore a blue dress. Her white hair, neatly pinned back, and her glasses combined to make her look kindly.

Puente kept getting up to refill their glasses. McCauley was little help. She had to do something soon.

The police had already found one body in the backyard. It was, the police discovered, an elderly woman, wrapped in cloth and a blanket, secured with duct tape. Puente knew the woman's name was Leona Carpenter.

"I told them I didn't know anything," Puente said defiantly to McCauley. "I didn't bury anyone."

McCauley nodded vigorously. He liked Puente and agreed with anything she said. "That's right, Dorothea. You don't know anything about it. That's the truth."

Puente sat down. She had been getting Carpenter's Social Security checks for some time and had placed orders for shoes in Carpenter's name long after the woman was dead. The police would find this out, Puente knew, and much more.

She had been taken to the police department Friday afternoon. They asked her about the dead body, about other missing tenants. She indignantly said she knew nothing and anyone who was missing would turn up alive and well soon.

She and McCauley had been put together, alone, in an

interview room. The police, Puente knew, were hoping one of them would say something incriminating to the other.

But she and her old drinking companion only lamented the destruction of the backyard flower beds, and she worried aloud whether the police would tear up her carefully laid down cement driveway. It was, she and McCauley agreed, terrible to have so much upheaval so close to Thanksgiving.

While they ate breakfast, the other tenants prudently stayed away, aware of Puente's sudden flashes of temper and her propensity to slap or punch anyone who angered her. McCauley had been slugged several times, cursed at, but he remained friendly to Puente.

"I better go get dressed," Puente said, shoving the soiled dishes aside. McCauley made no move to clear up. "I want you to be ready in a little while," she said.

McCauley, smoke curled around him, nodded. "Anytime you say, Dorothea. I'm all set to go."

Puente went upstairs to her bedroom. She had at least one great secret from the police that drove her that morning.

She knew that within a short time, if they kept digging, they would find six more bodies buried around the compact yard. Already she knew the police were trying to solve a puzzle and it would draw them on to other secrets of hers.

They had come on Friday looking for a missing tenant named Bert Montoya, but when they started poking around in the backyard, the body they did uncover was too old, too slight, to be the burly Montoya.

So over that last breakfast, Puente and McCauley got ready to take a bold step. Time for Dorothea Puente was running very short and she had none to waste.

Her bedroom was cluttered but orderly. There was a satinlike coverlet on the bed, shelves of paperback westerns and mysteries on one wall. She started dressing. Audacity had served her all her life. How else could she have buried seven people around the small yard only a block from the old Governor's Mansion, five blocks from the county District Attorney's office, practically within sight of the white state capitol dome itself?

How else could she, ex-con, ex-hooker, have run a boardinghouse in violation of the law right under the noses of federal parole agents, state probation officers, the social service agencies who sent her tenants?

As she carefully dressed, hearing the boisterous noise outside, Puente knew the bodies about to be unearthed were only a few feet from a busy street, in a bustling residential neighborhood, in plain view of dozens of people who passed 1426 F Street every day.

But appearances and deception had always been a key to how Dorothea Puente lived anyway.

She had yellow and white bottles of Giorgio Beverly Hills cosmetics and perfume on her dressing bureau. She applied them studiously, watching her face in the mirror, critically studying how the face lift had coarsened and stretched her mouth.

Then she put on a pink dress, purple pumps, combed her thick, stylishly set white hair. Everything she wore that morning, from her feet to her hair was paid for by her tenants, living and dead, without their knowledge. She added a red wool overcoat and took a purple rolled up umbrella with her.

Into her purse she dropped a little over $3,000, all she had around the house. In a single month of tipping cabdrivers for trips around Sacramento, she had once spent up to $2,000. Her own Social Security income was only about $600 a month.

Puente got up, finishing quickly. Lying around the bedroom were tins of butter cookies, just as there were downstairs. She had been filling them with clothing and canteen supplies of candy and cigarettes for mailing to old friends at the California Institution for Women in Frontera. But that morning, with the police already back to digging, there was no time to finish packing the tins.

She gave herself a final survey in the mirror. Dressed and expensively perfumed, Puente saw that she looked like a slightly too corpulent grandmother. Her glasses gave her a stern disciplinarian's gaze. Only her eyes, black and hard behind the glasses, hinted at the stark truth beneath the unthreatening veneer of her appearance.

The house trembled with the thudding of machinery near its walls, and the cacophonous voices were louder. Puente hurried outside.

Twenty or more men and women in black or drab overalls stamped either POLICE or CORONER on the back, swarmed around the backyard. Their high boots were muddy, their shovels busy. The lush flower beds in the center of the yard were gone, the newly planted fruit trees uprooted. A small gazebo a few feet farther up the yard had been moved, and men were starting to dismantle a metal toolshed at the far end of the yard. Heaps of dark, alluvial-smelling dirt lay everywhere. Too many people were crammed into the narrow space as the backhoe noisily worked. At the side of the house, Puente stood silently, umbrella hooked over one arm, and watched.

Detective John Cabrera, who had come the day before, strolled toward her. He had on a blue windbreaker and jeans, and his legs were spattered with mud. He was as polite, casual as he had been Friday morning when he came searching for Montoya. They chatted. They agreed it was very noisy and confusing.

The makeshift tent erected over most of the backyard to shield any evidence from the rain, consisted of a plastic sheet stretched over bare wood, and in the morning's drizzle and breezes, it sighed and crackled.

Puente moved a few feet up the driveway, away from the brick and wrought-iron fence in front. The crowd and alert reporters spotted her, and a murmuring grew across the street. Puente disdainfully avoided looking at the crowd or lights. She had bragged in the past to some of the people in the crowd about being famous. "I was in Hiroshima when they dropped the atom bomb," she told people. "I lived through the Bataan Death March," she told others. "I made movies with Rita Hayworth. I'm a medical doctor. I'm a lawyer," she said proudly.

Now as real fame reached out for her, Puente refused to acknowledge it. She grew anxious, nervous. She tapped her foot.

It was nearly 9:00 A.M. Cabrera and his partner, a bigger older man, Terry Brown, were talking and pointing around the yard. They did not believe her, Puente was sure. Cabrera had said she was lying Friday. She tapped her foot more quickly. The digging was too intense. She couldn't wait.

Puente went over to Cabrera and asked him if she could walk to the Clarion Hotel across the street, about a block away. She wanted to see her nephew, who worked there. "I want to get away from all this noise and everything that's going on for a few minutes." Puente sighed. "I'd like a quiet cup of coffee."

John Cabrera had been a police officer for fifteen years. He had worked Homicide/Assaults long enough to know a con when he heard one. He wanted to arrest the kindly little old lady beside him right then, but his superiors and the DA said there wasn't enough evidence. Keep digging and looking, they said. So Cabrera, who had dark hair and a mustache and an exuberant manner, listened to Puente as if he believed her. He examined her. She did actually seem worn out.

He left her and went up the yard to ask Lieutenant Joe Enloe about the request. Enloe, one of the supervising city cops on the scene, was balding, heavyset, and had on a white shapeless raincoat. The two cops talked briefly.

Cabrera came back to Puente. She asked him sharply, "Am I under arrest, Mr. Cabrera?"

Grinning sheepishly to put her at ease, Cabrera said, "No, you're not under arrest. And you can go to the hotel for a couple of minutes."

"Thank you. I'd like you to help me get through these reporters and people," Puente said politely, purse in one hand, hooking the umbrella over her wrist. "I can't do it by myself."

The two of them set off. John McCauley will come by, too, Puente said. Cabrera moved authoritatively, halting cars, taking her arm sometimes as they walked over rough patches of sidewalk. If he couldn't arrest her, Cabrera was determined to know where she was that critical morning. He would drop her off personally at the hotel.

They chatted about the weather, minor matters, like old friends, both solicitous and courteous to the other. A passerby would never have known that Cabrera had accused Puente of murder less than twenty-four hours earlier.

They walked past the old Governor's Mansion on the corner of 12th Street, a major tourist attraction, then across another street to the boxlike and ivy-covered Clarion Hotel. The gray sky was heavy with more rain as Cabrera left Puente and saw McCauley meet her. He watched them both go into the hotel to meet Puente's nephew, really her landlord at 1426 F Street and an old friend.

Cabrera walked back to the digging. He was positive something terrible had happened at F Street and more than ever convinced Dorothea Puente was involved. Enloe asked him when he got back if she was at the hotel now and Cabrera nodded. He went back to checking the yard for suspicious depressions in the soil.

Shortly before ten, after Puente had been gone about twenty minutes, Cabrera heard a shout from one of the digging groups. The other cops stopped, the backhoe idled. In another shallow grave like the one he had found Friday, Cabrera and his partner Brown saw a second wrapped body being uncovered. It too was buried about eighteen inches down, beside the wooden fence that ran along the lefthand side of the narrow backyard.

As he stared down, Cabrera saw that this body, like the first, was swaddled in cloth, dirt-covered, wrapped like a crude latter-day mummy, with a whitish sprinkling of lime on the cloth. The whole neighborhood was called Alkali Flat because lime existed close to the topsoil. But this layer of lime looked like it had been deliberately spread over the body, either in hopes of hastening decomposition or disguising any odor.

Cabrera's heart sank at the sight of the lime and the

second wrapped body. Simultaneously he, Brown, and Enloe realized there was suddenly abundant reason to arrest Dorothea Montalvo Puente. One body the wrong age, size, and sex for a missing tenant was too hard to pin on Puente. A second body meant there was a lot more going on at 1426 F Street.

Cabrera took off running to the Clarion Hotel. At Puente's old lady's pace, the two of them had taken ten minutes to walk there. He covered the distance in no time at full speed, cursing as he went.

He looked in the lobby dining area, the buffet. She wasn't there. Nor was McCauley or her "nephew" and landlord, Ricardo Odorica. In fact, Cabrera learned that Odorica didn't even work Saturdays.

With a sinking certainty, Cabrera checked the rest of the hotel, the grounds, the block around it, but he knew Puente was gone.

He ran back to 1426 F Street and put out a call for her arrest. She had about a half hour's start. Cabrera knew from experience with fleeing suspects that thirty minutes was a long lead.

At the crime scene as the news spread, there was a lot of swearing and anger among the cops, which spread back downtown to the police department, through the ranks of captains to the chief. To make the episode more embarrassing, Cabrera remembered he had been captured on film by the photographers and TV, gallantly escorting the white-haired suspect away from 1426 F Street.

But Cabrera's personal problem became Sacramento's shame. Within twenty-four hours a nationwide manhunt was begun for Dorothea Montalvo Puente, her pre-facelift, thinner, more bug-eyed driver's license photo spread on newspaper front pages, on the TV network news. The Sacramento Police Department was ridiculed for letting her get away.

In seventy-two hours, intense searches went on for Puente in Stockton, Garden Grove, and Glendale, California. She was reportedly spotted in Las Vegas, Nevada. The Attorney

General of California, who was in Chihuahua for a law enforcement conference, made a personal appeal to the Mexican police for help in finding the fugitive. Puente, with relatives in Mexico, was rumored to have fled south. She had tried to do so before, in 1982, when facing criminal charges.

At 1426 F Street, by the start of the next week, seven bodies had been unearthed, in various stages of decomposition, indicating some had been buried up to a year, others less than a few months. One victim, found beneath a shrine to St. Francis of Assisi in the front yard, was curiously robed in a white sheet, like a specter, buried in a sitting pose. The body was missing its head, hands, and lower legs.

Puente had been revealed as that rarest of killers, a female serial murderer. She was rarer still because even at the start of the investigation, the police rightly believed she killed not from passion but for profit alone. Night after night her white-haired bespectacled, plumpish face appeared on TV. She was a celebrity, a freak, a homicidal grandmother.

As the hunt for her went on, no one knew who the seven victims buried at 1426 F Street were. Nor did anyone know if these were the only victims. There was no sign of how any of these people had died or even whether they had been murdered.

As for Puente herself, the woman behind the haunting image, the object of law enforcement's frantic search from one side of the border to the other, the prime suspect in an unknown number of murders committed in the heart of California's capital, she had vanished into thin air as the long Veterans Day weekend ended.

2

JOHN CABRERA HAD STARTED OUT THE DAY BEFORE THINKING HE was just doing his job, trying to allay the worries of two social workers about a missing, retarded Costa Rican native.

So on Friday, November 11, 1988, five people crowded into the small office of the Homicide/Assault section at the Sacramento Police Department. Because it was Veterans Day, the old granite building was quieter than usual, quiet enough to hear the wind and dripping rain outside.

Cabrera was joined by his partner, Terry Brown, and Jim Wilson, a federal parole agent. Beth Valentine and Judy Moise were from the Volunteers of America, Outreach Social Workers.

Cabrera was informally running the early morning meeting. Brown, in his mid-forties, smoking sometimes, half smiling, let his outgoing partner handle the two social workers. Valentine and Moise had become very persistent in the last few days, urging the cops to do something about Dorothea Puente and the way she was acting about a missing tenant.

Cabrera had Wilson check his file on Puente and tell them what he knew about the woman.

Wilson had only recently become Dorothea Puente's federal parole agent, and he had never met her. He said she had been placed on federal parole in 1978 for forging checks and had been contacted thirty-five times by federal parole agents since she was released from custody on California state criminal charges in 1985. Most of those contacts had been at the federal parole office downtown. But on fourteen occasions, he said, flipping the file pages, Puente had invited agents to inspect her living arrangements as a tenant at 1426 F Street. No agent ever submitted a report that she was running any kind of boardinghouse or had other tenants living with her or that she was supplementing her assistance income in any way.

"She's not allowed to," Wilson pointed out. The conditions of her federal parole restricted her travel, banned contact with other parolees, and very specifically prohibited her from being employed by the elderly or emotionally handicapped.

Moise, light-haired, intense, said to Cabrera, "She's violating her parole. She gets people's Social Security checks, and she's got Bert living with her." The missing man Valentine and Moise were worried about was Alvaro "Bert" Montoya and he was retarded and mentally ill.

Valentine and Moise could completely not hide their frustration. They had told another Sacramento cop all about Bert Montoya and their fears for his safety with Puente that week. Now for the two homicide detectives and federal agent, they repeated what they knew about Montoya.

Unfortunately, they didn't know everything that had happened to Bert since he moved in at 1426 F Street.

Montoya was born in Costa Rica. In his mid-fifties in 1988, he was fat, with gray hair and a whitish beard or sometimes only a mustache. He was one of the two hundred or so clients Valentine and Moise saw every month in downtown Sacramento. Montoya had been living at the

Volunteers of America Detoxification Center on Front Street since 1982, and it was there the two women met him.

There was a forlorn but endearing quality to Bert that made him stand out for Valentine and Moise. Moise had seen a great deal of suffering and despair since joining VOA in 1986. Her territory downtown embraced Alkali Flat and the darker, older part of the city, thick with old trees and old houses and fading elegance from the era when it had been the home of governors and flour barons.

The governors and barons were long gone. Hallucinating, shouting drunks, men and women with diseases, poorer workers struggling to live, had taken over the crumbling fine houses and seedy apartments.

Bert, though, was big, and genial, and fearful, as if he didn't understand what was happening to him. At the Detox Center he was a rarity, mentally ill instead of alcoholic. He was a poor soul and easy to like. He spoke English better some days than others. Since he was a teenager, Montoya had suffered from hallucinations, some that spoke to him. He was frightened by the large cemetery near the Detox Center. Demons were calling to him from the graveyard where Sacramento buried its illustrious dead. Sometimes Bert heard his own dead father urging him to kill himself, so they could be together.

What Cabrera and Brown heard that far in the meeting sounded like the story of many of the lunatics and transients prowling downtown. They were around one day, gone the next. There didn't seem much to get worked up about in the case of this one missing man.

But Valentine and Moise argued for Montoya. For nearly two years he had been their special project. They contacted twenty-eight agencies trying to clarify his various legal and financial problems. He had been adopted, in a way, by the Detox Staff.

Bert would wave to the staff when they left in the morning, pat them on the shoulder when they returned. The big, confused, genial man sometimes was given a King

Edward cigar. Bert enjoyed the cigars immensely, leaning back, grinning, acting like he was worth a million dollars when he smoked one.

His major problem, Valentine and Moise said, was that he was easily led. He would just go along with a situation until it became intolerable.

What happened to Bert in February 1988 seemed like a blessing. Although neither Valentine nor Moise knew it, it was in truth his death sentence.

The two social workers had heard about Dorothea Puente's boardinghouse. They brought Bert to 1426 F Street, and Puente fastened on him immediately, talking gently to him in Spanish. She comforted him. She acted like she cared about him. She told the social workers she could make Bert better.

"She gave him a room, a TV. She said she'd make Spanish meals for him," Moise told Cabrera. For several months, everything looked fine. Every time Valentine or Moise visited Bert at F Street, he looked better physically. His hair was cut and combed, his clothes clean. He was being medicated for a skin problem. He sounded less suspicious of people.

But in mid-August, something happened. Montoya showed up again at the Detox Center, angry, confused, saying he didn't want to stay at 1426 F Street anymore. Dorothea was being unkind to him.

The Detox staff couldn't make much of what Bert said beyond his unhappiness, and having no place else to put him, they convinced him to go back to F Street. They drove him there. His old friends never saw him again. It was August 16, 1988.

What Puente did to simpleminded, trusting Bert Montoya was replicated over and over with other victims. First she won his confidence. Then she secured his money. Finally, she got rid of him because he became too troublesome. Bert was wearing out his welcome as far as Puente was concerned.

Part of the problem, for Puente, was that outsiders kept checking up on Bert. Lucy Yokota from the Health Department, for example, saw Montoya regularly from June 1987 through June 1988 about his tuberculosis. She wanted to "eyeball" him every two weeks and kept up with his life closely. She noted that Bert got better once he moved in at 1426 F Street, becoming more fit and talkative.

But Puente was a different story. By June 1988, the Health Department decided Bert's TB was cured and stopped his medication. This was not good enough for Puente who warned Yokota to stop coming by 1426 F to see Bert. In April, Puente had called Yokota angrily and shouted that she didn't want anyone visiting Bert. She threatened to send him back to the Detox Center and then hung up.

Puente had found other uses for Bert and his large size. Sometime in August 1988, after he returned to F Street, Bert was ordered to help Puente and another tenant unload sixty-five bags of cement. Bert, acting under Puente's sharp orders, stacked bags under the stairs at the front of the house. When the truck driver delivering the cement tried to talk to Bert, Puente instantly prevented it. She said Bert was retarded and she was the only one who could talk to him.

Puente had already taken Bert to the Social Security office, listed herself as his substitute payee, and thus gained control over the monthly checks he received. She stood over him as he signed his name and she entered hers as a relative. Puente had also gotten control of a trust account for Bert at the Bank of America and used it as a personal slush fund for herself. Puente bought fruit cake, Giorgio cologne at $110 a bottle and clothing, all for herself.

Although she wanted to keep him away from the inquisitive eyes of health workers and Moise and Valentine, Puente had no problem if Bert was kept close to 1426 F Street and people she knew. She set up a monthly account of about $80 for him at Joe's Corner, the bar at the end of the 1400 block. Puente knew the owner very well. She was a regular there herself, and brought in bundles of checks made out to her sometimes totaling $2,000. She never, though, came to drink with any of her tenants. They were the business part of her life, and she separated recreation and business.

Bert used the monthly account Puente had doled out to him to buy two or three beers and burritos once or twice a week. He said little, and struck most patrons and the bartender as shy. There was one disturbing incident in early August, shortly before Bert tried to flee 1426 F Street. He came to the bar about eleven-thirty in the morning, had his beers and burritos, and then passed out. He had to be carried back, half a block, to 1426 F Street. It was as if Bert had suddenly been struck by the effects of some drug.

He never came to Joe's Corner again. When Puente, grandly flourishing a batch of checks, arrived several weeks later and was asked about the absent Bert, she said he had gone to Mexico. She told the bartender to cancel Bert's monthly account. Plainly, she didn't think he would return.

But Bert's last known contact with the world outside 1426 F Street was chilling. The mask of pleasant, kindly concern that Puente wore slipped and revealed something wicked.

On September 2, a young woman working in the Consumer Affairs Section at the Main Branch of the Sacramento Post Office got a startling call around ten-thirty in the morning. A man identified himself as Bert Montoya. He was frightened, stuttering, nervous as he spoke. Behind him the young woman could hear another voice, yelling and raging obscenely. "I'll put his goddamn ass out on the goddamn street," a female voice screamed.

"What's wrong?" the postal worker asked worriedly.

"She's got my Social Security check and she's yelling at me," Bert stuttered back fearfully. "I can't give you my phone number. I live at 1426 F Street."

Trying to take notes, the young postal worker strained to hear Bert over the yelling woman in the background. Bert said the manager where he lived had taken his Social Security check. He couldn't even write down anything the postal worker told him. The manager, screaming and raging, wouldn't let him have a pencil. He talked for five minutes,

22

hung up, then called back twice in the early afternoon. It was quiet in the background on those calls. Bert insisted that something be done to get his Social Security check. The postal worker promised to look into it.

But no one ever heard from Bert Montoya again. He had tried to escape Puente in mid-August, failed, collapsed for an inexplicable reason just before his aborted escape, and then made one final, fearful call for help.

"He just disappeared," Valentine told the detectives and Wilson on November 11. She and Moise tried to find out what had happened to him.

In mid-September, Moise saw Puente. "Bert's gone to Mexico," Puente said, to visit her family. This struck Moise as highly unlikely. Bert had trouble navigating the streets of Alkali Flat and a transcontinental journey was far beyond him. "He'll be back in a few days," Puente assured Moise.

It was, Moise realized bitterly, just another of the innumerable lies Dorothea Puente had told.

Near the end of September, still without a clue about Bert's whereabouts, Moise again saw Puente. Puente was in a fine mood, happy to help. Bert had made a great impression on her family in Mexico. He was a favorite of her sister and brother-in-law, a respected banker.

"I want him to call me and tell me he's all right," Moise insisted.

"I'll make sure he calls," Puente replied.

But there was no call then or later, when Moise returned. "Bert's called me," Puente said. "He's doing just fine."

At first, Moise and Valentine believed that Puente had unwisely sent the retarded Montoya to Mexico where he had gotten lost or come to harm, and she was now hiding her actions.

It could not, they told themselves, be more sinister than that. Not that brisk, grandmotherly old woman. Not in the middle of downtown Sacramento.

But on November 1, the social workers confronted Puente. They found her on the front porch at 1426 F Street, looking stricken and tired. Moise used a ruse, telling Puente that Bert was being transferred to another social worker and he had to contact Moise immediately.

Puente began weeping. "I've just bought Bert a Christmas present," she said. Christmas decorations had gone up around 1426 F Street, including a macabre string of little white Santa Claus heads along the length of a wooden driveway fence. There were so many they looked like shrunken trophy heads.

Moise said Bert could stay with Puente until Christmas, but he had to contact her or Valentine and come back to Sacramento.

"If we haven't heard from Bert by November seventh, we'll report him missing to the police," Moise firmly told Puente.

"I'll go to Mexico and bring him back myself," Puente said stoutly. "I'll go Saturday. You can come back that afternoon and see Bert."

But on Monday morning, Moise got a call at work from a man who said he was Bert's brother-in-law. He was calling from Utah and had driven through Sacramento Saturday and picked Bert up.

Instantly suspicious, Moise demanded, "I want to talk to him."

"He's under the weather, he's a little sick right now," the man said. He went on to magnanimously decline Bert's Social Security. "We don't take charity," he said to Moise.

Dorothea, he said, had wanted Bert to stay with her. And Bert had very much wanted to stay. He'd had a tough fight to convince Bert to leave on Saturday. The man hung up.

Moise relayed the information to Valentine. Neither of them had ever heard of any Montoya relatives in Utah. Then a letter purporting to be from the same brother-in-law arrived, saying Bert would stay with him. It was mailed from Reno, Nevada.

The whole thing looked wrong, as if Puente was still trying to keep anyone from contacting Bert. Moise got on the phone to Puente. After a long, almost reflective pause,

Puente repeated the same story as the mysterious "brother-in-law".

"I'm calling the police," Moise announced, fed up with the lies and false leads.

"Could you wait until three o'clock?" Puente asked.

"No," Moise snapped. She called the Sacramento Police Department and filed a missing person report on Bert Montoya. A patrol officer later came to see Moise and Valentine and took down their information. There was no question for the two social workers. Dorothea Puente knew that something terrible had happened to Bert.

The patrol officer, later on Monday morning, November 7, went to 1426 F Street and talked to Puente.

Cabrera had seen the patrol officer's report. He and Terry Brown realized that the odd call and the letter meant Pucnte had at least one accomplice in any criminal activity.

Wilson was perplexed. A tenant, like Montoya, living with Puente? Four parole agents over time had visited her and she had manipulated the inspections in such a way that they never realized that the two-story Victorian house at 1426 F Street had tenants on the ground floor.

The detectives also now had information that on November 7 Puente had gotten an elderly tenant, John Sharp, to lie to the police about Bert leaving in a pickup truck on Saturday. The old man, however, had managed to slip a note to the patrol officer: "She's making me lie," it said, and the fear was obvious in the words.

Cabrera had also heard from a sometime prostitute and heroin addict named Brenda Trujillo recently. Trujillo had known Puente from their common time in county jail in 1982 and had lived at 1426 F Street when she was out of prison. Cabrera and Brown had discounted Trujillo's venomous denunciations of Puente, however, because Trujillo herself was a suspect in a murder (although the investigation was dropped). But the ex-con had said people were dying at the quiet house and Puente was burying them on the property.

25

With all of this information, Cabrera and Brown decided to do what the two social workers wanted, check out the house and Puente themselves, look around the yard for anything resembling a grave. At the very least, Cabrera hoped the search would finally satisfy the bothersome VOA workers who were threatening to go higher in the police department if he didn't do something.

"Okay," Cabrera said cheerfully, "let's go take a look," and a little before 9:00 A.M. a small caravan drove the twenty or so peaceful city blocks from the police department to 1426 F Street. The only other traffic was headed toward the Veterans Day parade set to start later that morning.

3

THINGS COULDN'T HAVE STARTED OFF BETTER WHEN THE SMALL expedition got to 1426 F Street. Moise and Valentine, concerned they might spook Puente, peeled off and parked a little distance from the house. Cabrera, Brown, and Wilson went up the front porch. It was cold outside, the sky leaden. Cabrera knocked on a paper Thanksgiving turkey stuck in the center of the door.

Puente appeared, smiling, in the doorway. She had on a blue dress with white dots, and a white sweater. She was courtly and soft-spoken, her plump little hands fiddling with the edges of the sweater. How could anyone who looked so sweet be guilty of even the hint of what Moise and Valentine suspected?

After making the introductions quickly, Cabrera went into the riskiest part of his sales pitch. He wanted her to agree to let them look around the property, talk to the tenants, try to get some idea where Bert Montoya might be. To Cabrera's relief, Puente, who could have ordered them off the property, only asked, "How can I help you?"

27

They all went inside where it was warmer. It was also stuffy, only a few lights on in the crowded living room against the dark morning. Puente offered them coffee, candy. They all declined.

Unconsciously, it was hard for Cabrera and the two other men to deal with Puente like a usual suspect. Nothing in their experience prepared them for her. She was kindly, cooperative, looked old, frail, and even timid. Making her out a killer or con artist didn't add up.

Now that they were in the door, Wilson dropped the hammer a little on her. He told her she had violated her federal parole by taking in tenants.

Puente nodded, arms folded. "I know it's wrong," she said contritely.

They walked through the living room toward the kitchen. Wilson advised Puente that her parole would be revoked. She took the news calmly. In the kitchen Cabrera noticed a wall calendar hanging on the door. It was almost too obvious. In early November, jotted in, was a note that Bert had gone to Mexico.

Cabrera turned to Puente. He asked about Bert. She was still calm. She said she hadn't seen him since September. Then, a little later during the house tour, Puente changed her story and told Cabrera she had gone to Tijuana to pick Bert up on November 4.

Both homicide detectives were interested in the number of pill bottles scattered throughout the kitchen. There were many bottles—sauces, liquor, medication—on tables, on counters. They had seen more pill bottles in the living room. Cabrera found a small cupboard in the kitchen; the rows of medications the tenants were taking in it.

Casually chatting with Puente to put her at ease, Cabrera also increased the pressure. "Now, Dorothea, I see you've got some felonies on your record. Drugs, forgery, things like that."

Puente nodded. "I did those things, but they're in the past. I'm trying to straighten my life out."

The three men split up and began talking to the six

tenants about Bert and another missing man, Ben Fink. No one had any information.

Cabrera was rapidly concluding that the visit was futile.

Finally, after an hour in the stale, tired atmosphere of what felt like a run-down nursing home, he asked Puente, "Dorothea, you mind if we check around outside? Maybe do a little digging?"

"No, no," Puente said helpfully. "Go ahead. There's nothing there." Just be careful of the new plantings, she said.

Cabrera, Brown, and Wilson returned to their cars, got metal probes and shovels, brought along as precautions, and went up the driveway into the backyard. Puente hovered like a bird around them. Over the wind came the faint sounds of drums and trombones and a cheering crowd as the parade passed the capitol building.

Cabrera complimented Puente on the lush, neat backyard. He was intrigued, like Brown, by the brick-bordered planter in the yard's center, just above the end of the concrete driveway, the stand of freshly planted small fruit trees in it, and thin, amateurishly poured cement around the trees. A metal toolshed was worth looking at, too. So was a tiny gazebo crowded into the upper part of the yard and an old sink turned into a planter beside the wood fence.

Trees, small plants, stones, statues, all made good unobtrusive markers for anything buried beneath them.

Peering around, Cabrera and Brown noted the ivy and flower beds arranged tightly in the narrow yard, with more flowerpots standing on the rain-damp cement, waiting to be planted. Cabrera knew Puente had a local reputation as an energetic and assiduous gardener, often working in the predawn darkness, digging and planting, tending the flowers and trees around the house, dragging heavy fertilizer bags behind her.

Cabrera was careful not to knock over any of the stone figures of cats on the cramped brick pathway between the flower beds. Puente stood, arms folded, face impassive, as he talked to Brown and Wilson, pointing out places around the yard to check. Everything was being done calmly, almost casually.

Once more, Cabrera asked Puente if it was all right to do a little digging.

"Go ahead," she said, nodding. Cabrera, as he turned to push his metal probe into the soil, wondered how a woman who had just been told by her parole agent that she would probably go back to prison, could be so cool.

The whole scene was incongruous, the grandmother waiting as cops poked in her flower beds for corpses, the gingerbread house so neat on the outside and so musty inside, concealing who knew what horrors. George Bush had just become President, people were starving in Sudan, Stanford was going to play UCLA in the Rose Bowl the next day. How could anything be very wrong at 1426 F Street in downtown Sacramento?

The fact was that Sacramento itself was a mix of incongruities, home of the legislature, cosmopolitan with a large airport, a cathedral, ballet and symphony, but also with nearby rice fields and almond packing plants. The city had three hundred thousand people, the county another seven hundred thousand. In the summer it could sweat for weeks over a hundred degrees, and in the winter, shiver under sheets of endless rain.

Sacramento was almost one hundred fifty years old in 1988, a Gold Rush boomtown that had become the state capital after rough bargaining. It had a busy port and yet lived in fear that the two great rivers that bisected it, the American and Sacramento, could flood it despite elaborate levees.

By 1988, Dorothea Puente had spent almost forty years, off and on, in Sacramento. Something about its deceptive appearance, its lust for past and future glamor and importance, must have attracted her predatory nature.

In fact, Sacramento was also a place of overlapping police jurisdictions. City police, county sheriffs, state police, federal agents, all worked in the city or county and frequently did not communicate on important matters.

Puente instinctively understood the possibilities in a tattered web of interlocking responsibilities. The Social Security Administration downtown might never talk to the city police. The federal court might never exchange information about her with the police or social service agencies. She could move about with ease.

She could in fact get away with murder.

The three men had been digging for a while. Puente stood in the cool wind, her white hair plucked at, but otherwise immovable.

Hitting on shallow roots in the thick, riverbed dirt that lay under Sacramento, Cabrera was growing tired.

A grizzled face appeared at the second-floor window over him. It was Mervin John McCauley, cigarette in hand. He called down to the three men, "You might find some garbage buried in there."

"Like what?" Cabrera called back.

"You know. Garbage. Junk." McCauley's face vanished from the window.

Cabrera and Brown chuckled. It was an odd thought, though. Why bury garbage in the backyard when the city picked up trash at the sidewalk every week? Why make sure the police know about it?

Wilson was digging in the upper left hand side of the yard, near the fence. Another lot, empty and weed-clotted, butted up against 1426 F. On either side of the property were aging Victorians, all occupied, and all able to see into the cramped backyard. Bury people out here? The idea was idiotic.

Then Wilson called to Cabrera. His shovel had struck something, and he wanted one of the detectives to dig for him, in case it was important.

Going to Wilson's shallow hole, Cabrera bent down and started digging. Brown paused and watched. Soon Cabrera hit what felt like a hidden tree root. It was, he saw looking closer, an object mixed with white powder, maybe the lime of Alkali Flat. A small fruit tree grew nearby, like a marker.

Cabrera was puzzled, so he turned the dark soil over more carefully, calling Brown over. It was not a root. Cloth, really only rags, was coming up from the narrow hole. He reached down and began plucking the material out, bits and pieces coming off in his hand. He could not tell what it was. Brown didn't know, either. It was dry and translucent and Cabrera could see the thin, elusive sun through the stuff when he held it up.

Just then, he realized he had not been pulling up bits of cloth, but dried skin. He poked down with his shovel. He uncovered a bone, white, still partly covered with skin, in some kind of shoe.

From the side of the house, as the three men turned to her, Dorothea Puente held her hands to her face, over her mouth. It was, Cabrera first thought, a gesture of shock, her eyes wide behind her glasses. From then until the day of her sentencing, it was the only surprise she ever expressed publicly.

As Brown and Wilson checked the find, Cabrera knew that this skeletalized body, whether human or animal, had been in the ground far too long to be Bert Montoya.

"We've got something to talk about, Dorothea," Cabrera said.

4

ON SATURDAY, NOVEMBER 12, AFTER SHE HAD GOTTEN TO THE Clarion Hotel, and was satisfied Detective Cabrera had left, Puente sent McCauley outside to see if any police officers were nearby. McCauley saw no one. He was an odd sight, skulking quickly around the hotel, smoking, bandaged hand, baseball cap on his gray hair, watery eyes behind tinted glasses.

When she was certain the police weren't watching her, Puente and McCauley immediately took a cab to Tiny's Lounge, a bar she knew in West Sacramento, across the Sacramento River.

The bar was not far from the Port of Sacramento, surrounded by truck stops, gas stations, busy freeways. Early morning drinkers liked it. Puente led McCauley to a table in the nearly empty bar. It was only nine-thirty, and back at F Street, the second body had not yet been uncovered.

She ordered and swiftly drank four vodkas and grapefruit

juice to calm down. McCauley limited himself to one beer. They stayed together about fifteen minutes, talking, brooding, Puente lamenting all the wrongs that were being done to her. McCauley later denied knowing what Puente was going to do, but he certainly didn't think she was going sightseeing in an industrial neighborhood on a gloomy holiday weekend.

They said their farewells. Puente had been good to McCauley, allowing him the rare privilege of living on the second floor of 1426 F with her, drinking with her, sharing meals. No other tenant was treated like that. They wished each other well as Puente got a cab for McCauley.

He left Tiny's Lounge around ten. Puente went back to the bar and called a second cab for herself. She had been planning what to do ever since Friday morning, through the long, restless night splashed with floodlights at 1426 F.

A Capitol City Co-Op cab arrived to pick her up. She told the cabbie to take her south, to Stockton, a city she knew fairly well, about forty miles away. It would cost her $70, but that's what she said she wanted to do.

The cabbie settled her into the backseat and turned south, heading for I-5. The woman he drove impressed him, umbrella at her side, as genteel, fashionable, almost regal.

Hurrying south, the rain starting again, Dorothea Puente saw green pastures and huge electrical towers along the freeway. The money she had with her was all she possessed in the world. She had lost control of the thousands of dollars of checks that came to the tenants every month at F Street.

She had told Detective Cabrera many lies in the last twenty-four hours. When he asked how long Bert Montoya had lived with her, she blurted out two months. She told Cabrera that Bert didn't want to see Judy Moise anymore; she bothered him. And she said that Bert's brother-in-law had come and taken him away the weekend before.

"If I had anything to hide," Puente blustered to Cabrera as they sat in the very tiny police interview room Friday morning, right after the first body was found, "I wouldn't have let you dig around the yard."

Cabrera, windbreaker off, in a shortsleeved shirt said quickly, "I think Bert's dead."

"He's not dead," she answered back as quickly.

"We found a body. I think, Dorothea, if we dig, there's others. What about Bert?"

"Sir, I have never killed anybody," she said, and told the man only an arm's length across the little table, how much she cared for poor Bert Montoya. "I haven't killed anyone. My conscience isn't bothering me," she said. Then to add weight to her claim, she told the detective she'd seen Bert several times in the week before he left with his brother-in-law.

Bert, she said, will come back. "I believe in God, and I know he's going to show up."

But Detective Cabrera didn't seem to believe her. He kept pressing on. He knew they would find more bodies, he knew Bert was dead, he knew she was lying.

"I always look like I'm lying because I'm nervous because I've been in prison," she said. "Once a person has been in prison, the police officers . . ."

Shaking his head, Cabrera said, "No, no," and Puente broke in sharply, "Yes, it is."

She tried to persuade him of her good intentions, "I want to get off parole. I've had a good record." She splayed her hands out, her white, flabby arms, before the skeptical detective. "I've got nothing to hide. I don't want to go back to prison. I'm an old lady. I'm trying to get off parole. I'm trying to get my life together."

But Cabrera went right back to saying Bert was dead and more bodies were buried with him in the yard.

Puente tried indignation. "Well, I didn't put them there. I couldn't drag a body anyplace. My health's bad. I have a bad heart and I can't lift anything very heavy."

Cabrera wanted her to take a lie detector test. She said she was too nervous, but she'd take one Monday.

She would be long gone by Monday.

Puente showed Cabrera a little diagram of a trench he knew about that had been dug in February. She drew more and said the trench was for a sewer line she was looking for, and it went down a foot and a half and traveled straight for four feet. It was not a grave, she told Cabrera. Then he asked about another sewer line she'd had dug that summer by parolees from a halfway house. It was near the little trees where the body had just been found. Puente said she had dug up the whole backyard unsuccessfully searching for that sewer line. She was not digging graves.

"What about the lime we found? There was lime all around the body," Cabrera asked, jotting down notes.

"The people at Lumberjack told me lime would soften the dirt for my plants. I don't know how it got around any body."

But, she knew they were all lies. The police would dig them all up, Leona Carpenter, Dorothy Miller, James Gallop, Betty Palmer, Vera Martin, and of course, Bert Montoya. He was buried with the rest of them in the backyard.

When the police got under the toolshed, they would find Ben Fink, too. And there were others Puente's lies would not conceal for much longer.

She got to Stockton about 1:00 P.M. Saturday and told the cabbie to take her to the Greyhound bus terminal. She tipped him, went inside, and bought a ticket on the next bus, leaving at 2:00 for Los Angeles. Puente sat down among the farmworkers and their families, a spark of color and style, standing out vividly.

The bus ride south, down the long valley of California and into the thicket of people around Los Angeles, took over seven hours. Puente kept to herself, as people slept or talked around her. She had a brother and sister in the city, but she wasn't going to contact them. One of her two children, given up shortly after birth, lived in nearby South Pasadena, but Puente decided to stay away from her, too.

Around 10:00 P.M. the bus pulled into the Greyhound terminal in Hollywood. It was rowdy and seedy on a

Saturday night, and Puente quickly checked into a nearby hotel for the night.

Early Sunday morning she took a cab to the Royal Viking Motel on Alvarado. The rents were cheap, Hispanics from many countries lived in the neighborhood, along with many people on government assistance. It was the big city equivalent of Alkali Flat, a place where Puente felt comfortable and could move around confidently.

She gave her name to the front desk clerk as Dorothy Johansson. It was a name she had used before and she had once been married to a man named Johansson. She got a room across from the manager's office, number 31. Puente carefully prepaid for two nights, taking her into Monday.

Once in her room, she got out of her heavy red coat and tight shoes. For the first time since Friday morning she could really rest. She had escaped.

A little later the maid came and asked if she needed anything. Puente only opened the door a crack, smiled, and said, "Just towels, that's all," taking them from the maid. No one else was allowed in the room while she occupied it.

Near twilight on Sunday she felt hungry, got dressed again in the red coat and walked down the street, past a whitewashed apartment building and tall palm trees, to the T.G. Express restaurant which sold "Thai Chinese Food." It was part of the Royal Viking. Puente ordered a beer, drank it and some soup, then got another beer and chop suey in a plastic tray to take back to her motel room. As she walked the short distance, she passed newspaper vending machines. The Sunday *Los Angeles Times* shouted in headlines: "Two Bodies Unearthed at Boarding Home, Manager Sought".

Dorothea Puente walked quietly back to her room, locked the door, and ate her dinner. She had gotten away from Sacramento, but she was not safe. She had to plan what to do next, how to get money and shelter from the police.

5

By Sunday evening Sacramento was in an uproar. The prime suspect in a widening murder investigation had been helped to escape by the police. And the number of bodies found in the yard at 1426 F Street had risen to five. Each body was like the others, wrapped in blankets, secured with rope and duct tape. All appeared to be old or elderly men and women.

While both Cabrera and Terry Brown continued to dig at 1426 F, they were also detailed to compile lists of missing people around Alkali Flat and past tenants of Dorothea Puente. The body count might go on and on.

Each time another body was brought up, the crowd along the street surged toward the barricades for a better look. Lieutenant Joe Enloe held impromptu press conferences; swarms of cameras and microphones shoved at him in the chill drizzle. "We're getting scared now," he said after the third body was found Sunday. He had already given reporters a description of the first body found Friday: "It's the entire skeletal remains of a gray-haired, rather petite elderly

38

female." It was buried only three feet down and a scant hundred feet from the curb of F Street. An early estimate from the anthropologist and coroner was that this unidentified victim had been buried since April.

By now, Enloe was also briefing reporters about Puente's criminal background. In 1982 she had gone to prison for giving drugs to people, robbing them, forging their checks. He told the reporters that none of the bodies showed any sign of violence. "We don't expect that was the case."

The questions that would persist through the case had already been raised: How did these people die? Did Puente kill them? Did she have help? Did she have help burying them? The police thought she had an accomplice, "probably male." That was just a guess.

Sprinkled among the crowd were friends of Dorothea Puente, too. A stocky, dark-haired cabdriver named Patty Casey watched the bodies and machinery at 1426 F Street with horror and fear. She and Puente had become friends during the many cab trips Puente took to buy cement for "home improvements" or carpeting for a room Puente said was cursed. People died in the room, blood flowing from them and staining the old carpet.

"God, I love that person," Casey said of Puente. "I'm sorry my friend might have done something so horrible."

By Sunday, the Sacramento County District Attorney's Office had been on the case for two days. Cabrera had called frequently, seeking legal advice about exactly what he could do as the investigation developed.

His contact was Tim Frawley, one of the deputies in Major Crimes and the normal on-call lawyer that week. It was sheer coincidence that Frawley had filed the original cases against Puente in 1982. When Cabrera first called him, he didn't even remember Puente.

Frawley was athletic, diligent, with a reputation among lawyers and judges for fairness. His first act had been to counsel Cabrera that Puente should not be arrested Friday. There was too little evidence pointing directly at her.

Frawley's next step was to start a search warrant for 1426 F Street. That was the best way to preserve any evidence Cabrera or other cops found from future legal attack.

On Saturday Frawley said Puente could be arrested for Bert Montoya's murder, even if neither of the two bodies found at that point matched him. The problem, as Cabrera ruefully admitted, was that Puente was gone by then.

So the DA and cops turned to Puente's closest associate. Frawley took Cabrera's information about McCauley and around noon Sunday, decided to arrest the shaking, watery-eyed tenant of F Street. McCauley had lied to the police about when the backyard concrete had been poured, and denied getting a call from Puente after she left 1426 F Street Saturday. Frawley instructed Cabrera to arrest Mervin John McCauley as an accessory to murder: he might say something about Puente's location. Frawley wasn't overly optimistic, though.

Cabrera then escorted the thin, blue-jacketed McCauley down the porch steps at 1426 F, holding him up a little. The crowd murmured at the sight. All Enloe said publicly was, "He was a confidant of hers. But we do not believe he was involved in the hands-on work involving the bodies." Frail, trembling, old McCauley couldn't have lugged any bodies anywhere, that was obvious. But it was equally obvious someone had.

By late Sunday the removal of soil and concrete from the L-shaped backyard was so complete that two dump trucks had joined the crowded collection of police cars, coroner's vans, and TV trucks in the street. The spectacle of lights, people, sirens, cameras, was bigger than Cabrera or any of the other cops could recall.

One man in the crowd shivered watching a tractor load dirt and uprooted little fruit trees into the dump trucks. He had almost rented a room from Puente. He was on Social Security disability, which interested her greatly. But he stayed away finally because the rumors around Alkali Flat were that she could be very rough. Tenants ate when she said, got their medicine when she directed, were punched, slapped, or screamed at if they crossed her.

The load of dirt fell into one of the dump trucks. "I'm glad it wasn't me," the man said.

Frawley worked at his office on Saturday and Sunday, reviewing the reports that were starting to come in, fielding calls from the police working at F Street or their supervisors downtown. The blocky beige DA's office had no heat on weekends, so it was chillier than usual.

He was also reaching out to people involved with Puente both in the present and the past. He spoke several times with John O'Mara, his supervisor in Major Crimes, about the course to take in getting the search warrant together quickly. O'Mara, a bluff, sometimes acerbic man with a beard, had also coincidentally been Major Crimes supervisor in 1982 when information came to him that Dorothea Puente might have murdered Ruth Munroe. For various reasons, he had concluded then that there was not enough evidence to go forward against Puente at that time and the Munroe murder had remained uncharged.

Both Frawley and O'Mara agreed on Sunday night that McCauley, now glumly sitting in the county jail, was not going to say anything harmful to himself or Puente. The case against him was brittle and he probably couldn't be held long in custody, either. It was just another of the frustrating realities Sunday night, with more bodies probably buried at 1426 F Street and Puente on the run.

It was decided to charge Puente with Bert Montoya's murder. No one held out any hope, given the developments of the last twenty-four hours, that he was alive.

Sunday night, Frawley called me. He had finally remembered Puente from 1982, when he had sent her crimes to me for prosecution. Now he wanted to know if I recalled anything from her 1982 crime spree that might help.

After six years, there wasn't much I could do for him. I felt shame that Puente had gone to prison in 1982, gotten out in

1985, and instantly returned to the scene of her crimes, picking up where she left off, with murder.

Frawley and I agreed to meet Monday morning at the DA's office.

On Monday, November 14, Frawley, O'Mara, and I took a strange, spur-of-the-moment walk from the DA's office to 1426 F Street under a suddenly blue sky, the ground still wet, the air sharp.

We had all known about Dorothea Puente since 1982, and we were going to the site of the murders she had committed.

The carnival look of the 1400 block had grown worse with good weather, and cops stood in front of the iron fence at 1426, while others tried to keep the crowd across the street orderly.

O'Mara was sour about the presence of so many TV cameras, several reporters recognizing him, so we hurriedly ducked past the police into the yard.

Joe Enloe, still in his shapeless white raincoat, called out teasingly to Frawley, "We have enough PC yet, Tim?" Frawley's caution on Friday not to arrest Puente without sufficient probable cause still rankled the police. The sixth body had just been found.

It was impossible, seeing the technicians, the activity, the crowd, not to realize something had gone very wrong. If Puente had been stopped in 1982, none of this would have happened. I had known Frawley since law school and later when we worked together at the DA's office. He, too, was unhappy that she so quickly and easily started killing again after prison.

Enloe acted as tour guide for us. The L-shaped yard was reduced to mud and packed ground, all flowers and grass stripped away. It looked like a battlefield. Men and women worked at holes, almost bumping into each other. The saddest site was a board near the center of the yard on which lay a red-cloth wrapped figure, the latest victim unearthed.

A detective wanted to know if we'd like to get in on the lottery. There was betting on how many bodies would be found. The highest estimate was fifteen. Frawley said a psychic announced on Sunday that Puente had buried a dozen people.

We passed the red-blanket wrapped body on the board, waiting to be carried out to the coroner's van, to the noisy notice of the crowd. It was apparently the body of another small woman, her shroud dusted with white lime, like sugar on a pastry. It was immensely sad seeing the body, buried like the garbage McCauley had warned Cabrera about.

Enloe was brisk as a guide. He pointed at the Berkeley anthropologist, down on his knees with three other people, beside another gravesite. "He sees all kinds of stuff," Enloe said of the blue-overalled man. "He found ground-down cigarette butts in three graves, a pack of cigarettes in one. We would've missed that."

O'Mara and I noticed a man standing under what had been the small side porch, now torn apart. It was the county coroner, in a neat pearl gray suit, talking to a cop. O'Mara was irritated that the notoriety of the Puente case was making officials feel the need to show themselves, as if they were finally doing something about Puente. "Fifty people all hanging around with nothing to do," O'Mara said.

We stopped with Enloe at the next door neighbor's yard, beyond a rickety wooden fence. A loose German shepherd barked and tried to reach us over the fence. "See, this house wasn't here two years ago," Enloe said. "It was just moved here. Look here," he pointed at a depression in the yard a few feet away. "We got one place already where she used to come out and dig here in the garden all the time."

"What is it?" Frawley pointed at the depression.

"Another body," Enloe said decisively.

It was not, though, only another false lead.

We stayed for some time, asking questions, the bustle of the diggers and machines going on around us. Finally Frawley and O'Mara had seen enough. But genial Enloe wanted us to see one more thing. He motioned toward the dry, unweeded grass of the next door lot. "This is where we found the teeth." He pointed upward to a second-story window in 1426. "That's her bedroom. We figure she threw the teeth out when she thought we were going to search the house Friday. We got one body without any teeth."

"What would she do with teeth?" Frawley asked.

"Hard to ID someone without dental work. It's going to be hard to ID these bodies anyway. They're in bad shape." Enloe's broad face broke into a grin. He knew Puente's past record now. "Besides, some of them were gold teeth."

That made perfect sense.

We left, passing the backhoe busily starting to churn up the tiny front yard, where the shrine to St. Francis had stood, and where the seventh and last body would be found on Monday morning. The stone birdbath and stone squirrels that had led to the shrine were dumped to one side.

So we were all back in the Puente case after so many years. We didn't talk about what had gone wrong. There was too much for Frawley and O'Mara to do. No one knew where Puente was or what she was up to, and the case was getting hotter by the hour.

6

FOR TWO DAYS, PUENTE HAD BEEN STAYING AS HIDDEN AS possible in room 31. She watched TV or rested, the motel room curtains drawn. She took towels from the maid and kept her out.

At night, wearing her purple pumps and red coat, Puente went only as far as the T.G. Express restaurant. She added barbecue pork to her menu of chop suey and beer. Then she hurried back to her room. She read the local newspapers and learned that McCauley was in jail, and she herself was reported in cities from Mexico to Nevada.

The only human contact she had had was with the night clerk at the restaurant, who found the old woman with white hair very gracious and pleasant, quite out of place on Alvarado with its dubious businesses, garish signs, and declining apartments.

But Puente was growing restless and fretful. The police were all over the map now looking for her; the knock on the door could come at any time. And her money was slowly and inexorably dribbling away.

She had to find a safe haven, and she had to get more money very soon.

She drank her beer and ate chop suey and planned, as she had planned for years, how to provide for herself.

On Monday night in Sacramento, Cabrera and other detectives, with a video camera and still photographers, used Frawley's just signed search warrant to thoroughly take 1426 F Street apart for evidence.

Cabrera, Brown, and the others divided the house up by rooms. Cabrera took Puente's bedroom. It was crowded, the bed filling half of it, pushed near the dresser-bureau, itself crowded with perfume bottles, cosmetics, and pictures. Puente had enough clothes, expensive but anachronistic dresses in styles decades old, shoes, to make herself appear rich.

On the bed he saw the plush, heavy bedclothes, a blue stylish handbag tossed on it, a sign of Puente's hasty departure on Saturday. The bookshelves filled with paperback westerns, lurid romances, and mysteries made Cabrera wonder if Puente arrogantly believed she had read enough to trick the police. She had, of course, been very successful at doing just that.

From the bedroom window, Cabrera looked down on the dark, nighttime ruin of the backyard. Three people had been buried almost beneath that window. All of the bodies, in fact, had been under some marker—a toolshed, a fruit tree, a commode, a driveway, a shrine—whether to remind Puente where a body was buried or gloat over a kill, Cabrera never learned.

He quickly began finding pill bottles all around the bedroom, many for the tranquilizer Dalmane. It seemed to be everywhere. He went through each drawer of the bureau, hunting specifically for the drug. It was already clear that none of the victims at F Street had died by violence, although the headless body in the front yard might change that fact. Cabrera himself suspected the dead woman in the front yard had been mutilated after death to hide her identity.

It made very good sense, given Puente's past criminal history of drugging people in order to steal from them, to look for something that might render victims unconscious, or, in large amounts, kill them.

Cabrera was on to a solid lead. In the back of one drawer he found Dalmane capsules. Intrigued, he upended the wastebasket, sorting through the tissues, papers, trash. He was delighted to find fifteen empty Dalmane capsules. Someone had opened the capsules to pour the tranquilizer out, probably so that whoever was taking the drug wouldn't know it.

All of the evidence went into plastic bags or manila envelopes with the detectives' names and badge numbers on them and was recorded on the search warrant. Even if Puente wasn't found for years, the Homicide detectives wanted to maintain a clear, legally perfect chain of evidence for use in a trial.

No one wanted to even think about the possibility Puente was gone for good.

Cabrera and the other detectives turned their attention next to the "cursed" room Puente claimed existed near the kitchen. The investigation had revealed that she told tenants the foul smell coming from the room some months earlier was from a broken sewer line. She had shampooed the carpet many times to get rid of the odor, given up, and bought new carpet.

There was not much to see in the small room. Cabrera noted a bed covered with a quilt, more shelves of paperbacks, mops, and brooms. But something did smell peculiar. With another detective, Cabrera moved the bed, then some of the mops and brooms. The new blue carpet looked all right. Then they pulled it up. Both men coughed at the stink.

The second, original carpet had a large bloodstain on it and the mingled smell of bleach and blood was powerful.

This had nothing to do with Bert Montoya, however. Cabrera's training and the investigation told him that a decomposing body had lain in the room, leaking into the carpet, and Puente had not been prepared for that. Another missing tenant, Ben Fink, had gotten angrily drunk one night months before, something Puente hated. After trying to bully him into being quiet, she told the other tenants she would take "Ben upstairs and make him better." They saw her lead the swearing, feisty little man to her room, and then he was never seen again. She told the tenants Fink had left during the night.

Several days later, one tenant noticed what he described as "the smell of death" from the room near the kitchen.

Cabrera was certain Puente had left Fink's body in the room until she could decide what to do with it. It looked as though his body had been rolled up in the original carpet at some point. The carpets were torn up by the detectives, and the sound of wood being pried, slamming drawers, echoed through the house. It was a thorough, professional search, because Cabrera and the others knew that everything they did, in light of Puente's escape, was going to be scrutinized closely.

Frawley came by, checking on the search. Cabrera showed him a handwritten manuscript from Puente's bedroom, a Western novel. Puente told people she was a writer, along with her many other stories.

The detectives collected photographs from bookshelves and drawers. There were family shots of her "nephew" Ricardo Odorica and his children. Cabrera, Frawley, and the others looked with greater interest at pictures of Puente —younger, stout, wearing scarves and jewels, her white-blond hair done up in a stiff, obsolete hairdo from the 1940s—with famous people. Puente was standing with George Deukmejian, California's Attorney General, then Governor. She was photographed with Sacramento's Catholic bishop, a judge in his chambers, Representative Robert

Matsui, a leader in Congress. In some photos she was being given awards or plaques for work in the Hispanic community. She looked like a wealthy matron doing good works. All of the pictures had been taken within the last ten years.

She was a woman of contradictions and mystery, who could kill on charm, mix with the powerful and important or spend her days with the lowest members of the community.

Before they left the house around midnight, Cabrera and the detectives located prescriptions for Dalmane in Puente's name, and strange things like a driver's license with the name Betty Palmer and Puente's photo on it. There were letters in a dining room sewing cabinet to Vera Martin, bank deposit slips for Leona Carpenter.

Then, in a large envelope addressed to "Dr. Dorothea Puente," they discovered material to help identify the seven bodies. There was a medical ID for Bert Montoya in the envelope, along with a bank statement for Puente and Montoya, and another health card for Leona Carpenter. Dorothea Puente had wanted to keep this special information separate, apparently in case she needed to produce identification for people no longer able to identify themselves. In order to continue to get Social Security checks, or use a dead man's health benefits, Puente had to lay her hands on just the right documents. The envelope also held Veteran's Assistance papers for Dorothy Miller, Supplementary Security Income material for James Gallop, more letters to Vera Martin, letters to Ben Fink, his health card, and a medical card for Betty Palmer. The large envelope, clearly, had been hidden in the sewing cabinet drawer.

Cabrera was puzzled by several additional photos found of a smiling white-haired man with glasses. There were many names and faces to put to Puente's victims, and when the detectives left 1426 F Street Monday night, November 14, they were sure they had made a good start. But no one knew who the smiling man was that night.

A rookie cop, flashlight in hand for company, was left to guard the strange house. Floodlights blazed against it on the bitter cold November night, and the curious cars slowing down to look at the empty graves finally stopped coming and the street was silent.

7

ON TUESDAY, IF PUENTE HAD ANY IDEA OF THE FUROR SHE had stirred throughout the country, she was undoubtedly pleased. She always liked attention.

From Sacramento to Washington, agencies started investigations of their behavior in her case. The Department of Health Services in Sacramento ordered an investigation of how Puente, an ex-convict on federal parole too, could get medical assistance for her tenants and their Social Security checks every month. The Social Security Administration wanted to know that as well.

The DA was busy defending the police decision not to arrest Puente on Friday and the fact they had let her walk away on Saturday. John McCauley was quietly released from jail for lack of evidence and went into hiding from the reporters and cameras searching for him.

As for Sacramento Chief of Police John Kearns, he was in Los Angeles attending a conference of police chiefs and was spared the public criticism that his department was enduring. He refused his captains' repeated pleas to hurry back to Sacramento to defend the beleaguered department himself.

Joe Enloe was replaced as police spokesman on the case. It was a cosmetic change to show the department was sobering up after the giddiness of the first few days of international attention. News reports of the crimes had appeared in Europe and Australia.

To appease the public, the new police spokesman gruffly said that "every square inch of the yard" at 1426 F Street had been dug up. As he spoke, furniture, chairs, sofas, a mattress, desks, cans, filled boxes, were hefted from the house and dumped into trucks. Only Puente's large liquor supply, mostly vodka, in her bedroom and kitchen, was left untouched. There was no sign of any bodies inside 1426 F Street.

Nor did it appear that any more bodies would be found in the yard. The crowds, though, ever hopeful, stayed vigilant in front of the house through the next few days.

By the end of Tuesday, in fact, all digging had stopped. There had been a question whether Puente might have buried bodies at another boardinghouse she had run at 2100 F Street. It was a large, spacious house now owned by the family who lived in it. A new patio had been poured after Puente left, and the police were reluctant to tear it up. Metal probing, though, showed no sign of hidden graves.

The only other issue was the vacant lot across the street from 1426 F. A woman, perhaps looking like Puente, had been seen digging there in the recent past. Cabrera wanted to search the lot, primarily for the missing head, hands, and lower legs of the seventh body. O'Mara told the cops to do so quickly to avoid a rush of crowds and reporters. Digging aimlessly around the Alkali Flat neighborhood would only make everyone, police and DA, look more foolish. Sacramento was already in a state of wild excitement about the buried bodies.

Although Cabrera was convinced a neat package of body parts was buried in the lot, a police captain declared he was "putting an end to this media circus" and prohibited any digging in the lot.

The police and DA, with the piles of furniture, photos, drugs, had a monstrous puzzle to sort through anyway without going after evidence that might not contribute much to proving Puente's guilt.

That, anyway, was the thinking on Tuesday.

The FBI had come into the manhunt because Puente was supposed to have crossed state lines. The Sacramento police had roused their Las Vegas colleagues to watch the airport for her.

But on Wednesday, November 16, 1988, Dorothea Puente was still in Los Angeles and restless enough to venture out during the daylight. It was cool enough so she needed her red wool coat, but not damp, and she left her umbrella in room 31 at the Royal Viking.

It was good to get out of the room. Without maid service the empty chop suey cartons, beer bottles, newspapers were stacking up. She made the bed by throwing the covers over it. The air was thick.

She walked down slightly uneven sidewalks, buses rumbling by, through a welter of voices in Spanish, Korean, and English. It was a city Puente had known twenty years earlier when she was working more or less consistently as a prostitute. On Wednesday she was on the prowl again.

In her purple pumps she walked about a mile and a half from the motel, past salesmen watching for customers from doorways, cheap electronic stores, bus stops. Anyone who saw her could have called the police.

It might have been that awakening fear of discovery that made Puente turn at mid-afternoon into a bar, the Monte Carlo I, a neighborhood joint very much like her old Joe's Corner.

Inside, the room was dim, the bar horseshoe-shaped. A woman sitting at the far end watched Puente, then went back to drinking.

Puente sat down on a stool and ordered vodka and orange juice. There was a man at the bar, older, with glasses, with a worn and tired look that echoed Mervin John McCauley or several others she knew. He was sitting alone, midweek, midafternoon, drinking in a bar.

She did not start the conversation. The man politely said to her, "The heat from the refrigerator motor comes right out where you're sitting."

She thanked him, ordered another screwdriver, and picked up her purse and drink and moved to a barstool near him. She told him her name was Donna Johansson.

She asked him his name. He said he was Charles Willgues, he was a retired carpenter. He lived alone in an apartment about two blocks away on West 2nd Street. He had just bought a glass cutter and thought that a beer would taste good.

Willgues was impressed by the woman's bearing, her intelligence, and fashionable appearance. He talked easily to her, listened as she listed her tribulations.

Puente was, by turns, charming and put upon. As she drank she told Willgues that her shoes needed work. She turned her leg to him. She had done a lot of walking in the last few days. Her husband had died a month ago, and she had come south from Sacramento on Monday. She wanted to put her grief behind her, get a job, start a new life in a new city.

Willgues nodded. He knew all about grieving and struggling with hope.

But, Puente went on, my luck's been terrible since I got to Los Angeles. "I can't find work. I'm all alone. Everybody's been taking advantage of me since I got here."

She warmed to the tale. "Why, the cabdriver who brought me from the bus station was a crook. Do you know the Royal Viking Motel on Third and Alvarado?"

"Sure I do," Willgues said.

"Well, that cabdriver who took me there drove away with four of my suitcases. I've only got an overnight bag left. My shoes are all worn down, I've been walking so long trying to find a good place to stay."

Willgues offered to have her shoes fixed. There was a repair store nearby. Puente thanked him, fished out three dollars from her purse, and sat quietly drinking while he took her shoes.

It wasn't long before Willgues came back. Smiling gratefully, Puente slipped her purple pumps on again. Willgues had another beer. She had another screwdriver.

"How do you support yourself? Since you're retired?" she asked.

Willgues said he was sick and got Social Security. He had arthritis and emphysema and had suffered two strokes. He got a monthly check for $576.

"You could easily get $680!" she said quickly. "I can show you how to do it." She slipped in information about assistance payments and social service agencies to show her expertise.

They had been together about an hour and a half, and the November afternoon was softening outside the bar.

Puente put a proposition to Willgues, who plainly enjoyed her company. "We're two lonely people in a big city. I've got no one left, and you don't either. I hate spending holidays alone. Thanksgiving's coming up, and you should be with someone on Thanksgiving."

Willgues nodded. "I suppose so. I suppose it's better."

"I'm a very good cook. Why don't I make Thanksgiving dinner for you at your apartment?"

"Well, maybe. I don't know."

"Why don't we share an apartment? I can make life easier for you, straighten out your Social Security. Together life would be a lot easier for us both."

Willgues wasn't instantly persuaded. He had lived alone for years. "I've got enough to think about with myself," he said. "I don't want to take on somebody else." He did say he'd think about it.

"How about tomorrow?" Puente asked. "How about getting together again Thursday?"

Willgues agreed. They could go shopping for new clothes to replace the stolen ones. They could go out in the morning.

He gave her one of his business cards, *"Chuck the Handyman,"* and in large, confident strokes, Puente wrote on the back, "Donna Johansson, #31, 2025 3rd." Willgues added her phone number and the name of the motel underneath.

He called a cab for her because it seemed wrong to wear down her only good shoes right after they were repaired. Puente asked Willgues to buy her two dinners at a nearby fast-food chicken restaurant. She wanted to take them back to the motel and eat one later rather than go out on the dangerous city streets after 5:00 P.M.

"No wings, please," she said with a smile, handing Willgues twenty dollars for the dinners.

He got the dinners and had them ready for her by the time the cab showed up. "Remember our date tomorrow," Puente said.

"I'll call you first," Willgues agreed.

It was after four when Puente, balancing her hot dinners, slipped past the manager's office at the Royal Viking, into her room and locked the door.

It had been a profitable afternoon. She had a change of menu for dinner, a place to stay until Thursday, the prospect of new lodgings, and a man with health problems and Social Security benefits as a fresh companion.

Charles Willgues did not stay at the Monte Carlo I much longer after Donna Johansson left in the cab. He walked two blocks back to his apartment, thinking about her. He was puzzled. The bar was dim, but he'd had a good look at her.

He had a strange feeling he'd seen her face somewhere before.

But where? Why did she seem so familiar?

8

A GLOOMY, DROOPY-EYED JOHN KEARNS, SACRAMENTO'S CHIEF of Police, finally faced the massed cameras and rowdy reporters in the small makeshift press room. He had come back to Sacramento and landed in the middle of controversy about his own competence and his department's professionalism.

He promptly blamed Cabrera and others for letting Puente get away. "The Sacramento Police Department made an error. As a result, we lost a suspect."

The reporters asked blunt, unpleasant questions about why Kearns had stayed in Los Angeles, why the investigation looked so amateurish.

"She should have been followed. There aren't any excuses, as far as I'm concerned, why the suspect wasn't kept under surveillance."

He had a ready explanation, based on Puente's grandmotherly exterior and pliant behavior. "She'd been talked to by detectives and established a dialogue, and I feel that what occurred was that we possibly became too familiar with the suspect and too trusting."

Homicide detectives are not supposed to be lulled into trusting a suspect.

Kearns was angry, sharp, defensive for the entire press conference. His words shook the department because the Chief was not supporting his detectives, but hanging them out as problems to be fixed.

Cabrera, Brown, Enloe, and others were veterans of enough police department politics to recognize the sound of management closing ranks against them. No captain or supervisor or the Chief would be blamed for Puente's escape, her long murderous activities, or the anger if she was never caught.

At the Sacramento County Coroner's Office, a dour modern building looking like a suburban bank, connected to the Crime Lab, the third body dug up at F Street was taken from its wrappings, and laid out on a white metal table under bright white lights.

The third body had been chosen because it was a man and matched, roughly, the description of Bert Montoya.

Four people worked carefully over the body, talking calmly, noting down what they saw and did for use in court.

The body was wrapped in a green blanket that was sprinkled with lime and tied with string. At the head, giving it a comic appearance, the knot was tied in a bunch.

What struck the pathologists and technicians first were the almost obsessional number of inner wrappings around the body, fourteen in all, cloth, plastic, secured with duct tape, then a quilt, and more plastic. Finally, in a pathetic revelation, the man himself lay under the merciless lights. He weighed, now, about 128 pounds. He wore gray trousers, jockey shorts, striped socks and a white T-shirt and looked to be between 50 and 60 years old. What hair remained on his scalp was light brown and wispy. He had been buried in such a way that his arms were raised, elbows flexed, at the side of his head, as if warding off something.

He was grotesque, in advanced decomposition, swollen, discolored and dripping fluids. He did have a bit of side-burns and mustache left, but most had rotted off.

With his clothes cut off, bathed in white light, stared at, exposed completely, dirt brown, the man looked almost like a giant russet potato.

His fingers were cut off to use in developing any prints. Dropped into a bottle of formaldehyde, they would be sent to the California Department of Justice's Latent Fingerprint Section.

The pathologists carefully removed the vital organs, noting some liver enlargement and hardening of the arteries. Brain tissue was preserved, and blood specimens taken. From these it might be possible to detect the presence of any drugs. Drugs tended to collect in brain matter or remain in blood, but the body's severe decay, like that of the other six from 1426 F Street, would make the task of detection very complicated and uncertain. The man's brain, for example, had decayed considerably, leaving a residue that had collapsed against the rear of the skull in a puttylike mass.

From the examination of fingerprints, a 1984 mastoid operation matched by body number three at the autopsy, the coroner announced that this was indeed Alvaro "Bert" Montoya.

Bert's eighty-two-year old mother, living in New Orleans, was notified. Moise and Valentine took the expected but still shattering news with a combination of resignation and bitterness. They had known something was wrong with Dorothea Puente and yet Bert had been forced to go back to 1426 F Street when he tried to get away.

Who else, they wondered, of their lonely, sad clients, lay on metal trays in the coroner's office, waiting to be identified?

For them and the police and DA, the questions remained stark. What had killed Bert? Or the others?

And who, Cabrera wondered, was the smiling, white-haired man with glasses in the photo in Puente's dining room? Why had she kept the picture hidden?

Worse, for everyone seeking answers, would Dorothea Puente ever be found? Earlier that day, at his raucous, uncomfortable press conference, Chief Kearns had allowed himself one bit of sensational speculation. In answer to a question, Kearns had said, "If someone's going to kill seven people, why stop there?"

Around 9:00 P.M. Wednesday night, Puente got a phone call. The local newscasts had again featured her face, her alleged seven murders, the vast law enforcement army seeking her across America.

It was Charles Willgues on the phone. He wanted to see how she was doing and whether they were still going out in the morning.

Puente said yes, they were, she had eaten the dinner he got her, and she'd be staying in that night.

When she hung up after Willgues's call, Puente was full and drowsy after a long day. She had been drinking screwdrivers and beer, eaten two chicken dinners. Her future security was shaping up. She could look forward to Thursday and her next meeting with Chuck the handyman who was apparently very interested.

PART 2

The mass murderer lies to himself.

William Bolitho,
Murder for Profit

9

WHO WAS DOROTHEA PUENTE AND WHERE HAD SHE COME FROM? Was there something in her early life, however much it was like that of millions of other people who never killed anyone, that set her toward murder?

There are mysteries around Puente, but some central answers, too.

The basic truth about her is that she always sought control. Her essential appetite was to control the people and situations around her. From an early age she was a practiced liar, graduating to minor crimes, then more serious ones, and finally murder. But the basic purpose of every criminal act was to control the world she lived in.

So Puente invented a glamorous past for herself, called herself a lawyer or doctor, and claimed a love affair with the Shah of Iran and a movie career. She was a smart, resourceful, and very attractive woman for much of her life, but also a very disturbed one.

In 1985, as she was about to be released back to Sacramento after serving time in prison for drugging, robbery, and forgery, a psychologist for the state Department of Corrections did an in-depth evaluation of the new parolee. He might have been describing Dorothea Montalvo Puente's entire life to that point:

> Montalvo appears to disassociate herself from any of the crimes for which she has been arrested and received time. She tends to minimize the importance of what she did or her responsibility for any of them [*sic*].
>
> It appears at this time that although Montalvo does not evidence any symptoms of psychosis—that is, hearing voices or having delusions of grandeur—that she is in fact, schizophrenic. . . .
>
> This woman is a disturbed woman who does not appear to have remorse or regret for what she has done, and who at least on two occasions has been involved with administering drugs and/or poison to unwitting victims. She is to be considered dangerous, and her living environment and/or employment should be closely monitored.

Puente told the psychologist she loved children and would enjoy being a baby-sitter, but the psychologist wisely concluded that she should be kept away from children and the elderly; vulnerable people were at grave risk when Puente was near them.

Yet this dangerous woman had shown great kindness and lavished attention on a number of orphaned or poor Mexican girls, helped sick people around Alkali Flat, and genuinely contributed to Hispanic community groups, even though she wasn't Hispanic.

But the anomaly evaporates in light of Puente's lifelong yearning for attention and control. As a rough boardinghouse mistress or civic benefactress, she achieved the control and respect she desperately coveted.

It was the same hunger that set her up for years as a

prostitute, where, paradoxically, her degree of control over others may have been the greatest.

The only problem for Puente as a great community leader and charitable donor was that her dream life required real money. She first got money through theft and forgery, then murder.

Why did Puente turn to murder? Her adulthood was cleft by two great calamities. In 1978 she lost her status as a well-off civic leader when she was convicted on federal forgery charges. This loss of position devastated her. When she was faced again, in 1982, with actually going to prison and losing her self-created role as a community figure, she first resorted to murder, killing Ruth Munroe in order to get quick money to flee the country.

After she got out of prison in 1985, Puente had no hesitation about killing again and again to protect her control, her dream image as a fashionable, important woman.

But where did the roots of murder lie? Killing for profit isn't predestined, yet in the mundane, sad details of Puente's unhappy childhood and later life, at least a fuller picture of this awful and driven woman exists.

"When I was 3 years old, I had to start picking cotton, potatoes, cucumbers, chilis, then fruits. I finally married when I was 18, he died after a few days."

So Puente began a letter to a judge in 1982, hoping to reduce her prison sentence. Like her life itself, Puente's letter mixes a little fact with much fiction in order to manipulate the observer. Her husband did not die nor was she married at 13. But her early years were hard and formative.

Born Dorothea Helen Gray on January 9, 1929 in Red-lands, a moderately sized city in San Bernardino County, California, Puente was the sixth of seven children. She later claimed to be the youngest of eighteen brothers and sisters.

Her father was Jesse James Gray from Missouri. Gray

fought in World War I and was severely burned by mustard gas; as a result he developed tuberculosis. The war, his continuing illness and debility, left Gray deeply depressed, which he sometimes expressed by saying he wanted to kill himself. He let his children, including little Dorothea, know that he thought life was vicious, mean, and he was the object of unfair treatment.

Puente's mother was Trudy Mae Gates and had come from Oklahoma. She was tougher, physically and emotionally, than her husband. A small-faced, pretty woman, she had a rough, rebel nature from the start of the marriage.

Because the Depression left the sick, despondent man Gray with little opportunity, the whole family worked at jobs around Redlands, sometimes moving with crops. It was an unpleasant, cold life, the children often left to fend for themselves when their parents argued bitterly, or more frequently, drank heavily. Trudy particularly, drank and stayed away from her husband and children. The older children took care of the younger ones, and Puente was essentially raised by her older brothers and sisters.

She had learned an interesting trick before she was six or seven years old. By faking illness or fabricating complex fantasies about her importance, Puente escaped the drudgery and terrors of early childhood. During the times she spent in school, Puente was often chastised by her teachers for lying.

In 1935, Gray was in and out of hospitals for increasingly futile treatment of his TB. While he was gone, Trudy spent much of her time with a motorcycle gang. She would lock Dorothea and an older brother in a closet for days at a time when she left. On her return, she threw up, made other messes, and Dorothea was expected to clean up after her. Trudy spent time in county jail, too, for drunkenness, leaving her seven children without either parent at home.

But when Trudy was at home, she lectured Dorothea about helping other people and the need to be of service to others. "Mother once made me promise to feel sorry for alcoholics and to take care of drunks," Puente said later in life. It is obvious that raised in a household in a constant uproar, with a mother often drunk or in jail, Puente early on formed her mixed detestation of drunks and her desire to make them better.

The family moved to Los Angeles in late 1936, where Gray's health faded inexorably and Trudy's drunken sprees continued, as did her time in jail. Dorothea joined her mother, and the remaining children who had not been split up between other relatives or neighbors, in February 1937. The household was coming apart completely.

Gray had gone back into the hospital in December 1936, and his condition never improved. He died on March 29, 1937, after Dorothea had been reunited with him only for a month.

Left with several children to raise, Trudy moved them to San Dimas, a smaller city, dry and dusty at the end of 1937. Her drinking was steady and brutal for Dorothea and the remaining children. When this became apparent to teachers and others who saw the children, Trudy lost custody of Dorothea in early 1938. Nine years old, with a sad-eyed, pretty face, Dorothea entered an orphanage run by the Church of Christ in Ontario, California. Her endless lying and imaginative fantasies were remarked on by the staff who cared for the unhappy, abandoned little girl.

On December 27, 1938, Trudy was killed in a motorcycle accident and Dorothea, now a true orphan, was desolated. No amount of dreaming or hard work had succeeded in saving either her mother or her father, keeping her brothers and sisters together, or preventing her from being left with strangers in an orphanage.

But Dorothea was not merely a little girl with a wretched childhood. She was also highly intelligent and had hardened around her a carapace of self-sufficiency. If she could not save others or trust them to take care of her, she would have to do it herself.

Sent to live with a succession of near relatives or older brothers or sisters, Puente rarely spent more than a few months in any one place, living a nomadic, unsettled life.

She was in Napa at the age of thirteen, then dipped for one semester into school in Los Angeles at sixteen.

At sixteen, Dorothea was dark-haired and slim, with hard black eyes, an appraising attitude toward people. By her lies and actions, she was going to shape the world to her wishes rather than let the world buffet her further. Her beauty was a tool, able to bend people to do as she wished.

World War II found Dorothea no better off than she had been in the thirties, until in 1945 she was sent back to Los Angeles to live with an older sister and her husband. But Dorothea, now alive to the possibilities offered by her own attractiveness, ran away, heading north. She was perceived by another sister, many years later, as having changed forever. "Sometimes," Dorothea's sister said in 1988, "when people have a hard childhood, their own world is so hard, they make up a pretend one."

Dorothea ended up in Olympia, Washington, in the summer of 1945, as the war was ending. She had invented a name for herself—Sheri—and worked as a waitress in a milkshake parlor. She had also begun working, for the first time, as a prostitute.

Prostitution was a simple way to capitalize on her physical beauty, make up any story she liked about her identity, and control her customers, too. As a prostitute, for the first time in her life, she felt she had a form of power.

It is also possible that Trudy Gray had worked, at least some of the time, as a prostitute, and brought customers home while Jesse was away or in the hospital. Trudy ran with a motorcycle gang, had trouble holding a job, drank heavily, and needed money. It was a recipe for prostitution.

Dorothea never had any scruples about being a hooker and since she learned so many things, or transmuted them like the advice about helping drunks, from her mother, it is possible she picked up prostitution as well.

After working for several months as Sheri, Dorothea met a twenty-two year old soldier coming back from the Philippines. His name was Fred McFaul and he was about six years her senior. McFaul discovered Dorothea and a girlfriend using a motel room as a trick pad. That did not bother him. He found Dorothea wildly attractive and even admired her ruthless desire to survive. She would do almost anything, he realized. Years later from a hospital bed, McFaul said, "She knew how to make a buck when she wanted to."

No matter what her problems were, McFaul determined to marry Dorothea and did so in November 1945 in Reno, Nevada. Although she was still sixteen, Dorothea listed her age as thirty on the marriage certificate and invented a fuller, imaginary maiden name for herself, Sherriale A. Riscile. The name puzzled her new husband, but he was getting used to her constant confabulations, the endlessly spun tales about her life, things she had done, the things she planned to do. When they met strangers, around town or at bars, McFaul marveled at his new bride's capacity to con anyone. She could smile, chat, tell a tall tale, and in a few minutes, convince anyone she had just recounted the honest truth. She was a fashion model, an actress, royalty, anything at all.

By 1945, having followed her mother's footsteps and married a returning soldier, Dorothea McFaul started drinking in earnest, and tried to start a family.

For the first two years of her marriage to McFaul, Dorothea lived in the remote, dusty little town of Gardnerville, Nevada. She had two daughters between 1946 and 1948, but couldn't stand to have either child around her. She and McFaul quarreled with the same intensity and bitterness as her parents had. The couple would not raise the children, Dorothea hated the idea, and McFaul was unable to prevent his strong-willed wife from doing as she pleased.

The first daughter was sent to live with relatives in Sacramento. The second, in 1948, was put up for adoption. Dorothea's second and last living child grew up as Linda and spent years tracing her biological mother, anxious to learn where she had come from.

The drinking and fights with McFaul, the strain of giving her second child to strangers, sent Dorothea to Los Angeles for about a month. She probably went back to prostitution to support herself. McFaul, even through the haze of their quarrels and many years, thought back on Dorothea in 1988 and said, "She was a good-looking female," with admiration.

After she went back to McFaul and the narrow life in Gardnerville, Dorothea miscarried, and it was this that apparently brought the marriage to a final end. McFaul had put up with her strange ideas, fancies, her lust for constant attention and compliments, and found that he could no longer trust her to tell him even the most basic truth. He left her in late 1948 and they later divorced.

For a woman with her difficulty maintaining a sense of self-importance and respect, McFaul's departure was a wounding blow. For the rest of her life, Dorothea Puente told everyone that her husband had died soon after they were married, sometimes as quickly as within two days.

She left Nevada and went back to California, heading for San Bernardino, another dry, dusty city in the southern part of the state, and near where she had been raised. Dorothea struggled through a succession of jobs, and at last embarked on the path of crimes that eventually took her to 1426 F Street and murder.

She began stealing checks in 1948 from a woman she had befriended. She used the checks to buy shoes, stockings, a hat, and purse. The next day she tried to buy $84.83 worth of shoes using a check drawn on the account of Sherriale A. Riscile, her imaginary name.

But Dorothea was not the practiced con artist she later became. Something in her nervous manner aroused the suspicion of the store manager and he refused the check. She hurried out and, almost in a panic, took a bus to the nearby city of Ontario.

But, by that time, the manager had alerted the police. They knew about the earlier forgeries and that Riscile was an alias. They were waiting when Dorothea arrived in Ontario and arrested her.

For the first time in her life, she was seen by a doctor. He was interested in her mental state, to see if she knew the nature of the charges and if she was mentally competent. Dorothea's lies to her woman friend and the store manager had apparently raised doubts about her emotional balance.

The county appointed doctor learned that the sometimes haughty, sometimes weeping young woman he talked to, had a "compelling need to buy clothes and re-establish her own self-esteem." It was a diagnosis repeated for forty years about her. She was not, the doctor told the court, "a true criminal," but really only "a situational offender." She would commit crimes only when opportunities presented themselves and she thought she could evade punishment.

Dorothea did not want to go to trial and expose her dream life to the rigors of cross-examination by a prosecutor or the judge. She worked out a plea bargain, as she would do again for forty years, and told the judge she was indeed guilty of two counts of felony forgery and one count of writing a fictitious check. She was sentenced to a year in county jail, based on the favorable report of the doctor, and actually served only four months.

In jail, faced with adult punishment at last, Dorothea's hardened self-sufficiency and survival instincts took over. She was respected by the other women for her brains, and her ability to get along with the guards. She begged or scrounged small favors, like candy and cigarettes, for herself and her friends.

When she was released, Dorothea moved north, having told her probation officer she lived in San Francisco. But in May 1950, only six months after her release, Dorothea disappeared. In Riverside County, which had jurisdiction over her probation, a judge issued a warrant for her arrest. While in jail, Dorothea had picked up useful knowledge about how the criminal justice system worked. Warrants for a routine small time forger would usually go to the bottom of a deep stack of other warrants for more serious crimes.

Dorothea was never arrested on the Riverside warrant. She changed her name again, kept moving, and even her relatives, the brothers and sisters she still wrote to, finally lost track of her. For a long time during the fifties, her family thought she was dead.

She was very much alive, though, and had probably returned to prostitution for easy money and to maintain her dream life. In 1952, Dorothea met and married Axel Johansson, who was as captivated by the smart, bustling, beautiful woman as Fred McFaul had been. He, too, was at first beguiled, then bewildered, then angry with her endless lies and stories.

Over the next few years the couple set up housekeeping in northern California in Sacramento or nearby cities. But Dorothea was restless and left for long periods, returning to Los Angeles, drifting around. When she did come back to Johansson, they fought about her absences and her being a hooker. Once again Dorothea was replicating her own home life with Jesse and Trudy.

But she was very much her own woman. She had learned a lot in jail, and while working as a hooker. By 1960, Dorothea had opened and run several brothels, sometimes employing several other women, or just herself and one other woman. She had far more business sense and fewer scruples than her mother ever did.

But boldness and brains, like luck, go only so far. In early 1960, Dorothea was once again the object of serious law enforcement interest.

The slim, lively young woman McFaul had married in 1946 had grown fat by 1960, still attractive, but over thirty years old, too. Dorothea was having considerable trouble working as a hooker, and no amount of makeup or carefully draped clothing could hide her diminishing sexual appeal.

It reached the point that she started brothels, acting primarily as the madam, only sometimes as a hooker. If Johansson protested, Dorothea still had her own money now and could keep away from him.

Her luck ran out in April 1960. The owner of a property on Fulton Avenue in Sacramento complained to the Sheriff's Department that what he thought was being rented as a bookkeeping service was actually a whorehouse. He was indignant and demanded something be done to stop it.

The phony bookkeeping service had a special telephone number for clients. The specialty of the house was a blow job for seven dollars and fifty cents.

Two deputy sheriffs staked out the address. They saw men coming in and out all day. The business, whatever it was, kept very regular hours, and closed promptly at 5:00 P.M.

Whoever was running the office had camouflaged it well and demonstrated they were clever. The sheriffs set up a sting to catch the operator in the act.

Two deputies dressed as truckers and rented a semitrailer and tractor. They coated twenty-five dollars in five-dollar bills with fluorescent powder as bait money. The deputies put powder on their hands, too.

They then went to a phone booth several miles from Fulton Avenue and used the special number to call the business. A woman answered and said they could come ahead. She would take care of them for the usual price—$7.50 apiece.

With backup squad cars nearby, the phony truckers drove their rig up to the Fulton Avenue address. The woman who met them at the door was in her early thirties, large built, with penetrating black eyes. She looked pretty in a fleshy way. She said her name was Teya Johansson, and she and her associate, Bonnie Lacoste, would happily service the two men.

Johansson told the deputies that she preferred giving blow jobs to customers, but would agree to a straight fuck if the men would use rubbers. Since there was only one bed, Lacoste would take the first trucker, and Johansson would give his friend some coffee while they waited. Johansson then reconsidered. She would only give a blow job after all.

She took fifteen dollars in fluorescently marked money from one of the deputies. He abruptly asked if her breasts were as big as they looked. Johansson smiled and said both men could fondle them, for free, if they liked. One deputy, to complete the sting, put his hand inside Johansson's dress and rubbed a breast, coating it with powder.

The two deputies followed Lacoste to the lone bed and watched her undress. As she raised her skirt, one deputy touched her legs and buttocks to mark her. Then a surprised Johansson and Lacoste were arrested for prostitution. The marked bait money was retrieved from an annoyed Johansson. Other evidence seized from the office included Johansson's trick appointment book, which listed regular customers at rates varying from seven dollars down to fifty cents.

Taken downtown, to the old county jail, a matron stripped both women. Johansson did not protest much. Using an ultraviolet light, the matron passed it over Johansson's naked body, the fluorescent powder glowing blue on her breast, back, and knee.

Dorothea Puente, using the false name Teya Johansson when talking to people face to face, had employed a different phony name when she called a month or two earlier from Los Angeles to rent the Fulton Avenue property. She had said she was going to be doing business in bookkeeping, mostly with men from Reno.

Puente had progressed very far from the simple motel room she used as a trick pad in 1945.

Still clinging to the false Teya Johansson name, Puente was charged finally with being in a house of ill repute, a misdemeanor. She had sidestepped the tougher charge of pimping and pandering by agreeing to plead guilty quickly. Like her 1948 forgery plea, Puente calculated that a quick plea, a lighter sentence, was better than risking cross-examination. She had a sophisticated sense of survival and what the criminal justice system could do to her.

Standing before the judge, looking puzzled, contrite, and motherly, Puente said she had been visiting a girlfriend when the deputies arrived. The judge didn't believe her and gave her ninety days in county jail.

She served her time without incident and continued to lie about the crime for thirty years. The actual arrest report, she knew, for a misdemeanor charge, would sink swiftly under the tide of new cases, so she could lie about it with impunity.

When she got out of jail, Puente went back to Axel Johansson, who must have been furious she had used part of her married name as a hooker. They went on fighting, Puente spending more time away from Johansson. The couple moved to Broderick, across the river from Sacramento, and lived there for three years. Puente held down a series of short-term jobs, a cook, a dishwasher, anything that came along, while buying clothes and make up constantly.

Finally, as McFaul had done before him, Johansson could not stand the mysterious absences of his wife, her erratic behavior, lies, drinking, scheming, and he sued for divorce in 1966.

This ended the first phase of Dorothea Puente's life. As the sixties and her second marriage came to a close, she had reckoned that prostitution was too small-time and risky for her. Nearly forty years old and growing quite fat, she turned to what became her life's occupation: looting health care businesses while elaborating a continuously imagined past of glamor, danger, and sacrifice.

10

Casting a predatory eye around the landscape of Sacramento in 1968, Dorothea Puente searched for the elderly, ill, or alcoholic. These were people left largely on the margins of society. But they still got bountiful state and federal checks, payments that could add up if one bundled these people all together in one place.

So Puente, who had learned how to operate a business profitably as a madam and hooker, opened the first of several unlicensed health care operations. She called it "The Samaritans," and it specialized in alcoholics, those people Trudy had made Dorothea promise to help. The bonus for Puente was that she could siphon off a little bit of money paid to each client and have a steady, untaxable income.

It was not a large operation. It was a testing ground for Puente, who learned as much from her mistakes as her successes. She supplemented "The Samaritans" income by hiring herself out as a twenty-four-hour-a-day caretaker and "nurse" for the elderly or invalided.

Working from a small building at the Capitol Guest

House on Alhambra Boulevard, Dorothea Johansson, as she now called herself, impressed every social worker who came by with her kindly manner and her concern for the alcoholics she tended. But Puente was also a stern woman, physically taking the drunks in hand, making them follow her schedule of meals and medication. She seemed, thought the social workers, so *motherly* in her compassion.

Puente learned to curry favor with city inspectors and social workers who came by. They could always find a sandwich waiting or a fresh piece of pie. She threw montly dinners for them, the whole groaning table of alcoholics and social workers, presided over by a beaming hostess.

In return for all of the attention she gave to others, Dorothea Puente only insisted that she be made payee for any money due her boarders and she have complete control over their checks.

If her public face was benign, orderly, secure, Puente in private was in disarray. She had ballooned up to nearly 200 pounds on a five-foot-eight-inch form, and she was drinking consistently and constantly in the evenings.

She began courting younger men, especially Hispanics. At the same time that she discovered the financial rewards of helping others, Puente also found that Hispanics were having a hard time in Sacramento. As a child in Redlands, working in the fields, she had known many migrant farmworkers. She had grown up around Mexicans and had learned some Spanish. People who were struggling to make a decent living, facing neglect, ostracized, were Puente's people. She could both comfort and master them, and these were always her intertwined compulsions.

She met and married a young Hispanic named Roberto José Puente who was twenty-one years old. She was thirty-nine. The disparity in their ages was matched by a collision of interests and attitudes. Dorothea dressed as fashionably as possible to hide her bulk, and acted like a great lady in public. She assumed she was important. Her new husband was boyish, without noticeable skill at any job.

The marriage was a flop from the start. The two, married in Reno, went back to Sacramento and fought every day. For perhaps the only time, Dorothea Puente misread another person's hopes and found herself on the short end of a bargain. She liked to use others as a meal ticket, not the other way around.

After only two bitter weeks, Roberto left her. She sued for divorce in 1969. Recounting this misadventure later, Dorothea said she had gotten married in Mexico after she visited relatives there. She claimed the man turned out to be a homosexual and they were married for seven years.

Shaken by the experience with Roberto, faltering in her motherly facade, Puente's business foundered. "The Samaritans" was $10,000 in debt, and she declared bankruptcy the same time as divorcing Roberto.

But she had picked up lessons in management, how many boarders she could handle, how to con outsiders, and most important, how to fully control the daily lives of her boarders and their money.

Within a short time, Dorothea was back in business as a board-and-care operator, in much larger quarters, with a more ambitious program.

She had leased a large three-story house at 21st and F Streets. It was a white, square house, Victorian and grand. It had sixteen small bedrooms and bathrooms and each room, like a hotel, contained a bed, television, and closets. Puente appropriated the entire third floor as her own residence, living literally over her boarders, as she would do again later at 1426 F.

In the ground floor she put the more affluent boarders who were on federal assistance. She relegated the poorest, county-assisted tenants to the basement in what one former tenant called "little cubicles with just curtains separating them."

But the change from the first operation was dramatic. Puente had up to two cooks permanently on staff, and on holidays she threw lavish parties for the social workers who sent people to her. Since the tenants Puente accepted did not require any specific medical or psychological program, she did not have to license the operation.

A cozy relationship developed between her and the social workers. Their perpetual problem was finding someone who would care for alcoholics, and Puente was happy to do so, provided she gained control over the assistance checks that came in.

It was a neat, nearly immaculate house. The dinner table was set carefully, gleaming with glassware. Even the refrigerator looked spotless. Keeping a place so clean with up to thirty problem drinkers going in and out was a tough job. Puente again impressed any official visitors with her loving care toward her tenants combined with a willingness to swear at them, push them, and compel them to take medication or follow her direction. She appeared to be the answer to a social worker's dream.

The only slight defect many people saw in her was a wild imagination. Not content to run a large alcoholic board-and-care facility well, Puente described herself variously as a medical doctor or a lawyer. She claimed acquaintance with famous actresses and public people, and said she had not only been on the Bataan Death March, but had survived the atomic bombing of Hiroshima as well.

Her official guests, eating a piece of pie she had offered, watching her sympathetically pat a troubled drunk, invariably decided to simply discount the lies and concentrate on her real accomplishments.

She had, though, gone a little further than many realized. In an office downstairs at 2100 F Street, Puente hung phony printed medical diplomas, bought medical equipment like blood pressure cuffs and syringes, and held herself out as "La Doctora." She gave what she claimed were vitamin shots to people who came to her informal clinic. Most were from the surrounding Hispanic neighborhood, and Puente provided an easy, friendly service.

One physician who stopped by 2100 F Street every month to examine the people living there found a willing assistant in Puente. She told him she was a qualified doctor, too, but he brushed that aside because he was impressed with her management of the business.

The two of them would set up in the kitchen, at the long table, the real doctor at one end, Puente at the other, and each tenant would come in, be checked over, then given a prescription if necessary. Puente acted as a stern lecturer, warning the tenants to take the medicine.

She could, though, blow her top. Sloppy drunks infuriated her.

If she saw a drunk in the house, Puente would rage instantly, her voice raised, cursing loudly and furiously. Her salty language startled people like the visiting physician, but he noticed that her rage had one salutary effect: the drunk never came around the house under the influence again.

Both the physician and other social service workers who dropped in unannounced to check on Puente's operation, conceded that she ran a tight, efficient business at 2100 F Street. Out of sight of these visitors, though, Puente had fights with tenants at night, especially when she had been drinking, and sometimes either she or the tenant ended up bloodied.

By the mid-seventies, Puente embarked on the two major enterprises of her life that transformed her into a woman of importance and compassion. She became a civic leader and she took struggling young Hispanics, usually women, under her wing.

"My impression was that she was a lonely person," Puente's lawyer in 1975, Don Dorfman, recalled. Busy with 2100 F Street, she nevertheless seemed to need something more to make her happy.

Puente solved her problem by devoting her considerable energy to making a mark in the downtown Hispanic community. She already served it as a "doctor," now she opened her purse as well.

Meeting a young Hispanic announcer without a job, Puente used her contacts in the community to launch his career on Spanish-language radio. She sponsored events, for medical aid or housing and donated money generously. No one cared where the money came from. The well-dressed, matronly Puente told anyone who asked that she was a rich woman who owned homes all over the world.

One of her pet charities was Hispanic performers, singers and musicians. Puente sponsored their entry into the United States, got them airtime on Spanish-language radio or television, acted almost as their agent.

By 1977, Puente's relentless promotion and good works had earned her a genuine place among Sacramento's Hispanics. She was always available to give money, make a phone call, or organize an event.

But she didn't limit her activities to charity. Puente also became a major contributor to political candidates. Her lawyer recalled one event when she bought an entire table at a fund raiser for Democratic Congressman Mervyn Dymally who was running to become California's Attorney General. Puente, dressed in her most elegant gown, her hair beautifully set and shining, sat at the table while the hundreds of politicians and other donors swirled around and stopped by to pay their respects.

She was always gracious, grand. Dymally came over, warmly embraced her and kissed her. They talked like old friends about his chances for election and the wonderful things he would do.

As people began dancing, California's Governor Jerry Brown, strolled over, also clasping the white-haired smiling Puente. He kissed her too, and, taking her hand, the two of them danced out among the important and wealthy campaign contributors. Puente had gone far on audacity and willpower. She had been in jail, worked for years as a hooker, and now danced at the pinnacle of California's political establishment.

Along the way, Puente did not limit herself to one political party. She also gave money lavishly to Republican candidates and posed for pictures with George Deukmejian, then Attorney General, later Governor. Bishop Francis Quinn praised her for her work in the Hispanic community and had his picture taken with her. Puente found herself the subject of glowing articles in Spanish-language newspapers published in Roseville and Sacramento.

But public honors and attention did not satisfy her. She hungered for something else, too. Her loneliness struck many people who saw her in 1976 and 1977. She frequently went to bars at night dressed in expensive fashions, made up with the most costly cosmetics, and struck up conversations with people she met, telling tall tales about her exploits. Some tales, though, were true.

If she didn't go out at night, and was sure that no one would drop in, Puente drank heavily and became that violent, obscenely cursing drunk that her mother had been and she herself detested.

Starting in the mid-seventies, Puente had begun accumulating hard-pressed young women, who found in her the mother they themselves did not have. One summer she took in twin sisters, both nine years old, and tutored them on how to be proper young ladies. She gave them motherly love as well, and protected them from their own abusive home lives. It was a story repeated a dozen times.

Puente's lawyer was surprised, at first, when she appeared in his office with children in tow, sad-eyed little girls in bright dresses.

"This is my stepdaughter," Puente would declare proudly, "Rose." The names changed: Catherine, Maria, Deborah. Sometimes Puente said the children were her adopted daughters, although she never went through any legal process to make it so. In her own mind, the dozen or more little girls were her children, stand-ins for the two real daughters she had given away and lost track of entirely.

Puente wanted her lawyer to take care of all kinds of legal problems for the girls and their parents. Credit problems, divorces, bankruptcies, she paid for all of them. The impression Dorothea Puente made on these people, especially the girls, was deep and loving. Later, as grown women, many credited Puente with saving them from jail or death.

She showed them how a caring, motherly person acted and spoke. She instilled self-reliance, a strong sense of femininity. "You are in my mind and my heart," one now grown-up protégée of Puente's from those years said recently. Another summed up the feelings of all of them: "I just hate to think about where I would be today if this woman had not touched my life."

Puente, always hard to unravel, was a contradictory collection of compassionate impulses and radical selfishness. These were contradictions that grew worse, more extreme, as the years went on.

Around 1977, Puente entered a hospital for surgery. Her weight had grown morbid and she needed a jejunal-ileo bypass to close part of her intestine to prevent her from gaining more weight and to shed a lot as well. As she had done since childhood, Puente exaggerated the illness. She had told visitors to 2100 F Street that she had a fatal heart disease and various forms of cancer. The only real cancer she had was a basal cell growth on the tip of her nose, which was treated successfully. She did have her thyroid removed, leaving a neck scar, but her health was actually quite good, given the amount of alcohol and stress she subjected herself to.

Puente summoned her lawyer to her hospital bedside before her corrective surgery. She had asked the Seventh-Day Adventists, who sent tenants to her, to pray for her. She told them she was going to die.

Propped up in bed, alternately feeble, then domineering, Puente ordered her lawyer to draw up a will. She named each of her "stepdaughters" with a bequest. Then she set up educational scholarships for them. Her lawyer dutifully scratched down the will. It was a document fit for a grand lady, a political force, a wealthy woman who had homes everywhere.

The catch lay in the fact that Puente had nowhere near the money needed to actually make the bequests. It was another fantasy. She did have money, but it was all stolen. At $200 to $300 per month per tenant, Puente had been keeping most of the assistance checks sent to her tenants, using the cash to finance her grand style in politics and her charities. Her alcoholic tenants got only room and board while she took their money.

After her operation she went back to 2100 F Street. By now her dreams of glamour and the financial demands on her were getting out of hand. A day of accounting was drawing down on her.

But before the blow fell, Dorothea Puente fell in love and married for the fourth and last time.

Puente had started noticing a young Mexican laborer working the grounds at 2100 F Street. His name was Pedro Angel Montalvo. He was bouncy, almost too high-strung and excitable, and by July 1975 he had lived at the boarding-house for a year. Puente began spending more time with him, inviting him to the third floor, taking him to her favorite bars. She even introduced him to some of the management of the business, careful to keep all of the financial pieces in her own hands.

They got married in 1976, again for Puente, in Reno. Montalvo apparently started having second thoughts as soon as the ceremony was over. Dorothea was about ten years his senior, yet she wavered strangely between acting much older, especially for visiting social workers, or trying to act much younger. She had a constant need for clothes, trips to the beauty parlor, shoes.

As for Montalvo, he did not impress others. Puente's lawyer Dorfman candidly thought Montalvo was crazy, jumping around the office, talking loudly, bragging, acting excitable. The physician who saw the tenants at 2100 F Street agreed with Dorfman. He believed Montalvo had married this chunky, tale-spinning older woman simply to get permanent residence in the United States and access to her money and her car. Both men, like others who observed Dorothea Puente at this time, were utterly amazed that the sober, if quaintly fibbing woman, who mothered and bossed others, would marry someone so different from herself.

Montalvo had his own worries. He believed that his new wife was lying about her wealth. She lived as if she were rich, but he suspected she was stealing to support her grandeur.

As she had with Roberto Puente, Dorothea started quarreling with Montalvo at once. They separated soon after the Reno ceremony, got together again briefly, and then Montalvo agreed to an annulment. If he hoped to tap into a rich woman, he had struck fool's gold instead.

Dorothea Puente claimed Montalvo was physically abusive from the moment they were married. He beat her, she said, and stabbed her between the eyes. In their first married week, she alleged that Montalvo killed her pet cat, broke windows at 2100 F Street, and slashed the tires of her car. However much of this was invention, theirs was not a happy marriage, and Dorothea Puente was certainly incapable of having one. Her pattern, from McFaul through Montalvo was invariant, and always replayed the scenes she had been part of between her own father and Trudy. So in 1982 when she wrote to a judge, seeking leniency, she wrote with absolute falsity, "All my problems started when I married Mr. Montalvo." They were much older, more intractable than a sour late-life marriage could cause.

Through the harrowing stress of running a business, playing mother to surrogate daughters, sponsoring Hispanic causes, Puente also whisked in and out of homes as a nurse. She stole small things, sometimes checks, from her sick or elderly patients. But she always came through the door with a smile.

Everyone—bartenders, cabdrivers, tenants, social workers, and her housebound patients—praised her. A portrait of Puente, describing her at this point in her life, appeared later in a Sacramento magazine: "She was an attractive woman, striking some would say. She had the countenance of a fairy godmother and Florence Nightingale rolled into one. Her silvery hair was perfectly in place, her stylish clothes fit well . . . [she] always had a pleasant word for everybody even though she herself, poor thing, was suffering from cancer." The last comment was, of course, a sarcastic reference to Puente's susceptibility to sympathy-attracting diseases.

This strange, wonderful figure lived in a dreamy state herself. One of her "stepdaughters" loved going into Puente's bedroom. It was the prettiest room in the house at 2100 F Street, ladylike, frilly, soft, with drapes and curtains and bright pillows. It made the young girl feel like Cinderella, an effect Puente enjoyed too.

But in mid-September 1978, Dorothea Puente's dream life and real life came tumbling down. The Social Security Administration had started an investigation of forged checks paid to her and turned the matter over to the Treasury Department. Until then no one in authority had bothered to ask how a woman who'd been convicted of forgery and prostitution could reliably run a boardinghouse for alcoholics on government assistance.

Now the questions were being sharply asked, and the answers set in motion a murderous series of events that ended on a rainy Friday morning in the muddy ground at 1426 F Street ten years later.

11

THE IRONY WAS THAT PUENTE WAS BROUGHT DOWN BY A JAIL inmate, someone as familiar with a cell as she was.

Robert Davis was doing time at the county's Rio Consumnes Correctional Center in 1977. He had been living at 2100 F Street for about three years, and he'd spent time in and out of county jail for minor offenses. He was in jail, waiting for his Social Security check and got very angry when it was late, and angrier still when it turned up with his signature on it. He had never seen it until after it was cashed.

The ensuing Treasury Department investigation uncovered thirty-four more checks to tenants at 2100 F Street, all with forged signatures. And all of the signatures were written by one hand: Dorothea Puente, the socialite and political gadfly.

When questioned by Treasury agents, Puente said that Robert Davis had asked her to come out to RCCC and bring his check. "He asked me to cash it for him. I went there to have him sign it." Puente puffed up defiantly. "The guards were standing right there while Davis signed the check over to me."

It was an audacious lie, but typical of Puente.

So Pedro Montalvo, whom all of Puente's professional associates considered a kook, had been right after all. She was an outright thief.

The Treasury Department did not probe every transaction Puente had conducted over her years at 2100 F Street and stopped totaling forgeries when they got to about $4,000. It was enough for a felony conviction.

As she had in the past, Puente hated going to trial, and so pled guilty to federal forgery. Because of her age and the nonviolent nature of the crime, she was not sent to prison. Instead, she was put on five years formal parole and ordered to undergo psychiatric counseling.

The last condition of parole was a wise one. Puente suffered what amounted to a nervous breakdown in 1978 because of her conviction.

Crying constantly, confused, angry, dazed, Puente kept up her appointments with her parole agent and always dressed very well, but she had trouble living from day to day. As part of the plea bargain, she was forced to give up 2100 F Street, lost her position as a civic leader, and was now shunned by the political figures who had courted her and kissed her so publicly.

Suddenly she was nothing and nobody. And worse, she had no money and no grand house or staff. Her life may have been mostly lies, bought with stolen money, but some of it was real. Now it was all gone, the truth and lies alike.

She took odd jobs again, as if starting over. Dishwashing, cleaning, cooking—menial jobs for people she thought below her. She could do nothing for her "stepdaughters" or the Hispanic artists she cultivated.

Puente left Sacramento, going south to Stockton. She lived alone, going to bars at night, still elegant outwardly, but struggling mightily to maintain the mask. She was brooding a lot. She had been stupid to make herself so vulnerable, to put herself in a position where everything could be taken away from her.

Next time it would be different. She blamed the whole thing on Montalvo, as she told a judge in 1982. "It was during this time I started writing checks," she said brazenly, ignoring years of previous criminality and forgery. "I just wanted you to know I'm not a street bum."

She also began seeing a psychiatrist for the first time. He was appointed by the federal court and it was a fateful pairing for Puente and him. Dr. Thomas Doody became enmeshed in her life from 1978 until 1989 when he found himself, because of her, in court, trying to maintain the confidentiality of his patients.

But what Dr. Doody first observed in 1978 was a seriously unbalanced personality. She was, he wrote, "a schizophrenic, chronic undifferentiated type." It was a catch-all diagnosis, merely saying that Puente had a severe emotional problem. The truth was, over the years, that Dr. Doody really had no clear idea what he had on his hands. Dorothea Puente was unlike any patient he had seen in nearly twenty years of practice. No one matched her ability to lie, manipulate, and deceive.

Even while she was cooperating with the court, seeing her parole agent and a psychiatrist, Puente could not resist forgery. In 1978 in Stockton she passed another Treasury check. She made repayment quickly and there was no prosecution. The incident should have signaled that even in the most dire circumstances, Dorothea Puente would break the law if she thought it would help her. But she was being so helpful that her latest criminal act was overlooked.

She disliked Stockton, a smaller, cramped city compared to Sacramento, and in mid-1979 she went north again. She had apparently decided to concentrate on individuals rather than a big operation like 2100 F Street. She would be a nurse.

And she had also apparently decided that she would risk

much more than a few months in jail rather than lose her money, dreams, and respect again.

Ricardo Odorica was a small man, not quite five feet tall, with black hair, and a wizened, prematurely aged face. He had come from Mexico in 1967, met his future wife, Veronica, and had married. They both had been born in Zacatecas.

Odorica got one of his first jobs in California at the Mansion Inn, which later became the Clarion Hotel. He worked long hours as a gardener. He and Veronica saved their money, did without trips or luxuries. By 1975, Odorica had saved enough to buy the family's first home, a run-down two-story Victorian at 1426 F Street.

He and Veronica worked on the house for years, fixing the buckled floors, the cracked walls, planting flowers, painting. They spent their time on the first floor, living there with their two young daughters. The second floor remained a mess.

At night, after work, Odorica sometimes went over to Joe's Corner for a drink. Veronica often didn't join him. He was sitting there one night in 1979, drinking a beer, when a silver-haired, kindly woman approached him. She was dressed beautifully. "I heard that the second floor of your house is for rent," she said.

Odorica was dazzled by the genteel, well-bred woman. She was charming, smart, and she liked him. "The second floor's in terrible shape," he stammered to her.

"I'd like to rent it."

"Are you sure? You haven't even seen it."

"I like the neighborhood. I used to live near here," she told him.

They walked the two doors from the bar to 1426 F Street. The woman, whom Odorica called "the lady" as if she were royalty, said her name was Dorothea Montalvo. She made an immediate impression on Veronica and the two little girls. She chatted sweetly with them, hugged them, talked intelligently about her medical training. She promised to help Veronica with tips about getting the best schooling and clothes for the kids.

Odorica thought a fairy godmother had walked into his life.

She rented the second floor for $200 a month and moved right in. Dorothea began making small improvements on the second floor, adding a decent bed and bureaus, trying to turn the peeling, dusty apartment into a version of her rooms at 2100 F Street.

She spent many nights with Veronica when Ricardo was at work, babysitting the little girls, tutoring them in English, gently chatting with them in Spanish. Dorothea said that she had been very wealthy and that Pedro Montalvo had stolen all of her money. "I've lived in castles," she told Veronica and Ricardo soon after they met, "but I'll sleep on the floor if I have to." She told them about her fine house in Cuernavaca, and the many relatives in Mexico, of her ex-husbands, all of whom she said she supported.

Ricardo and Veronica were so entranced by the grandmotherly and warm older woman that they asked her to be the sponsor for one of their daughters at her first Holy Communion. Dorothea was with the Odoricas for almost every holiday meal, for almost every dinner, and for every special occasion like a christening. She became, in very short order, one of the family.

For Dorothea Puente, the Odoricas represented a vision of family life she never had, and a ready conduit for money that she herself, as a parolee and ex-con, would have had trouble explaining to authorities. She was also not above using her new friend Ricardo as an accomplice.

Where had penniless, but ruthless Dorothea Puente gotten money not only to rent from the Odoricas but to buy things for herself?

Since her return to Sacramento, besides doing odd jobs as a cook or dishwasher, she had occupied her time going from one private nursing business to another, passing herself off as a trained live-in caretaker for the sick or elderly. She had the brusque professionalism, the matronly stance, of a longtime nurse. Several businesses bonded her, meaning they vouched for her bona fides. They did not, though, do any background checks on Puente. No one knew she was an ex-con on parole.

So she was sent out to feed and clean up after vulnerable, older shut-ins. Rumors began that she was stealing from some of them, little things that would not be missed or chalked up to fading, elderly memories.

But in one house, Dorothea Puente found someone she could control and steal from. And Puente was willing to cross over the line to harming people.

For the first time, social workers who had been so fond of Puente started believing she was capable of murder.

12

SOMETHING TERRIBLE WAS WRONG WITH ESTHER BUSBY. HER doctor thought so; her social worker, Mildred Ballenger, did, too. But no one could figure out what was happening. Busby's kindly nurse Dorothea seemed always distraught and worried when the old woman became suddenly sick.

Busby was in her seventies, a frail, smallish woman with a generally bright temperament, living in a small home. She was cared for by Dr. Jerome Lackner, who had been Director for Public Health in California under Governor Jerry Brown. With a handlebar mustache, abrupt manners, Lackner was an alert, careful doctor who knew his patient was in the grip of something very odd.

In late 1979, Dorothea Montalvo had started providing live-in nursing for Busby. The job required Dorothea to sleep in Mrs. Busby's house. By early 1980, things started happening.

Busby was frequently admitted to Sutter General Hospital for emergency treatment of medical problems that had no suspicious cause. Dr. Lackner certainly never noted one.

Mildred Ballenger was curious. She began keeping track of Busby's acute attacks. Large, open, with gray hair, Ballenger was Lackner's equivalent, keenly aware of her clients' well-being and tenacious on their behalf. Once Busby got to the hospital, Lackner and other doctors would stabilize her and her condition would improve almost overnight; the source of the medical problem stayed unknown. Busby herself was frightened and bewildered. She was old but not stupid. She tried frantically to get someone—her doctor, her social worker—to tell her what was going on. No one knew.

One telling fact emerged. Busby, getting better in her hospital room, would relapse into medical emergencies soon after solicitous visits of Dorothea Montalvo. The doctors would rush in, get Busby's heart beating normally, her breathing regular, and the crisis would pass. She rebounded quickly, too, and was discharged and sent home.

But, soon after she got home, with Dorothea feeding and medicating her daily, Mrs. Busby suddenly fell ill and would have to be brought, by speeding ambulance, back to Sutter General.

Mildred Ballenger worked for Adult Protective Services and felt her professional duty required her to dig deeper into the peculiar pattern of Esther Busby's hospitalizations. She called Peggy Rossi, who was responsible at Sutter General for scrutinizing the discharge records of elderly, potentially vulnerable people like Mrs. Busby.

"What's going on?" Ballenger asked pointedly.

Rossi checked her records. "I don't know. Everything should be fine. Mrs. Busby's getting her medication regularly, she's fed. With a caretaker like Dorothea, I don't understand it."

Ballenger chose her words carefully. "I've been hearing rumors from my other clients. About Dorothea. She uses different names. That may not even be her name."

"What rumors?"

"She poisoned her last two husbands."

"Oh, my God."

"It hasn't been proven," Ballenger said. "But don't Esther's illnesses sound like poisoning?"

Rossi said, "I'll call Dr. Lackner."

Lackner, after talking to Rossi, was perplexed. Busby's emergencies had all been attributable to some prosaic cause: too much salt in her food, too much digitalis, her heart medicine. An overdose of salt, for a woman with Busby's fragile heart, could be fatal. Too much digitalis, instead of stimulating her heart, could stop it. If this was poisoning, it was diabolically clever and simple. The victim had access to these substances herself.

But what about this Dorothea Montalvo? Lackner recalled how Dorothea always came with Mrs. Busby when she was rushed into the emergency room, then followed along to her hospital bedside. How is she, will she get better? The poor woman, how terrible, Dorothea wrung her hands, begged to help. What can I do, tell me, Dorothea would plead, her face contorted with worry.

Dorothea was in and out of Mrs. Busby's room all the time. She was, Lackner thought, the perfect friend to Busby. *I wish every elderly patient had a friend like this, someone to look out for them,* Lackner thought as he watched Dorothea bustling into the room.

He was familiar with Montalvo, too. She had been his patient for a short time and he treated her for potassium retention, an ulcerlike condition, and heartbeat irregularities. She did not take digitalis, though.

But Lackner changed his mind. Busby kept going into the hospital and he kept thinking about Rossi and Ballenger's fears. It was, he realized, only by the grace of God that Esther Busby didn't die in the emergency room. The next "illness" could kill her.

Plaintively, Mrs. Busby asked her doctor, "What's wrong with me?" and he couldn't answer her.

Lackner startlingly concluded that Dorothea wasn't worried about Busby's health during those tearful, hand-wringing visits at the hospital. She was worried Busby would recover completely. She's got Esther at home or in the hospital, he thought, keeping her alive, but sick so she's got access to everything, checks, whoever came by. It was an ideal setup for cold blooded theft.

Lackner paid a visit to Mrs. Busby after her recovery from one of the strange medical episodes. Esther was apparently not suspicious of Dorothea and liked having her there at home.

Dorothea proudly said to Lackner, "I make sure she takes her digitalis on schedule," pointing to the table of medicines for Esther Busby.

Later, Lackner presumed that Dorothea didn't show him everything she was dosing Busby with.

His home visit had aroused Dorothea Puente's keen sense of danger. The next time Mrs. Busby had an emergency illness, Lackner was surprised to find his patient rushed to the University of California at Davis Medical Center about twenty miles away rather than to the much closer Sutter General. Lackner realized why immediately. At UCDMC Busby was a new patient and the treating physicians wouldn't be suspicious of her unusual illnesses. Dorothea could start her lies all over with a fresh audience.

He talked again to Peggy Rossi, reporting the odd development.

Rossi said, "Esther Busby's being poisoned."

Like a bolt, Lackner saw it all. "My God, Peg, that's exactly what's going on."

At UCDMC, the doctors and nurses had quickly observed a marked deterioration in Busby's condition following visits by Dorothea Puente.

Lackner got a call from a friend at the hospital to discuss his sick patient. "I want you to run a tox screen to see what's in her blood," Lackner said. He believed a toxicological examination would show something.

Sure enough, Busby's blood contained phenobarbitol, a drug he had never prescribed for her. This fitted Busby's comalike appearance whenever she first arrived at the hospital, too. Lackner was certain Busby was being poisoned when the tox screen showed digoxin in her blood. Digoxin was a heart medication, not prescribed for Esther Busby but being taken by Dorothea Puente.

Lackner and Ballenger heard that Puente was calling Mrs. Busby's relatives, telling them the old woman had terminal cancer and more money was immediately needed for her care. She doesn't have cancer, Lackner thought. Dorothea's lying. *To get the money.*

When he knew Dorothea would be out, Lackner went to see Mrs. Busby. Bluntly he told her that she had high levels of a strange medication in her system. He said Dorothea was poisoning her. "She's calling your family, too. She says you're dying and need money," Lackner told Mrs. Busby.

Frightened and angry, the old woman asked, "What should I do?"

"Fire her," Lackner answered.

Mrs. Busby nodded. Dorothea Puente was dismissed immediately to her shocked, quarrelsome chagrin.

There is no indication that anyone contacted the private nursing companies that continued to send Dorothea out to see patients. Puente's homicidal career is a record not so much of her unmasking, as her slipping away from pursuers.

She had taken on two dedicated foes in 1980, Lackner and especially Ballenger. Working on parallel tracks, they notified the Sacramento Police Department that a dangerous woman was loose among sick people.

The tip came to Sergeant Dave Schwartz in Homicide. Slight, self-confident, with a thin black mustache, Schwartz heard all of the suspicions Lackner and Ballenger had documented and built up. He agreed that Dorothea Puente's behavior looked sinister and that she might have been poisoning Esther Busby, but these suspicions wouldn't support sending the matter to the DA's office or doing much more. It was mostly conjecture.

When Esther Busby died in a nursing home in 1981, Schwartz reported her death as possibly suspicious, and noted that the woman's doctor and others thought she had been poisoned in the past. Schwartz, like Lackner and Ballenger, intended to keep an eye on the busy, courteous, and grandmotherly Dorothea Puente.

In 1980 Dr. Thomas Coyle at Sutter General began noticing that one of his patients had an unusual pattern of acute illnesses and recovery. He made a note in his medical record that it looked like intentional poisoning.

The patient, an elderly, generally solitary woman like Busby, didn't get better. Coyle talked to Peggy Rossi about the case. Very quickly Rossi's fears were heightened. "Is someone looking after this woman?" she asked.

"She's got an attendant. She got her through an agency, a bonded one. I don't remember the woman's name offhand."

Rossi thought, don't tell me it's Montalvo.

She told the doctor it was imperative to find out who was looking after this elderly woman. Coyle and Rossi hurried to the patient's room. "I think the attendant's name is in this address book," the doctor said, picking up a slim book on the bedside table.

Rossi fearfully waited as they checked. Under *M,* they found the name Dorothea Montalvo, 1426 F Street.

Rossi hurried back to her office and called the Nursing Office at the hospital. She was angry that another elderly woman had fallen into Dorothea's web. "I want Montalvo reported for poisoning this woman," Rossi said emphatically.

But the Nursing Office, unpersuaded, refused, based on the scanty information, to take any steps against Dorothea.

Shaking her head, angry, frustrated, Rossi placed an anonymous call to Mildred Ballenger, who had made no secret of her accusations about Dorothea Puente. Rossi told Ballenger that another old woman was being poisoned.

Ballenger wasted no time. The patient was told, just as Busby had been, and Puente was fired.

Ballenger made it a point to keep Schwartz at SPD apprised of what Puente was doing, where she went, what patients she saw. Maybe they could catch her in the act, or at least prevent something fatal from happening.

A bitter Ballenger found her path blocked at the county counsel's office when she reported Puente. The county counsel refused to go to the Sacramento County Welfare Department to have Puente barred from working with the sick and dependent. The answer was the same one Rossi had gotten: not enough information.

What Ballenger did accomplish over the next year, was to turn up four more patients of Puente's who experienced health emergencies under her care. One woman, according to Ballenger, died after repeated heart attacks "within minutes" of eating or drinking food Dorothea had prepared for her. Still, Schwartz wearily insisted that the link from Puente to poisoning was too tenuous to justify arresting her.

Mildred Ballenger, tracking Puente like a Fury, and Schwartz realized that what they needed was for Puente to be caught pouring something into someone's food or actually seen stealing from someone's home or passing a forged check.

In early 1982, Ballenger and Schwartz got all three from an unwittingly obliging Dorothea Puente.

PART 3

Night air and gardening are the great tonics. There is nothing so stimulating as bare contact with rich mother earth. You are never so fresh as when you have been grubbing in the soil—black hands, black nails, and boots covered with mud.

E. F. Benson,
"Mrs. Amworth"

13

"KEEP AN EYE ON HER," DAVE SCHWARTZ WARNED ME ON MARCH 2, 1982. "She's dangerous. I haven't even sent over the good case yet."

He meant Dorothea Montalvo and the series of cases he was then submitting to the Sacramento County District Attorney for prosecution. Puente, then using the Montalvo name, had been very busy in early 1982 and through the spring and her tenacious enemies, Ballenger and Schwartz, had finally caught up with her.

The Homicide detective wanted to avoid letting a deputy DA like me get fooled by Montalvo as so many had been before. I sat in my office, poring over the files that started showing up on her, chilled by the almost vampiric parasitism of this seemingly gentle white-haired grandmother. She really was like Benson's vampire, Mrs. Amworth, who looked like a jolly, motherly woman and trapped her victims through deception.

In 1982 I had been with the DA's office for about five years, handling everything from disturbing the peace to murder. I had quit in 1981 to write full-time. Then about a year later, the office needed an immediate replacement for about eight months for a deputy going on maternity leave. Although I wanted to write as a career, I was still close enough to the good spirits, high-mindedness, competitive routine, and courtroom antics to want to continue as a DA for a little longer.

So I ended up with Dorothea Montalvo Puente by accident.

The office felony bureau was divided into five trial teams. I was assigned to Team Four. Tim Frawley, my old law school friend, was the supervisor and he sent me the more volatile cases, the ones which might require special handling, like Montalvo. I could devote the time to them unlike a regular deputy. Since I was only going to be in the office a short time, Frawley knew my judgment would be unclouded by thoughts of career advancement.

Team Four was a cluttered crush of little offices on the third floor of the squat, very ugly new building the DA had moved into from the courthouse across the street. The courthouse was an enormous white rectangle without exterior decoration, like the most graceless, cold hospital imaginable. The Montalvo crimes would play themselves out in courtrooms in that coldness.

"Don't drop the ball on this one," Schwartz admonished me over the phone in March. "There's a lot more going on than you think. She's worth the time."

I discovered, through the files, that Dorothea Montalvo had been very active lately. She moved like a shark among the older, weaker people in downtown Sacramento.

The first case I saw established Montalvo's capacity for predatory heartlessness.

Malcolm McKenzie went out drinking at the Zebra Club in late January. In his seventies, McKenzie enjoyed going to bars, and he was a regular at the Zebra Club. He was a two-drink customer, lingering and talking for hours.

On the night he sat down near the door, McKenzie was

delighted when an attractive, very well dressed older woman came in and struck up a conversation. She swept into the bar, her manners and brightness almost out of place among the usual drinkers. She told McKenzie her name was Dorothea. They moved to the bar. It was late in the evening and they had time only for two drinks. McKenzie let Dorothea know that his apartment was nearby.

"I'd like to see it," she said, flattering him with attention.

"Well, let's go," McKenzie said happily. The bartender saw them get into a cab.

By the time they got to his apartment, McKenzie felt distinctly unwell, strange. He had never experienced sensations like this before, a paralytic numbness that froze his arms and legs. As Dorothea stood over him, he lay down on the sofa. In another moment, McKenzie found he couldn't move his body at all. He was conscious, able to see and hear, but he couldn't talk.

He watched in stunned amazement as Dorothea began a thorough, businesslike search of his apartment. She opened drawers, went through closets, checked his clothes. She found a small red suitcase and started putting things into it, including a collection of wheat pennies worth some money. Smaller items, like cash, she just stuffed into her pockets.

Then McKenzie saw her glance around and come toward him. She grabbed his left hand and tugged at his pinky ring, finally pulling it free. McKenzie couldn't resist in any way. With a last, acquisitive look around the apartment, Dorothea, red suitcase in hand, left as casually as if nothing had happened.

McKenzie stayed frozen on the sofa for another hour, then found he could move a little, got to the telephone, and called the police.

It hadn't taken long for the police to catch up with Montalvo after that. She tried to pass two of McKenzie's checks at Joe's Corner several days later. "He gave them to me," she insisted to the police, even though only her handwriting appeared on the checks. She claimed to be seventy-two years old. She was really only fifty-three, but her appearance matched that of a much older woman. "This man wanted to go steady with me," Montalvo said, "but I wouldn't do it. I didn't take anything from him."

But she hedged. "I've got a psychiatric condition. I sometimes forget my actions." She said she was being treated.

I went to Frawley's office on the second floor. "What's so special about this?"

Frawley leaned back. "It didn't look like much to me. Dave Schwartz called me. He says she's very dangerous and he's got a lot more cases coming over."

Frawley said that Schwartz was also talking to George Williamson, who was in Special Investigations in the DA's office. "We'll have to handle her carefully," Frawley told me.

I wondered why Schwartz, a Homicide detective, was so interested in a thief. I got a better idea when her other crimes popped up.

Not long after apparently drugging and robbing Malcolm McKenzie, Montalvo struck at an eighty-two-year-old woman living alone at the St. Francis Mansion.

Irene Gregory was frail, ill, and needed outside help to get through the day's routine. One morning in the spring of 1982 she was visited by a kindly, professional-sounding woman named Betty Peterson. "I'm from the Sacramento Medical Association," the white-haired woman, wearing glasses, carrying a medical bag, told Mrs. Gregory. But Betty Peterson also looked odd. She wore a floral-print dress and a lot of makeup, her nails painted a flashy, loud red. She said she was a nurse and she had come to help Mrs. Gregory. She even produced medical gear and competently took Mrs. Gregory's blood pressure. Betty Peterson looked, sounded, and acted like a genuine nurse, perhaps a slightly eccentric one.

Mrs. Gregory had seen this nurse before. One of the few things Irene Gregory did regularly was go to Marcene's Beauty Parlor to get her hair done. On a recent trip, Mrs. Gregory had fallen down as she got out of the chair, and

Betty Peterson had been there to help her up, check her for bruises, comfort her, and get her address in case there were further problems. Mrs. Gregory had a granddaughter and a small circle of friends who looked out for her, but she was by herself a lot of the time.

"How are you feeling after that fall?" the nurse asked, putting away the blood pressure gauge.

"Oh, better. It wasn't really too bad."

Peterson was sympathetic and nodded. She said, "Well, I think I have something for you," Peterson said. "Your blood pressure tells me that you're keeping too much water. You need to get rid of it to feel better and recover faster."

Mrs. Gregory nodded. Peterson pulled out a bottle of pills from her medical bag. "I know your doctor," and she named Mrs. Gregory's treating physician. It wasn't unusual for her to know the name: the doctor's medications were nearby on tables in the apartment.

"These are water pills," Peterson told Mrs. Gregory. "Take a couple of them and lie down."

Dutifully, Mrs. Gregory swallowed the pills. She watched the smiling, reassuring nurse. Then Mrs. Gregory lost consciousness.

When she woke up, hours had passed. Betty Peterson was gone along with a valuable diamond ring in an elaborate setting and about one hundred Dalmane pills Mrs. Gregory took as medication.

Feeling faint, Mrs. Gregory stumbled to the telephone and called her granddaughter. Then the two of them reported the incident to the police. The problem was that Mrs. Gregory couldn't identify Betty Peterson beyond giving a description.

But luck was with Irene Gregory. Several days later she went back to Marcene's to have her hair shampooed and set. Sitting in a chair, bold and brazen, was the false nurse, Peterson. "Call the police," Mrs. Gregory spluttered, but before SPD arrived, a perfectly calm Betty Peterson got up, tidied herself, and walked out after telling her hairdresser that she was going to Mexico.

The hairdresser, though, knew Peterson's real name was Dorothea Montalvo, and the police quickly arrested her at 1426 F Street. Montalvo maintained she had done nothing, and none of Irene Gregory's jewelry was ever found. The whole experience shook Mrs. Gregory to her core. She locked her door tightly at the St. Francis Mansion, was fearful of going out, and terrified of people.

This Montalvo, I realized, was a very special criminal. It took a rare callousness to drug two old people and steal the rings off their fingers.

Then Schwartz called and solved the puzzle of his interest in Montalvo. "We're pretty sure she killed someone," he said. "The problem is we probably can't ever prove it."

"The case is bad?" I asked, ready to credit almost anything to Dorothea Montalvo.

"There's a lot of possibilities, but there's nothing to work up. I just wanted you to know about it."

"Who was it?"

"A sick lady, someone she was working for," Schwartz said sourly. "Like the ones you're getting now."

I didn't know it for several months, but he was talking about Esther Busby. "Are there more cases coming?"

"You bet. We're digging back, too. I bet we find some old ones she's good for."

In rapid succession, more Dorothea Montalvo crimes appeared.

Claire Maleville and Lauretta Chalmers were elderly women who employed Montalvo as a live-in attendant or occasional helper. The two old women never met each other, but their identical experiences bound them together. Montalvo was working through the Quality Care Nursing Agency, apparently a reputable, trustworthy person to have around old people. But both Maleville and Chalmers discovered checks and personal belongings missing after Montalvo was in their homes. The checks began appearing with forged signatures on them.

I was starting to set up court dates to put Montalvo's

crimes in front of a judge. In California the first step in taking a serious crime, a felony, to trial, is a preliminary hearing held in a lower court, the municipal court, before a judge without a jury. My job was to present just enough evidence at the hearing to show that a crime had been committed and that the defendant likely committed it. The case would then be sent to superior court for trial.

But Maleville and Chalmers showed me how hard it was going to be to nail Dorothea Montalvo.

Claire Maleville called me first, days before the preliminary hearing. "I'm so sorry," she said, her voice thin and quavery. "I simply can't come to court."

"You're the only one who can tell the judge that Montalvo took your checks without permission."

"And if I don't testify?"

"Well, the judge needs to hear from the victim, Mrs. Maleville. Without you, I have to dismiss this charge." I hated pressuring the infirm, nervous, and fearful old woman.

"Can't I just send in a statement? She did steal those checks from me."

I explained the law of forgery. "You have to be on the witness stand, so you can be cross-examined, too."

"I can't do that," Mrs. Maleville said anxiously. "I'm far too ill. I'm in bed all the time."

She apologized again and again. I had her under subpoena but I couldn't force a sick old woman into court. Lauretta Chalmers called soon afterward. She, too, was bedridden and unable to make it to court. Suddenly the Montalvo prosecution was coming apart.

The police had uncovered an earlier crime, committed in August 1981. It was the same story. Dorothy Gosling, eighty-four years old, hired Montalvo as a nurse and cook. Then the elderly woman discovered $3,500 worth of gold rings and other jewelry missing. Montalvo had the run of the house, preparing meals, cleaning up, conscientiously tending to Mrs. Gosling. But several times, Mrs. Gosling went to bed and woke up later to find more of her possessions gone, including checks. The pattern of deep, sudden sleep followed by missing property looked suspect, too. Schwartz said that no drugs were found in Mrs. Gosling's system, though. In 1981 the police hadn't been looking that closely for drugs.

I didn't have any drugs at all to show a judge, much less a jury later. I only had people who ate or drank near Montalvo, lost consciousness or their ability to move, and later found they'd been robbed.

When Mrs. Gosling pleaded with me in early April that she too couldn't stand the strain of coming to court, I was left with Malcolm McKenzie. The preliminary hearing was scheduled for April 12. The appalling possibility existed that Montalvo, having chosen her weak, helpless victims so well, would benefit from their frailty and walk away free.

14

IF I WAS FEELING PRESSURE AS THE PRELIMINARY HEARING GOT nearer, so was Dorothea Montalvo.

Since January 1982 she had been arrested four times, and now faced a long prison sentence if convicted. Each time she was arrested her bail rose, from $15,000 to $30,000. She had to keep finding more money on very short notice if she wanted to stay out of custody until the preliminary hearing.

I tried to make her life as miserable as possible that spring.

My own life wasn't happy. After talking with George Williamson, who was also tracking the Montalvo cases in the DA's office, we concluded that there was no way to get legally useful testimony from the reluctant, sick old victims. My only hope was to use McKenzie to send Montalvo to trial, buy some time to re-file or shore up the other cases. As Schwartz and Mildred Ballenger reminded me several times, Montalvo had to be taken off the streets.

It was with a lot of relief that I brought Malcolm McKenzie into my office the morning of April 12.

He turned out to be a spry, bright-eyed man in white pants and a white windbreaker. His gray hair was carefully combed and he smiled often. He seemed high-spirited.

We went over the limited purpose of the hearing. I told McKenzie I wouldn't ask him every possible question. He got a little nervous thinking about cross-examination, but perked up quickly.

"Is she going to be there?" he asked.

"If she is, I'm going to have her arrested after the prelim," I said.

He grinned. "That should be fun. Is it on my charges?"

"No. We turned up some more checks she'd written." I didn't tell McKenzie that he was the single thread keeping the Montalvo prosecution together. I gathered up my files, took McKenzie in hand, and we walked across the street to the courthouse. I hoped for the best.

The schedule of cases in a criminal court is called the calendar. Morning calendars in Department D were crowded, noisy, chaotic. I left McKenzie in the courtroom's audience section. He stood out in his white outfit among the children, darker clothes, the mass of sour-faced people waiting for court to start.

I needed to find Montalvo's lawyer. The time had come to try for a deal, since I only had one victim available.

Al Hess, Montalvo's public defender, had been a criminal lawyer for years. He wore glasses, slouched a little, and had a cynical smile. "Are we going to get rid of this?" Hess asked me. He never looked like he took his cases seriously, but he was an effective trial lawyer.

"Is she here?" I asked. I thought she might avoid court.

"Didn't you see her coming in?" Al grinned wryly. "She's the little old lady, the sweet one sitting in front."

"She can plead to a four-eight-seven point two straight up," I said, bluffing a little. I was offering a guilty plea to grand theft from the person of McKenzie, short of robbery with force. It was a felony and Montalvo probably would go to prison.

Hess knew a bluff. He snorted dismissively. "She won't take it. You have your victim?"

I nodded. Hess wanted to see McKenzie testify before accepting any plea bargain. Maybe he could walk Montalvo free completely. He already knew, because I had told him, that I couldn't produce the other victims that morning.

"He gave her the stuff," Hess said. "He just doesn't remember. They got drunk together. Look, the judge's going to drop this down to a misdemeanor after the prelim."

"No deal for a misdemeanor," I said.

Hess shrugged. Montalvo was merely another case in the pile of files he carried that morning. "Let's see the judge."

As we walked into the judge's chambers, I passed Montalvo for the first time. She wore a black dress, her white hair in a grandmotherly bun. She was stout, pale-skinned, with glasses, as meek and harmless-looking as Mrs. Butterworth on the maple syrup bottles.

There was a mob of lawyers, all talking, in the judge's chambers. The judge was Kate Canlis, a bright, sharp-tongued former deputy DA I had known for a long time. She was trying to work out which prelims would actually go to a hearing and which would plead.

She gave me a fish-eye. "Why are you going after that cute little old lady?" she demanded.

"Wait until you hear my witness."

Canlis turned to Hess. "Is she going to take anything?"

Hess shook his head. "I asked her. She says she hasn't done anything. No deal." He smiled at the judge. "You'll drop it down to a misdemeanor after you hear the prelim anyway."

"Maybe, Mr. Hess," Canlis said, moving to another case and another brace of bickering lawyers in front of her.

Back in court I was annoyed and nervous. Canlis might decide that Montalvo had done very little or that McKenzie was confused, or McKenzie might freeze on the witness stand. Anything could happen. I would have to dismiss the last case, arrest Montalvo outside of the courtroom on additional forged checks, and then re-file everything and try for a second and last time. In California, the prosecution could re-file a case only once after dismissal.

That would leave Dorothea Montalvo on the street, free to roam among the gullible and vulnerable.

There was almost no one left in Canlis's courtroom when *People v. Dorothea Montalvo* was called. Still fussing with a small purse, as she had while waiting for the case, Montalvo sat down beside Hess at the counsel table. Canlis, sitting on the bench, told me to call my first witness.

I asked for Malcolm McKenzie. He came forward, a little jittery, took the oath, and sat down on the witness stand. Montalvo stared at him. Canlis stared at me. It was obvious she thought I had misread the facts of the case.

McKenzie turned out to be that blessing among witnesses, unflappable and concise. He answered my questions easily and simply about what had happened to him on the night of January 29, 1982. He pointed out Montalvo as the woman who stole the ring off his hand. Canlis now stared at Montalvo.

Hess cross-examined McKenzie, concentrating on the drinking, the small amount of property taken. When he was finished, he gave Montalvo a little smile. She nodded, blinked, frowned. McKenzie stepped off the stand, much more confidently.

"I have no further witnesses," I told Canlis.

"In view of this evidence, I'd like the court to deem this case a misdemeanor instead of sending it to Superior Court," Hess said.

He waited, pen over his file. I crossed my fingers mentally.

Canlis swept her penetrating, hard gaze over Montalvo and Hess. "No, I'm going to hold the defendant to answer to the charge in the complaint," she said.

That was a victory, I thought.

But Judge Canlis went on, "I'm also going to hold her to answer for violations of sections 211 and 470 based on what I heard this morning."

She had added charges of robbery and forgery. It carried a great deal of weight about the strength of the evidence when the judge did that. Hess and his client realized there was definite prison time involved.

Hess tried to reassure his irritated client as they got up and started walking out of the courtroom. The stout, black-dressed figure of Montalvo bustled to the courtroom's doors, unaware of the detectives waiting in the hallway for her.

Canlis called me to the bench as another prelim set up. "She's a monster," the judge said as Montalvo passed out the doors.

When I got into the hallway a few minutes later, Montalvo was in handcuffs, complaining, drawing a circle of fascinated people, obviously wondering what this harmless little old lady could have done to make these burly cops put her in handcuffs.

Montalvo was taken away. Hess was furious and turned on me. "That was chickenshit," he snapped angrily. "You should have told me."

"Then you would have had to tell her." It would have been Hess's ethical duty to inform Montalvo that she would be arrested. I didn't want to risk her escaping from the courtroom.

McKenzie waited, delighted at the scene. He was chipper and enthusiastic. "How'd I do?" he asked.

"You did exactly what we needed," I said. Both he and Canlis had given me much more leverage over Montalvo than I'd had going to court that morning.

I was busy trying to get more victims before a judge over the next few days, sorting out which of the cases against Montalvo could be re-filed.

Hess was also busy. After Montalvo had been in jail for several days on the new arrest, he managed to have a second judge release her on her own recognizance. I knew what must have persuaded the judge: *Look at her, Your Honor. She's old. She has ties to the community. She's made all of her court appearances. The other cases against her have been dismissed."*

And one more official would have been fooled by Montalvo's act.

She went home to 1426 F Street on April 16, worried and desperate. She faced prison, and she couldn't deceive a judge if one of her victims actually testified.

Dorothea Montalvo needed enough money to get out of the country immediately. She couldn't pull her nurse routine now, though, because the agencies wouldn't use her.

Unfortunately, a source of easy cash was living with Montalvo at 1426 F Street. As I was working hard to resurrect the cases against her, Montalvo in the last weeks of April 1982 planned and carried out her first murder for profit.

15

I NEVER MET RUTH MUNROE, BUT SHE HAS HAUNTED ME FOR A decade. She was an utterly innocent victim of Dorothea Montalvo Puente. I have learned what happened to Ruth in her last weeks of life and it is as bad as anything one human being can do to another.

Ruth Munroe was a genial, pleasant woman in 1982, stocky, carrying her one hundred seventy-nine pounds on a five foot four inch frame. She wore glasses, had white hair, and occasionally put on a wig if she didn't feel like fixing her hair. She looked in many ways like Dorothea Montalvo. The difference was that Ruth actually had grandchildren, a family, a career. She was genuine, not an impostor.

Ruth had retired from the Gemco department store on Broadway and Riverside in Sacramento, after working as a clerk in the pharmacy for ten years. Oddly enough, Gemco was within a few yards of the cemetery where Bert Montoya would go, years later, and hear spirits calling to him from the grave.

Less than a year earlier, Ruth had married her second

husband, Harold Munroe. It was a periodically rough marriage. In late 1981 Harold was diagnosed with terminal cancer. They sold their home for about $20,000 and devoted the next few months to living as merrily as they wished, a last fling. They took a trip to Alturas, gambled and drank over a long weekend, and spent over $400. There were other trips, too. Ruth, never much of a drinker, now tried to keep up with her dying husband.

But he of course got worse, and they quarreled more often. Harold went into the Veterans Administration Hospital in Martinez in the early spring of 1982. Ruth remained upbeat, optimistic during this ordeal. She had just gone into a business partnership.

Harold had been drinking in various bars before he got too sick to go out. At the Flame Club he met Dorothea Montalvo, who was working there part-time as a cook and dishwasher. Harold, noting the similarity to his wife, brought Ruth along on a night out and introduced the two women.

Montalvo took the initiative and proposed that Ruth and she go into business as caterers. They would sell ready-made dishes to parties. "I've picked up a lot of business sense from the restaurants and bars I've worked at," Montalvo said.

The idea appealed to Ruth. She was down to only a few thousand dollars. The business would supplement her income, provide something to do as Harold became weaker and she needed a distraction.

Montalvo went to the owner of the Round Corner bar and bargained for use of the kitchen for about $150 a month. The bar's owner knew Harold well, and liked Ruth. She was a cheerful, hardworking, robust woman. Montalvo, with her sharp business sense, looked like an ideal partner.

Ruth then made a fatal mistake. To finance her share of the business, she withdrew money from her savings account. She and Montalvo, again at Dorothea's insistence, opened a joint bank account.

Ruth was proud of her new venture, certain it would be successful. Her only worry was Harold. He had started calling her from the hospital, querulous, bitter, and his continual depression made Ruth believe a divorce was inevitable. "You shouldn't be alone," Dorothea said helpfully. "I've got a lot of space where I live. We're in business together. Why shouldn't we share our living expenses, too?"

Dorothea must have used her most caring, sincere pose, because Ruth agreed, and on April 11, 1982, Easter Sunday, Ruth's three sons helped her move into 1426 F Street.

Ruth Munroe had a wide circle of close and old friends and four grown children, Allan, Houston, Bill, and Rosemary. Raised a Catholic, Ruth abhorred suicide and had a "fear of God," Allan said later.

Ruth threw herself into the new restaurant business. She worked long hours, cooking and washing up. Her children came by 1426 F Street to see her, talked to her on the phone, and found she was very happy and excited. She never mentioned any legal problems her partner was having, and apparently didn't even know about Dorothea's criminal background or her current crimes. Ruth, of course, never saw any of Dorothea's elderly victims around 1426 F Street.

If she had heard about Dorothea's legal pressure, Ruth probably would have tried to help her. Everyone who knew Ruth agreed she was a large-hearted, open woman. She always tried to help others. She trusted people.

During her last weeks, Ruth maintained her regular schedule of seeing friends and family. On April 14, she stopped by Nadine Nash's home. Nash, slight, with coppery-colored hair, had been like a sister to Ruth. It was natural to share good news with her.

Ruth had brought along a lot of money. It surprised Nash to see over $1,000 in Ruth's purse. "It was for the business," Nash remembered Ruth telling her. And Ruth was effusive about Dorothea, her partner. As an old friend, Nash sometimes called Ruth at 1426 F Street. She didn't know that the visit in mid-April would be the last time she saw Ruth. They had been close for over fifteen years.

Usually on Sundays, Ruth and her children got together or talked on the phone. She liked holding her grandchildren and hearing about their first steps or what they'd done. Her son Allan called Ruth on Sunday, April 25, to talk about her grandchildren, and she was as interested as she'd ever been. She didn't tell Allan, though, how poorly she felt.

But Ruth had told an old friend, Carmella "Camy" Lombardo about her terrors on April 24. The two women had worked at Gemco together in the pharmacy. Since Munroe retired, the two only saw each other about once a week, usually at the Tallac Village Beauty Salon where they both got their hair done.

Lombardo was shocked at Ruth's appearance. She was dazed, frightened, very worn. She seemed to be confused. They talked briefly about Harold's illness, and Lombardo offered to drive Ruth to Martinez. "No, Mrs. Puente can take me," Ruth answered.

Then, around someone she had known for years, Ruth broke down. Lombardo had trouble connecting the terrified, sick looking woman with her Gemco friend. Ruth said, almost in tears, "I can't talk to you. I think I'm going to die."

Lombardo was frightened now, too. "You've got to go to an emergency room or see a doctor," she said.

"I can't. I can't do anything," Ruth said, in terror. "I don't remember what I'm doing. I don't remember eating dinner or going to bed. I don't know where I am."

This was not the Ruth Munroe whom Lombardo had seen two or three weeks before. Something awful had happened and Ruth couldn't understand what it was. She said again that she thought she would die.

When she watched Ruth stagger out of the beauty parlor, Lombardo assumed she was going home, to bed. Camy Lombardo did not know that Ruth was living at 1426 F Street, alone, with Dorothea.

* * *

On the last night of her life, April 27, 1982, Ruth Munroe was visited by two of her children. Rosemary, called Rosie, came by early in the evening. She found her mother upstairs, in a deep, unrousable sleep. It was very unusual for Ruth to sleep so heavily. Rosie asked Dorothea, who hovered in the downstairs living room, what was wrong with Ruth.

"The doctor at the emergency room just gave your mother a shot," Dorothea said. "To calm her down."

"What emergency room?"

"At Davis Medical Center," Dorothea said.

Worried, but reassured by Dorothea's soothing calm and concern, Rosie went home. Ever since she met Dorothea, Rosie, like the rest of the family, had been impressed by her care for Ruth, her almost motherly worrying and fussing over her new roommate. Besides, Rosie felt better knowing that Dorothea was a nurse who had been trained to care for ill people. Ruth was certainly, Rosie believed, in good hands.

Sometime later in the evening, Bill Clausen stopped by after work. He was quite anxious about his mother's sudden health problems. In the last few years the two of them had grown very close.

Bill was brown-haired, with a dark mustache, medium sized and sometimes intense. Everything had seemed fine with his mother and Dorothea, living contentedly at 1426 F Street, until about three days earlier.

On April 24, Bill came by after work. He found Ruth sitting in the living room, propped up in a chair. He noticed his mother was drinking something. "What's that?" he asked.

"Dorothea fixed me a drink to calm me down," Ruth said. She was agitated. Harold had been calling. In fact, as Bill and she chatted, the phone rang. Bill answered it. It was Harold, complaining, angry, wanting to bother his wife again. Bill told him to stop calling.

Ruth went on drinking. Bill, unlike Rosie, was unaware his mother drank alcohol. He was also unaware of the bar-hopping weekends Harold and Ruth had taken in the last six or seven months. So he was startled when his mother told him the green, minty-smelling stuff she was sipping was crème de menthe.

For the next two nights when he came by, Ruth was sitting up, more stuporous each night, drinking a crème de menthe cocktail made by her friend Dorothea.

On April 27, Bill was met by Dorothea who invited him in. She wanted to brace him. "The doctor's just been here and given your mother a shot," Dorothea said.

"Why?" Bill asked quickly.

"She was very upset and nervous."

"I better see her." Bill noticed that Ruth wasn't sitting in the living room. She must be upstairs in her bedroom.

"I don't think you should go up there," Dorothea said, her hands clasped. "She's sleeping. You shouldn't disturb her now."

For the first time, Bill disregarded Dorothea's professional nursing advice and went upstairs to see his mother for himself. He found her in bed, facing the wall, on her side. Her eyes were open. She didn't appear to notice him. He gently shook her. She didn't respond. She seemed drugged, just as Dorothea said.

"Don't worry, Mom," Bill said softly, leaning to her. "Everything's going to be all right. Dorothea will take care of you."

He was anxious when a tear came out of his mother's eye. "I'll come back soon," he said. He left the bedroom, and on his way out of 1426 F, Dorothea, patting him, comforting him, said that all Ruth needed was some rest. "I'll be here to look after her," Dorothea said, closing the front door.

Nadine Nash called that evening, hoping to talk to Ruth.

"She can't come to the phone," Dorothea said.

"Why not?"

"The doctor's been here and given her a shot. She's sleeping."

"Tell her I hope she feels better." Nash hung up, a feeling of unease troubling her.

* * *

Rosie was jolted awake by a ringing phone around 5:30 A.M. April 28.

It was Dorothea. "Something's wrong with your mother. I've called the paramedics. You better come over."

Rosie jumped from bed, dressing hastily in the pre-dawn. She called Ruth's other children.

When she hurried into 1426 F Street, Rosie noticed the police squad car, the emergency vehicles parked on the dark street, curious neighbors standing on the sidewalk.

A tearful, anguished Dorothea met her in the living room. "Your mother died," she said.

Officer Robert Nichols, a patrol cop, was first on the scene. He got to 1426 F around 6:00 A.M. in response to a casualty call. When he arrived, he was met by Dorothea Montalvo. He started making notes about what had happened. "She was all right around four this morning," Dorothea told Nichols. "I checked on her. Then about forty minutes ago she wouldn't wake up so I called the fire department."

Nichols said he wanted to see the deceased person himself. As he walked upstairs, Dorothea told him that Ruth Munroe had a heart condition and she was suffering great emotional stress lately because of divorce proceedings against her husband.

Nichols went to the upstairs side bedroom. He quickly determined that the pink nightgown–clad woman in the bed was indeed dead. He came back downstairs and called the coroner and his supervisor.

Within a few minutes, more people appeared, frantic and crying family members of the dead woman. They stayed in the living room, talking to Nichols or to Dorothea, who tried to comfort them. Dorothea told Bill and Rosie she had gone to see Ruth around four, and given her a drink of grapefruit juice and water. But she mentioned to others that she gave Ruth an injection. It did not sound strange, given Dorothea's nursing background.

The house was brightly lit up, filled with grieving people,

men in uniform, as the sun started coming up. The coroner's assistant arrived to remove Ruth's body. He also talked with the tired but firm Dorothea. "She was having pains in the left side of her arm," Dorothea told the coroner, with a medical person's specificity.

The coroner went to the bedroom. He made a point of looking for unusual items in the room. Dorothea plainly believed the woman had died from a heart attack, and yet subtly suggested she might have killed herself. On a table near the bed the coroner found a prescription bottle of Miltown, a tranquilizer, for Ruth Munroe. He did not find any other bottles or medications in the room. Nor did he find any suicide note.

Rosie, Bill, and other members of the family could not believe Ruth was dead. They wept with Dorothea. Since Ruth had no known serious medical problems, Dorothea's suggestion that perhaps suicide was the explanation for this sudden, horrific death, fitted what the family saw at the house. Perhaps Ruth had been more anguished over her divorce than they had realized.

Knowing nothing of Dorothea's legal problems or Mildred Ballenger's efforts, the monstrous idea that someone had deliberately, cold-bloodedly drugged and then poisoned Ruth Munroe for money never entered their minds on April 28, 1982.

Looking at the sad, sympathetic, grandmotherly face of Dorothea that terrible morning, how could they have suspected murder?

Ruth's body was taken downtown to the coroner's office. Since her death was from an undetermined cause in a home, without any physician present, an autopsy was mandatory.

Later on April 28, a pathologist examined the body of the sixty-one-year-old woman and found no visible external trauma. Even after Munroe's body was cut open, Dr. Gwen Hall saw nothing to explain sudden death, although Ruth's liver was enlarged, and she had a slightly enlarged heart and mild hardening of the arteries.

But the liver bothered Dr. Hall as she examined it. There had been fatty damage to the liver, the kind associated with either alcoholism or chemical toxicity. This might be significant. Dr. Hall took tissue samples from the liver, stomach, and kidneys.

When she opened Ruth's stomach, Dr. Hall discovered a dark green mint-smelling material. There was no evidence the dead woman had eaten any solid food for several days. Dr. Hall had found the remnants of Ruth's crème de menthe cocktails.

Dr. Hall reviewed Ruth's medical history through the records of her family doctor. She had seen him often for cold-type symptoms. In January he prescribed meprobamate or Miltown for the anxiety Ruth was feeling. Other than that, she had been a healthy woman when she saw her doctor last on March 26.

Dr. Hall packaged up the tissue and blood samples and sent them to a toxicologist for analysis. The results came back within two weeks. Ruth Munroe's blood and stomach contents showed she had died from a massive overdose of acetaminophen and codeine, in other words, Tylenol and codeine. There was also a high but prescription level amount of Miltown in her system. She had not had a heart attack.

It was, Dr. Hall realized, a puzzle. Miltown and the gram-amounts of Tylenol and codeine would suppress breathing. The Tylenol and codeine alone were sufficient to kill. None was found in her bedroom.

The coroner's office classified Ruth's death as being of "undeterminate cause." Suicide was not ruled out, but nothing else, including homicide, fitted the clinical evidence. There simply wasn't enough information to rule the death anything at all.

A melancholy, shocked family got together at Allan's house on April 30. The unthinkable had happened, and they were still trying to grasp it.

Rosie's husband, John, was there. Tall, black-haired, and

intelligent, John did not share Ruth's children's high opinion of Dorothea Montalvo. There was something wrong with that woman, a skewed aspect to the caring grandmother he couldn't quite put his finger on.

Rosie said they had to accept the real possibility that Ruth had killed herself. "She didn't want to get old," Rosie said sadly.

Out of the blue, Houston's girlfriend blurted out, "I think Dorothea Montalvo killed her."

John then had an epiphany, his suspicions and disquiet coming together in an angry burst. "I believe the same thing," he said suddenly.

But neither Bill nor Rosie, Allan, or Houston could face that horrific, almost unimaginable possibility.

John intended to see where the evidence went. He worked on Rosie, and gradually she came around to his thinking. She called UCDMC and found out that Ruth had never been to the emergency room there on April 27 or any other day. No doctor had come to 1426 F either. Dorothea was lying.

John got in touch with the DA's office on May 1. A receptionist told him to talk to the police if he had a possible murder to report. So John called SPD Homicide and was connected to Sergeant Dave Schwartz. "What you've got to do first is get everyone to write down a statement of what happened," Schwartz told John.

Wasting no time, John went back to Ruth's other children and had them recount, on paper, everything they had seen or heard over the last few days. He turned the statements over to Schwartz, but after reading them, the detective wasn't encouraging. "Unless you saw Dorothea Montalvo give this woman a lethal drug or she told you she did that, there's not much I can do."

"You mean there's not enough evidence?" John asked incredulously.

"There's no case here at this point."

John was furious. He had become Ruth's champion. He said to Rosie, "I'm going over there and I'm going to kill her," meaning Dorothea. He did angrily confront Dorothea at 1426 F, but did nothing else.

The police reaction to the facts strengthened Bill and Rosie's judgment that their mother had killed herself.

Several weeks later, Bill went to 1426 F Street and gathered up his mother's clothes. He talked to Dorothea briefly, the two of them commiserating over the loss of a sweet woman.

It was a tragedy that Ruth's family determined to put behind them.

They did not realize that the money Ruth had drawn out for her business with Dorothea had vanished. The joint bank account was emptied as well. In early May, with a date in Superior Court to answer robbery, forgery, and grand theft charges racing toward her, Dorothea bought a plane ticket for Mexico.

The unanswered mystery remains, though. Why did she not leave Sacramento as soon as she had what she wanted? Instead, she acted as if she hoped to be caught.

16

"I'M DRUNK," DOROTHEA SAID, SLURRING HER WORDS. "Everything's going wrong. Everybody's taking advantage of me. You've got to come over."

Dorothy Osborne listened to the worried, clearly drunken woman on the other end of the telephone. Osborne, forty-nine, had known Dorothea Montalvo for about a year, and had been cared for by her. It was midmorning, May 16, 1982. "Well, I don't really want to go out, Dorothea," Osborne said.

"You've got to come over. We can have a few drinks, talk about life. Things haven't been going well." Pause. "A woman died."

"I'm sorry about that. But I can't come to your house."

Dorothea, anxious, muttering said, "All right, all right. I'll come to you. I've got to see someone."

It was a strange call, unlike any other Osborne had gotten from Dorothea. She waited, wondering what was so upsetting the usually calm, almost cold Dorothea Montalvo.

* * *

128

Osborne lived at 1620 G Street in apartment 10, only a few blocks from 1426 F. It took Dorothea only a short while to show up around eleven. Osborne had been thinking. Who had died? What woman? Dorothea had never mentioned a death that disturbed her.

Dorothea came to see Osborne dressed plainly, in a simple solid-colored dress, her hair pulled back. She brought over a bottle of Korbel brandy and some vodka.

"I'll make some drinks and we can talk," Dorothea said. "I've got a lot on my mind."

Osborne followed her into the kitchen. Dorothea opened cabinets, got out grenadine, grapefruit juice, apple and cranapple juice. "No, no," she hustled Osborne out, "you go watch TV. I'll bring everything in."

While Osborne sat in the living room, Dorothea worked alone in the kitchen, finally coming in with a large glass of the peculiar cocktail she had mixed. Osborne didn't like the biting, strong taste. "It's very sharp," she said, complaining.

"It's good," Dorothea said.

"Why don't you have some?"

"I only want vodka right now," Dorothea said, sipping from her own glass of straight vodka.

Dorothea launched into a monologue. She didn't say anything specifically about the mysterious death, but wailed and complained that people were lying about her, using her, putting terrible pressure on her. Osborne listened, finished her drink, and left Dorothea briefly to go to a nearby liquor store for something other than the brandy or vodka. She drank a little more, switched to iced tea to get the persistent sour, stinging taste of the first cocktail out of her mouth.

Dorothea never stopped complaining. She paced the living room, then sat down opposite Osborne, moaning about the wretched way she was being abused.

It was a little after noon and Osborne, listening to the incessant voice sitting near her, suddenly began to grow hazy, dim. The last thing she heard was Dorothea, whining. Then she passed out.

It was twilight outside when Osborne came to again. She

staggered around the apartment, trying to wake up. It was then she noticed that some of her checks were gone, and her credit cards, and six rolls of pennies with her name and phone number on them.

Osborne intuitively realized there was something wrong with the drink Dorothea had made for her. That weird mixture of juices and liquors could hide any strange taste. Osborne got into the kitchen, and found some of the reddish liquid remaining in a blender. She scooped it into an empty pill bottle, along with a white powder she noticed. She called the police at once.

When the police arrived, Osborne explained what had happened, who had done this to her, and gave them the pill bottle of liquid and white powder.

"She said she's going to Mexico," Osborne alerted the police. "Dorothea told me she's already got the tickets."

When Dorothea Montalvo was arrested on May 19, she still had Osborne's credit cards and rolled pennies with her. She also had the damning plane tickets.

She was taken downtown to jail, and denied bail. No judge would let her out again. She had committed a crime while on bail for another offense, and she had obviously made plans to flee the country. Dorothea Montalvo would stay in jail until her case was in Superior Court for trial.

I was delighted when the reports and files came to me. At last someone had caught Montalvo in possession of a drug. Osborne's physical effects were identical to McKenzie, Gosling, Gregory, Chalmers, and Maleville. So was the reason for drugging: theft.

I sent the pill bottle and powder over to the Crime Lab for analysis. My theory, based on the symptoms the victims experienced, was that Montalvo had used chloral hydrate, called a "Mickey Finn."

It was a terrific disappointment when the results came back. There was no controlled substance in either the reddish liquid or powder. But I found out years later that the

Crime Lab in 1982 was comparatively primitive. It could not, in fact, detect chloral hydrate or a whole range of barbiturate/tranquilizing drugs. Nor could they test for flurazepam, the generic name of Dalmane, which had been stolen from Irene Gregory.

Montalvo and I appeared before a judge later in May. She looked different, an orange jail sweatshirt giving her a sporty look. She pleaded with the judge that she had not been planning any escape, only going to visit relatives in Mexico. She would definitely be in Sacramento on the day of her Superior Court arraignment on the other charges.

I only pointed out the obvious—a plane ticket, another crime—and argued that the defendant should stay in jail to ensure the community's safety and her presence in court. The judge agreed.

Hoping for the best, I went ahead and re-filed Gosling, Gregory and added Osborne. I wanted Montalvo and her lawyer to face as many charges as possible in Superior Court and perhaps realize that a plea was preferable to a trial.

By early June, though, negotiations with Hess were going nowhere. I had not, however, heard of the terrible events at 1426 F Street on April 28. Ruth Munroe's death would have instantly resolved the question of what to do with Dorothea Montalvo.

There were a few problems. The DA's office was in convulsions in June, throwing out the incumbent, and electing a new District Attorney. I was going to debates, moderating events, acting as impartial arbiter between the two candidates because they knew I'd be gone in a few months.

Frawley and I had been working out what to do with Montalvo once things calmed down in the DA's office. The objectives were simple. First, get as much time in prison as possible, to keep her away from more victims. Second, have her plead to enough separate crimes so her rap sheet, her criminal record, reflected what she had done. As Mildred

Ballenger impressed on me, Montalvo had gotten away for so long with so much largely because her rap sheet only faintly suggested her true criminality.

To help speed this plea bargaining along, I filed a charge, section 222 of the penal code, citing Dorothy Osborne as the victim. That felony was known as "administering a stupefying agent for the purpose of committing a second felony," robbery or theft. I didn't know what drug Montalvo had used, but she certainly had drugged her victims. She would have to plead to the 222 to have it on her record for the future.

The major problem, though, was that Hess thought Montalvo should get a much better deal. I had offered him three felonies involving Osborne, Gregory, and McKenzie. In return, Montalvo would have no other charges filed against her, based on what the DA's office knew at that time, and she would serve about four years in prison.

"She's helping the cops," Hess told me. We were in Superior Court, Department Four, waiting for Judge Roger Warren. "Give her something more."

We had been going back and forth with offers for weeks. This latest development threatened everything. I still had shaky victims and no solid proof of drugging, but I didn't want to make Montalvo happy.

I called the Sacramento police and got referred to Schwartz. "What's going on, Dave?" I asked. "Montalvo's lawyer says she's working for Vice."

He laughed. "Well, what's happening is that she's over in the Women's section in jail," which was miles from downtown Sacramento, isolated, "and the younger girls are coming to her with their problems. Boyfriend troubles, things they've done. She's kind of the mother confessor for these younger inmates."

"So what is she doing for you guys?"

"These girls are telling Montalvo about crimes they've committed, crimes their boyfriends did, and asking her advice."

"Montalvo wants to trade this information?" I asked. That sounded likely.

"Right. She'll give up these kids, whatever they told her, in return for a better deal on her cases."

Schwartz and I both laughed at Montalvo's limitless duplicity. "The stuff is no good," Schwartz said.

I told him Vice couldn't use her, either.

"We shouldn't give her anything," Schwartz said firmly.

I told Hess that while I still wanted to resolve all of Montalvo's cases at once, she wouldn't get a better offer. He nodded. He was, he said, getting out of representing her. He had too many other clients. A private lawyer would come in and take over.

It was extremely frustrating. Montalvo was balking at pleading to anything, trying to twist a deal all the time, and now I had to start all over with a new lawyer.

Montalvo's next lawyer was Dennis Porter, in his twenties, a nervous, uncertain man who smoked a lot. We met on June 25. He instantly repeated Hess's belief that Montalvo should get a break because she was helping the cops. In fact, he thought she should get immunity in return for turning over so many other defendants.

Porter didn't think he was going to have much client control, based on his initial meeting with Dorothea in jail.

We set another plea negotiation for July 13. I didn't want to string this out forever, especially if I had to go to trial. My victims didn't improve as time went on. I needed something strong to use against Montalvo.

I talked to Schwartz. I thought I could push Porter. "You better send over whatever you have on Montalvo's bad one-eighty-seven," I told Schwartz, using the penal code section for murder.

"Okay. You know it's no good. You can't use it in court."

"I don't want to use it in court. I want to have it handy."

Schwartz warned me there wasn't much. He sent over a one-page face sheet on Esther Busby's poisoning. It was, I saw, completely useless as a case, but very powerful as a bargaining chip to persuade Dorothea Montalvo to plead guilty to the other crimes.

The only defect in my reasoning was that Dorothea Montalvo had on her mind the murder of Ruth Munroe, not Esther Busby.

On the morning of July 13, 1982, Porter and I met in Department Four. We went to the sunlit hallway behind the courtroom so he could smoke. He had just been in the tank, the courthouse jail cells, to see Montalvo. "She doesn't want the deal," he said.

"I thought she was interested."

"She thinks she deserves immunity. I told her what you said, but she says she's helping the police, and I believe her." He squinted at me nervously. Montalvo was giving him strict marching orders.

I realized I had to push as hard as possible. "All right. Before we leave court," I said, "you should know that the Sacramento police think she's responsible for a homicide."

"Oh, Jesus," Porter sighed, his cigarette hanging from his hand.

I showed him the one-page Busby summary. He read it quietly.

"The offer now would be that she pleads to all four victims, four separate cases. I'll agree not to prosecute any other crimes known to my office now."

"Including this," he held the Busby summary page.

"Including that," I took the page from him. I sent him a copy of it the next day.

"I'll talk to her again," Porter said. He looked white and shaky.

We were back in court on July 14, the following day. "She'll take the deal," Porter said, after he came out of the tank. "And she agrees that the maximum time she can do is four years."

"Four years eight months in state prison. That's my recommendation to the judge."

We went back into Judge Warren's chambers and told him the proposed disposition. Warren was a younger judge, with no criminal trial experience, but he had good sense. He said he'd abide by this plea bargain unless he saw something very bizarre in Montalvo's probation report before sentencing. Then he'd reject the whole deal and we'd start over, ready to go to trial.

Porter stood beside Montalvo in the dock. Judge Warren went through the mechanics of gathering the re-filed cases into his courtroom, postponing the actual pleas until July 21. Montalvo whispered to Porter and answered hesitantly, with a nervous, wary stare at the judge or me whenever she was asked if she understood the proceedings. Judge Warren asked if she agreed to continue the trial status conference to the new date.

"Yes, sir, I do," Montalvo answered in her quavery, old lady's voice. I had never seen a more incongruous defendant in an orange jumpsuit than this timorous, bespectacled, old, white-haired woman.

Dorothea Montalvo's appearance, either in municipal court or in Judge Warren's courtroom, usually caused a murmur of astonishment among the spectators. It was always difficult to reconcile the white-haired woman with what she was charged with having done.

On July 21, Porter and I were back in Department Four. I crossed my fingers and hoped Montalvo hadn't grown stubborn again and decided to throw the plea bargain out.

Porter and I spent some time back in chambers with Judge Warren, explaining the plea bargain. I told him my reasons for it were simple: I had sick victims, and this arrangement gave the sentencing judge enough latitude to put Montalvo in prison for a long time. I didn't want Judge Warren to state in open court, though, that the DA was forgoing prosecution in a homicide in order to get these pleas from Montalvo. The less I had to explain about

Busby's case and the police assessment that it was unprovable, the better.

If Montalvo heard me say that I wouldn't pursue her on a homicide, Judge Warren would probably ask, in front her, why I was doing so. I knew if Montalvo heard me say how bad the Busby case was, she'd insist on going to trial, having also heard that her living victims were too sick to come to court.

It was a delicate hide-and-seek game when we got into open court. Judge Warren, dubious about it all, agreed not to mention the homicide in any fashion.

The courtroom was nearly empty. Montalvo and Porter seated themselves at the counsel table. We began when the judge asked Montalvo a series of required questions.

"Do you understand the crimes with which you've been charged, in other words, the nature of the charges against you?"

She glanced at Porter who nodded. "Yes," she answered.

"Have you discussed the charges, your possible defenses, and this suggested disposition with your lawyer?"

Another glance at a nodding Porter. "Yes," Montalvo said, her hands clasped in front of her.

Every so often, Montalvo would look over at me. Her mouth was set. She had an inscrutable, but cold look behind her glasses. I was not one of her favorite people.

I gave a factual basis for each plea and then Judge Warren, a careful man, asked her four separate times if she was pleading guilty knowingly to each charge. Four times Montalvo said she was. She pled guilty to drugging Osborne on May 16 in order to steal from her.

The judge then put on the record that no other crimes known to the District Attorney would be prosecuted. Montalvo nodded solemnly.

Leaving the courtroom after she was taken back to a holding cell, I told Porter he had done the right thing, tying all her cases into one deal. I felt satisfied. I had gotten all four victims some justice and had used an unprosecutable suspicious death as a bargaining lever. Dorothea Montalvo would be off the streets for years.

Judge Warren set the sentencing for August 18. I thought, as I walked away from Porter out of the courthouse, I had accomplished a lot.

In fact, the white-haired, nervous old lady had out-smarted me.

The local press started picking up on Montalvo. Her grandmotherly exterior and the nasty nature of her crimes were irresistible during a slow news summer.

In a front page story on July 22, the *Sacramento Bee,* the area's largest daily, jokingly wrote that Montalvo had robbed "an elderly chap" in a bar after slipping him a Mickey Finn. I made the mistake of adding to the light-hearted spirit of the coverage by saying that Montalvo was "the most mild, pleasant appearing grandmother you could possibly think of. But I wouldn't sit down and have a drink with her."

I called her "the quintessential granny." Six years later I would cringe in disgust, seeing that stupid remark repeated as the *Bee* reported on the first bodies dug up at 1426 F Street.

The TV stories were also hitting the comical aspect of a larcenous old lady.

But I didn't treat Montalvo lightly when I got back to my office. Her files were going to the county Probation Office for the preparation of a pre-sentence report. This report would guide Judge Warren in making his sentence or rejecting the plea bargain. I wanted him to follow the plea bargain, but be starkly aware of how dangerous and malign Montalvo was.

It is unethical for a DA to send letters or call a probation officer without letting defense counsel know about it. The defense then has a chance to offer any opposing arguments.

But in difficult cases, or especially vicious and unusual situations, the normal practice was to write a detailed file memo that included every statement the DA intended to make before the judge. The memo also highlighted parts of the file, so the probation officer could go right to the heart of the crimes.

Ballenger and Schwartz had sensitized me to Montalvo's slippery abilities and I didn't want her fooling the probation officer.

I wrote a lengthy file memo, hoping to influence how the probation officer wrote his report for Judge Warren. My major point was to stress how Montalvo preyed on the most vulnerable and helpless members of the community.

When the report itself came back weeks later, I was pleasantly surprised to see how much Montalvo had cooperated in making herself look bad.

I showed Frawley the probation report Tony Ruiz had prepared. We agreed that he had caught on early to many of Montalvo's tricks. For example, he wrote that although she made remorseful comments during the interview, "in this officer's opinion her expression of remorse was diluted by her attempts to manipulate the interview."

She was pretty blatant, too:

While this officer was explaining the purpose of the interview, the defendant, after noting this writer's Hispanic surname, interrupted to explain that she, too, was of Hispanic descent. Further, although the defendant appeared distraught and tearful throughout the interview, it was apparent to this writer that she was extremely observant of the notes that were being made during the interview and, at one point, asked for an explanation of a particular word this writer had written in his notes. The defendant attempted to read, upside down, the officer's notes, as she sat on the opposite side of the interview booth.

Then Montalvo gave her version of the crimes she had committed. She felt badly, she told Ruiz, that the victims had lost some of their possessions. "She could see they were needy people or had a right to continue to possess their property. She indicated that she, too, had suffered as a child and disliked seeing other individuals suffer likewise."

But as far as admitting doing much of anything, Montalvo tried to have it both ways, being caught and innocent at the same time. She denied taking anything from Dorothy Gosling, although she agreed she had forged the woman's checks. "She was quick to point out that she made restitution, but she could not reasonably explain her actions as she reportedly did not need the money that bad."

Nor could Montalvo admit doing much to Irene Gregory. "She was confused as to her actions in this offense," Ruiz wrote, "but she nevertheless denied that she had ever been in the victim's apartment and denied taking any items from her. She indicated she had only seen this victim at the beauty shop they both patronized."

Frawley and I had wondered how Montalvo would explain away the Osborne drugging. First denying everything, Montalvo told the probation officer that she "admitted administering a drug but could not recall what it was composed of. After first indicating she had no explanation for her behavior, she then changed her story and denied administering any drug at all." Osborne, Montalvo said, invited her over to drink and gave her the wrapped pennies to buy beer.

What about Malcolm McKenzie's encounter with Montalvo in the bar? She claimed now she had only taken and forged two checks. She never took his coins or ring. "However," as Ruiz wrote again and again in the report, "she could not explain her actions."

Montalvo told Ruiz that "she pled to certain counts made against her as it was simply part of the plea bargain arrangements."

In other words, she lied to Judge Warren throughout the taking of those pleas when he asked her direct questions.

There was nothing in the report about Esther Busby, nor did Montalvo bring up the death of Ruth Munroe.

"She doesn't like to admit anything," Frawley said, with

characteristic understatement, when he gave me back the report.

I was back in front of Judge Warren on August 18. Porter was unhappy, and so was Montalvo, who muttered and shook her head as she sat at the counsel table.

She was annoyed because Warren had informed Porter and me that he found Montalvo so bad, he intended to give her the maximum possible sentence based on the four charges—five years in state prison. Ruiz had called her "callous and unconscionable" in what she did, and Judge Warren emphatically agreed.

Warren asked Porter for his thoughts. Porter argued that the judge should pick a shorter prison term. Warren was firm. Either he would give her five years or the whole plea bargain would be set aside. Neither Porter nor I wanted that.

I didn't know that Montalvo had written two letters to the judge, trying to influence his opinion of her. On June 8 she told him, "I admit I'm a forger," then said she had been a civic figure, made many charitable contributions, helped worthy political candidates with "clean money," and was burdened with a rough early life.

She wrote again on July 25, apparently sensing that the young judge wasn't so pliable as she assumed and her efforts to manipulate Tony Ruiz had failed. Montalvo told Warren that the plane tickets found on her were so she could take care of her dead sister's needy family in Mexico. No sister, of course, had died. Montalvo hoped the judge would give her the shortest possible prison time so she could help her family in Mexico by sending them "money to buy meat, eggs, milk." Her surviving brothers, she said, were too old to provide for the family.

"I don't mind if I have to report each day or what," Montalvo offered helpfully.

"I know I have done wrong," she went on. "These months in jail have been terrible on me. But worse on my family, as I have not been able to send them any money. I feel so terrible for the poor people I did wrong to."

Judge Warren, however new he was to criminal trials, was no fool. He had read the probation report's detailed summaries of what Montalvo had done and he knew that lurking in the background was something worse, even if the DA couldn't prosecute it.

He sat on the bench, spoke calmly, directly, shortly to the frowning Montalvo in front of him. He sentenced her to five years in state prison, with credit for the few months she had already been in county jail. "Do you understand the sentence?" he asked her.

"I do," Montalvo nodded sulkily.

The bailiff escorted her back through the clerk's office, down to the second floor holding cell, and then she was processed and put on a state bus and sent to the California Institution for Women in Frontera to do her time.

I left the courtroom assuming I would never see Porter or Dorothea Montalvo again. I got back to my office, called Dave Schwartz to tell him the sentence and to pass along the good news to Mildred Ballenger. We could all breathe a little easier.

On August 19, 1982, the *Bee* ran another big story on the thieving grandmother. It was more sober than the earlier stories. The headline was: "Woman Who Slipped Mickeys Draws Five Years." She was described as being handcuffed, calm, wearing a yellow jail T-shirt when sentenced.

It looked like a nice windup to the case of Dorothea Montalvo.

On August 20, 1982, I got a phone call in the afternoon. "We just read your name in the newspaper," the unknown man said. "About Dorothea and her sentencing. We think she poisoned our mother."

17

WHAT HAD HAPPENED? I WONDERED, SHOCKED BY THAT CALL. I thought I knew everything about Dorothea Montalvo's criminality, but she had kept the worst secret to herself.

It was Bill Clausen who called me and I asked him to come down to the office immediately.

That afternoon, with his brother Allan and sister Rosie, I met for the first time with Ruth Munroe's children. They sat in a semicircle in my small office and told me everything that had led up to April 28 and their mother's death.

Bill did most of the talking. He had the *Bee* article with him that had pointed them to me.

"What killed her," Bill said intently, "was a lot of codeine. The combination of pills. That's her husband's medicine, it wasn't hers. There was a lot stronger stuff around the house if she was going to kill herself." Until they saw the story about Dorothea's other crimes that spring, they believed she was a kindly, caring woman, trusted by Ruth Munroe completely. Ruth's children didn't stop bitterly blaming themselves for listening to Dorothea the whole time they were with me.

When we finished that afternoon, I was deadened and self blaming too, realizing Dorothea had fooled me as well.

I shook hands with Bill, Allan, and Rosie, and agreed to meet again early the next week. I wanted to see any documentary evidence they had, like bank statements, notes, or reports. I asked them to bring Ruth Munroe's death certificate.

As soon as they were gone, I muttered about their revelations to everyone in Team Four. What a disaster.

I talked to Frawley, O'Mara, and a bureau chief, telling them what had just happened. I went back through the Montalvo files, trying to see if Ruth Munroe's name was mentioned anywhere. It was critical for two reasons. First, I couldn't prosecute Dorothea for the murder if the DA's office had known about it before the plea bargain on July 21. And second, I needed to reassure myself I hadn't let a horrible murder slip through my hands.

But there was nothing in the files on Ruth Munroe from the police. I took a mental deep breath of partial relief and wrote a memo to O'Mara, as head of Major Crimes, alerting him to the Clausens' allegations.

Then on August 22, I called Schwartz at SPD.

I only had a little over a week left in the DA's office. My temporary job was ending before Labor Day. The investigation of Ruth Munroe's murder had to be started before I left. I owed the family that much.

The Clausens came back on August 30, bringing the death certificate. Rosie had some additional information, too. In March Munroe had lent Montalvo $600 secured by two rings. Montalvo took the rings back when she claimed she was going to see a sick relative. Munroe was never repaid. It occurred to me suddenly that the rings might belong to either Malcolm McKenzie or Irene Gregory. Montalvo didn't want stolen property in someone else's possession and so got them back from Munroe as soon as she could.

Telling me about Ruth's last days was terrible. Rosie broke down and wept.

"Dorothea told us," Bill said, pointing to himself and Rosie, "that Mom was having a nervous breakdown. She said a doctor had just come out and given her a shot, and that's why she wasn't awake or wouldn't talk to us."

Dorothea had told the patrol officer and assistant coroner that Ruth was having heart problems and had suffered a heart attack. Dorothea would say whatever it took to throw the listener's attention away from her.

It was another grueling, tense meeting. At its end, all I could do was to promise Bill and Rosie that I would make sure their information got to the police and Major Crimes.

Finally, after years as a prosecutor, I realized there isn't much you can really do for the survivors. Evil, when it hits a family, leaves an ineradicable injury.

The only bright spot I saw was that Ruth Munroe's killer was behind bars and would stay there for years. It might just be possible to get some justice for the family and Ruth. Montalvo could be charged with murder.

I typed out more memos for Schwartz and O'Mara, including the death certificate. Frawley and I talked about the best way to proceed, and putting it all in the hands of Schwartz and Major Crimes in our office was the best path to follow. I talked to O'Mara, and he agreed to check out the Clausens' information.

It turned out that my meeting with the Clausens was the last one I had as a deputy district attorney. I had to clean out my desk by September 1.

O'Mara put a seasoned investigator in Major Crimes on the case. He also got in touch with Schwartz, reviewing the statements the family had made in early May. It looked like suicide, given the divorce, Harold's illness, the lack of more evidence about Ruth Munroe's final hours, was as likely a possibility as murder. When the DA's investigator submitted his report several months later, corroborating suicide and relegating Munroe and Montalvo's connection to coincidence, O'Mara concluded that even if he did file a murder charge, he was not likely to get a conviction.

It was better, all around, to drop the matter, secure in the knowledge Dorothea Montalvo was in prison.

The story of Ruth Munroe's ugly murder sank away into limbo until 1988 when more bodies were brought up from 1426 F Street and the whole heartless past of Dorothea Montalvo, then called Puente, would be exposed to view once again.

PART 4

18

When Charles Willgues finished talking with Donna Johansson on the phone on Wednesday night, November 16, 1988, he was not alone in his apartment. He had a newsman from a local TV station with him.

All into the remainder of that afternoon and early evening, Willgues had been trying to recall where he had seen Donna before. It was not her name that tickled his memory, but her features, the white hair, glasses, the penetrating dark eyes and set mouth. "I know this woman," he thought. "I've seen her before."

Was it on TV? Around seven-thirty that night, Willgues remembered seeing Donna on the TV that morning. He called KCBS-TV and talked to the assignment editor. He described Donna and her interest in his benefit payments, his living alone. The newsman, Gene Silver, came to Willgues's apartment a little later, bringing a newspaper with a photo in it of the fugitive Dorothea Puente.

More than interest in a great story drew Silver to Willgues. "This woman could have been trying to prey on him," Silver said later. "He was disabled and drawing a pension." A prime target. Silver thought Willgues was in real danger.

The two men talked for an hour, going over what Puente said, how she acted, what she said about her plans. Willgues told Silver about the Thursday date and the tentative plans for Puente to cook Thanksgiving dinner. The two men realized how close Willgues had just come to heading down the same road with Puente others had traveled.

Willgues was fairly sure, after he saw the newspaper photo, that Donna Johansson and Dorothea Puente were the same person. He and Silver watched the 9:00 P.M. news on KCBS and again saw a photo of Puente. Willgues had no doubt now about who he had been drinking with. He called her at the Royal Viking, making sure she was in her room.

It was time, Willgues and Silver agreed, to call the police.

Puente, after the call from Willgues, had stuck to her routine of the last few days and stayed in room 31 at night. Perhaps she really felt unsafe around Third and Alvarado after dark. If so, it was an enormous irony, given her murderous propensities.

She passed the time watching TV, dozing, reading the newspapers scattered over the bureau.

After 11:00 P.M. there was a flurry of hard knocks on the door. Puente opened it. Several detectives and police officers from LAPD came in quickly, using her real name.

"I'll go with you," she said, almost meekly. In her purse the detectives found her driver's license. They had her picture from Frontera in 1982. They knew who she was. For the first time, Puente was arrested, handcuffed, and in custody for murder.

Shortly after midnight, Wednesday blending into Thursday in the city's darkness, Puente was driven in a small caravan of police cars to the Rampart Division station. She had said very little getting ready at the motel room or sitting in the squad car. She wore her red overcoat and scarlet pumps. Her white hair straggled somewhat, and when she was put into a cell, she was bowed and tired. "She's very quiet and peaceful," a police sergeant told the crowd of reporters at the station, "looking at the floor, and has her head down."

There was a burst of calls back and forth to Parker Center, the headquarters of the Los Angeles police. The decision was made not to question Puente. The LAPD was fearful that haste might jeopardize any admissions Puente made. She was, of course, rightfully a Sacramento prisoner and needed to be returned to the capital as soon as possible. There is a local jurisdictional rule in Los Angeles that suspects arrested within city limits must be arraigned on charges within five hours. Puente would have to be in court by Thursday morning.

LAPD fervently wanted to get her out of the city and back to Sacramento to avoid any future legal problems if she was arraigned in one city, then re-arraigned in the capital.

In Sacramento, Chief Kearns held a brief press conference, at last able to announce good news in the case. He was happy she had been captured. As he spoke, John Cabrera was already making arrangements to bring Puente back for trial.

Cabrera discovered that a regular charter from Sacramento to Los Angeles couldn't be set up until later Thursday morning. By that time, Puente would have been tangled up in the Los Angeles courts. There was, though, an unorthodox transportation method available, and he got permission from his superiors to use it.

Cabrera didn't know he was setting himself and the police up for as much criticism as they had gotten by letting Puente get away on Saturday.

Sacramento's NBC-TV affiliate, KCRA, was prepared to fly a cameraman and reporter Mike Boyd south as soon as Puente was arrested. Boyd wanted to get pictures of the places she had visited, the motel, Monte Carlo I, the T.G. Express. A photographer from the *Bee* would also be on the chartered plane.

Boyd and KCRA offered space on the Learjet to the police if, as Puente was flown back, they could take pictures of her. Cabrera liked the speed of the trip. He would bring another detective with him.

There were ground rules, Cabrera told Boyd. Puente was not to be asked any questions about the case, the investigation, the bodies unearthed, or her arrest. "Ask her general stuff, anything that's not about any crimes," Cabrera said. "Or else I stop all questions for the rest of the flight."

Boyd agreed to the condition. He and the *Bee* would scoop every other news organization in the country just by carrying Puente on the plane.

Cabrera spent the time until the flight talking to the L.A. police at Rampart, then, when Puente was taken downtown to Parker Center, discussing her treatment. When she was brought to Rampart earlier in the evening, head down, hands cuffed in front of her, two women officers at her sides, Puente was bombarded by shouted questions from the swarm of TV reporters that followed the squad cars from the Royal Viking. Cabrera wanted to make sure Puente stayed in a cell, away from reporters, until he arrived to take custody.

He thought LAPD agreed. But instead, to satisfy the local media, the police "marched her back and forth to her cell," Cabrera said, annoyed, as he looked at the TV pictures. "Someone hit her on the head with a camera. Accidentally." During the garish exercise, Puente said nothing. Sometimes she had on a belly chain that kept her hands tightly at her sides or in front of her with restricted movement. She had been turned into a performing bear. The attention she had craved for so long—real lights, microphones, cameras— engulfed her, even reached out and struck her.

At 2:30 A.M. Puente was taken from her cell at Parker Center, wearing a bellychain, marching head down between uniformed women officers and detectives in lockstep. As she got out of an elevator to head for a squad car, a mass of reporters and cameras surged toward her. Then the whole clumsy parade backpedaled as she was hustled forward, several reporters tripping over each other to get out of the way.

She was put into a squad car, head pushed down awkwardly, clambering into the backseat, and rushed to the Learjet and the return trip to Sacramento waiting for her.

The original flight plan for the KCRA chartered jet was to Los Angeles International Airport. Boyd had the impression they would be on the ground for a while, long enough to get the local pictures he wanted.

At the last minute, the police changed the destination to Burbank. And Boyd was now informed they would be taking off again almost immediately.

He was startled by the speed and byzantine twists of the trip. He felt caught up in a maelstrom himself, like the police and Puente, unable to do much more than go along for the ride.

The Learjet touched down at Burbank airport in early morning blackness, lit only by the bright airport lights. As Boyd talked to Cabrera about what was going to happen, a truck began pumping jet fuel into the plane.

As if on cue, Puente appeared in her procession of squad cars, followed by cameras and reporters. She looked, to Boyd, wan, white-haired, ridiculous almost in her belly chain. She was formally transferred to the Sacramento detectives from LAPD, like a spy in a prisoner exchange. Boyd told his cameraman to get some shots of Puente being handed over.

Cabrera, who still smarted badly from her Saturday deception, believed he had some rapport with Puente. He said to her, "Are you ready to come home?"

She showed him the bump on her head from the camera. He asked, "Do you want anything, Dorothea? Tell me what you want to do now." It was not, Cabrera knew, a sincere question. He was taking her back no matter what she wished.

Puente, though, tired and sagging, her head low, said, "I want to go home."

Cabrera helped her into the jet. He mused about how she

had greeted him a few moments earlier, just like they had stepped from the porch of 1426 F inside for coffee.

Inside the jet, Cabrera sat by the window, his partner on the far side, Puente in the middle, also wearing a seat belt. The reporters sat opposite them. Cabrera advised Puente of her Miranda rights. She said nothing in reply, made no movement at all, a chained and seat belted granny. Her handcuffed hands lay in her lap as the jet took off.

The small passenger compartment was cramped and very loud with engine noise, and no one spoke for some time. The gaudy, colorful lights of Los Angeles slipped past below them in the darkness heading northward. It was about an hour flight time. Puente asked for a cup of coffee and got a half-filled plastic cup.

Boyd's cameraman began taping her and the *Bee's* photographer snapped off pictures. She peered out toward the window into the darkness, the random tiny city lights far below.

Gently, conversationally, Boyd began talking to her. He didn't know if she was guilty of anything, but he had been a reporter long enough to sense when someone was trying to use him. Puente a few moments before had initiated the chat. "I know you," she said to Boyd, long a local celebrity. "You probably know me. We've been acquaintances for a long time."

Puzzled, Boyd listened, nodded. He had never met her before, and he knew a con job when he heard it. She was trying to establish a friendly past for them both. He let her. They had, she said, been at some political and charitable functions together. They were, she seemed to imply, equal celebrities.

So, Boyd figured she'd broken the ice. He asked her, "How do you feel about going back to Sacramento? How do you feel now?"

His probing revitalized Puente. She spoke firmly suddenly, combatively. "I used to be a good person," she said, perhaps thinking back a long way to the halcyon days at 2100 F.

Then she turned to Cabrera, "I told you that. I have not killed anyone. The checks I cashed, yes." She repeated this several times to make sure everyone heard her, then lapsed back into silence, not even bothering to work Boyd or Cabrera anymore. She held the plastic cup and complained about being tired.

A little after 4:00 A.M. the jet landed at Sacramento Metropolitan Airport, and Puente was taken first to the police department for booking on the warrant charging her with Bert Montoya's murder, then to the orange and white block of the county jail. Boyd was fatigued, happy, delighted with the exclusive story he'd just gotten.

Cabrera, too, basked in momentary satisfaction that his misjudgment of Saturday had been blotted out by an efficient recapture of Puente. And she hadn't had time to commit any more crimes.

The early morning triumph turned sour almost as quickly, though, like so many illusions about Puente.

It was left to Cabrera's partner on the flight to sum up most people's reaction to Puente's capture. At the Burbank airport he said, "In twenty-three years of law enforcement, nothing is beyond the realm of believability when you're dealing with human beings."

He added with a nod, "We're relieved to get her off the streets."

19

THURSDAY MORNING, SACRAMENTO MUNICIPAL COURT, BEFORE Judge John Stroud, Dorothea Puente appeared in an orange jail jumpsuit, behind the railing guarding the jail tank. She held on to the railing for support and answered only two brief questions put to her by the judge: Was her name Dorothea Montalvo Puente? Yes, she said. Did she have the money to hire her own attorneys? No, she said.

The judge appointed two Sacramento County public defenders, Peter Vlautin and Kevin Clymo, to represent Puente. They conferred with her hastily at the railing, taking a copy of the one count murder complaint passed from the deputy DA to the clerk to the judge to them. Puente, Vlautin announced, would not enter any plea at that time. She had been arraigned by Judge Stroud on the single charge of killing Bert Montoya. Further investigation, more consultation were needed by her lawyers before she said whether she was guilty or not guilty.

Stroud set December 15 for her next court appearance.

Puente, tired, small, stout, was taken back into the tank.

The murmuring, fascinated courtroom turned to the normal cases that were called up in quick succession.

Left hanging in the air, just before Puente left the courtroom, was the announcement from the deputy DA that a new set of charges would be filed against her soon, charging her with all the murders she was believed to have committed.

In an almost angry bustle, Vlautin and Clymo hurried from the courtroom, followed by a line of reporters, stepping into the hallway, into another blaze of camera lights and shouted questions.

The overarching question on everybody's mind was just how many people had this white-haired woman killed?

Although it took only a few minutes, the arraignment in municipal court had been choreographed carefully. The judge ruled on requests for cameras in the courtroom, listened to the deputy DA in chambers officially state that new charges were coming, and then called Puente out of order on the busy morning calendar. Stroud had also made sure that two senior public defenders were ready to instantly take over Puente's representation. Although she had about $3,000 on her when she was arrested, everyone assumed Puente would claim indigency and be entitled to the free services of the county public defender.

California, almost alone in America, requires that two lawyers represent a defendant in a death penalty case. One lawyer puts on the defendant's case during the first part of the trial, the guilt phase. If the defendant is convicted, the jury must decide whether he dies in the gas chamber at San Quentin or is sentenced to life in prison without the possibility of parole. It is the sole job of the second lawyer to present mitigating evidence during this penalty phase of the trial.

Clymo would take charge of Puente's guilt phase defense, and Vlautin would try to keep her out of the gas chamber if she was convicted on multiple murder counts with special circumstances. Both men had been public defenders for over a decade and were familiar courtroom figures. Both had also earned a degree of respect from their adversaries in the DA's office.

It was assumed on Thursday morning that Tim Frawley would prosecute Puente, but O'Mara, as head of Major Crimes, could elect to keep her case and another serial killer trial for himself.

In the courthouse hallway, Vlautin made a good effort at mastering the stammer that afflicted him at times of stress. Red-faced, wearing black-rimmed glasses, with a receding hairline, looking more like a banker than a defense attorney, he spoke with greater authority than Puente's other lawyer, Clymo. Clymo, bald, his hair long and dangling in back, with a deep, slow voice and large, coarse frame, seemed a holdover from the sixties beside Vlautin.

They were thinking alike, though. It appeared they were embarking on a public relations campaign for Puente. During a series of press conferences they conducted throughout the trial, Vlautin and Clymo attacked the gaping unknowns in the case against Puente, and counter charged that she was being hustled through the legal system.

Vlautin, with Clymo towering beside him, worked himself into indignation over the media attention Puente was getting and the way the Sacramento police had carted her back to the capital.

"It's unheard of to have a suspect transported with reporters and cameras on the plane before she even has a chance to talk to an attorney."

Clymo broke in. Puente had "no opportunity to talk to anybody who had her interests in mind," he said.

"I don't know where the blame lies," Vlautin said, "but it isn't right." Puente, he said, had been upset and frightened since the ordeal.

The reporters and camera crews from all over the United States, France, and England, recorded the defense's irritation and paradoxical scorn for the "circus atmosphere" around Puente even as they fed it. "Our client denies killing anybody," Vlautin said clearly. "The true facts will come out in the courtroom, not in the courthouse hallway." He would subpoena everyone on the plane, all the film and videotape. The prosecution was so eager to get at Puente, Vlautin said, it had compromised the case against her. "I'm surprised she wasn't on the Geraldo Rivera show this morning," he snapped.

With a wave, more questions shouted after them, Puente's two lawyers strolled down the corridor, their first skirmish fought on her behalf.

Vlautin and Clymo were not alone in holding a press conference Thursday morning. A tired, visibly cranky Chief Kearns faced another ring of hostile reporters and cameras. He had been compelled to meet with some of them earlier, behind closed doors, to apologize for leaving them out of Puente's capture and flight back.

He was adamant in the press conference that he knew nothing about Cabrera's plan to use the KCRA jet. Several reporters were openly disbelieving that a lower-level police official, acutely aware of how bad the department looked after Saturday's escape, would take a major decision alone. But Kearns wouldn't budge. No one had told him about the flight beforehand. He wasn't responsible for any legal problems that developed.

"I'm ordering an inquiry into the matter. I'm not going to answer any more questions."

The only agency not heard from publicly was the DA. Frawley kept his own counsel as the week ended, and he tried to sort through the cascade of reports, files, and packages Puente's investigation created.

I went to see him, to urge him to file Ruth Munroe's murder against Puente.

He was a little weary, but cheered, his desk cluttered. The Coroner's office had just announced that the autopsies of two more F Street victims had been completed, without establishing a cause of death. The two still unidentified victims were described as an elderly woman, without teeth, dressed in a long-sleeved blouse, jacket, and low shoes. It was her body Enloe referred to on Monday, whose missing teeth the police thought they had found scattered below Puente's window. In fact, the police now believed the teeth were unconnected to Puente and had been deliberately put there merely to grab attention.

The second victim was a fifty-year-old woman, in a red blouse with narrow black stripes and another light-colored blouse over it.

The two victims underlined Frawley's problems. First, he still didn't know who these people were. The evidence collected from 1426 F might identify them, but for the moment, he was blind. He also had to worry that no cause of death would be listed. To convict Puente, it was essential that how she killed these people be discovered.

"You've got a cause of death in Munroe," I said when I saw him.

"It's kind of a weak case," he replied. "I'm looking at it."

I was very anxious, after the horror of what had happened, that Puente answer for Munroe.

We talked about using Munroe's cause of death, a drug overdose, to help explain what had happened to the other victims. It was a possibility.

Frawley was also exploring two other possible homicides to tie to Puente. One involved fleshy-lipped, doughy-faced Eugene Gamel, about to go on trial for child molestation in the summer of 1987. Gamel died in front of the F Street house, an apparent suicide, and Puente notified the police. It had definite echoes of Munroe's death.

"What's the other case?" I asked. Bodies seemed to turn up everywhere Puente went.

"It's a man she was going to marry," Frawley said.

"You're kidding."

"He lived with her at 1426 F for a while. The problem is to link him and a body they found a couple years ago."

Frawley had solved one mystery already, the smiling white-haired man in the photograph Cabrera seized from

Puente's dining room was Everson Gillmouth. The remaining mystery was why Puente kept his picture. Unless she thought she was above suspicion in his disappearance.

Frawley needed to connect Gillmouth's smiling photo with a John Doe body found in a makeshift coffin on the bank of the Sacramento River in January 1986.

20

EVERSON GILLMOUTH WAS A HAPPY MAN IN AUGUST 1985. HE was going to meet a woman he had been writing to for some time and he was going to marry her.

What happened to Gillmouth is tragic and horrible because it demonstrates that literally as soon as she got out of state prison, Dorothea Puente went right back to murder for profit.

Gillmouth was a lonely widower in his late seventies, a large-featured, avuncular looking man in glasses. He was the cousin who would come to holiday meals and not be seen for the rest of the year. He had retired from Martin Marietta, got a small pension from them, and lived for several years near his sister Reba and her husband in Sweet Home, Oregon.

He lived in an Airstream camper attached to a red Ford pickup truck. He did small jobs and for some time devoted himself to wood carving or leather working. Gillmouth's wood work was elaborate, totemistic, like the polished, intricate work of a tribesman. He exhibited and sold some of his work.

But living near his sister wasn't enough. Reba was also sturdy, large-framed, looking like she could run a frontier farm. She and Everson were not as close as they could have been, although she was very fond of him and proud of his talent.

Since his wife died, Gillmouth felt sour toward doctors, and although he was treated for significant heart problems and phlebitis, which required hospitalization, he never told Reba about it. When they both lived in Maryland in the seventies, they didn't see each other very much. It was from his loneliness that he parked his camper near Reba's home for several years.

He started writing to women in prison, too. He very much wanted to marry again, have a wife for his last years, and the intimacy of a home of his own. Gillmouth was a regular correspondent with a woman in an Oklahoma prison, and another in Banning, California. He offered to marry a woman prisoner in Oklahoma who had a child.

He also began writing to Dorothea Puente, then an inmate in Frontera. Their letters were friendly, then more personal, and Puente confessed to Gillmouth that she, too, wanted to settle down once more, straighten out her life and start anew with someone she could love.

They kept up this conversation by mail for a year, and Puente told Gillmouth that the prison would be releasing her to a halfway house in Fresno, California, for the last few months of her sentence. She was getting out early, after about three and a half years of the five-year sentence, because she had been an excellent prisoner and earned work credits, too.

Would Gillmouth like to meet her and the two of them could drive back to Sacramento? They could both live at her house on F Street. Puente had Gillmouth get in touch with Ricardo Odorica to set up the details of when to come to Fresno to pick her up.

Puente left the love struck Gillmouth with the clear belief she would become his second wife.

Gillmouth's sister Reba had read some of her brother's mail, so she knew about several of the women he was writing to. She did not, though, know about Dorothea until Everson told her. And startled her with the news that he was packing up his carvings, loading everything into the camper, and driving south to pick up his fiancée.

"If everything works out all right," Gillmouth happily told his sister, "Dorothea and I are going to get married."

Reba knew a little about Dorothea and did not share her brother's unabashed enthusiasm. It struck her as a risky, uncertain thing to end up in a strange city, no friends or family nearby, living with a woman he had never met.

But Everson was a very lonely man. When Reba saw him a few days later, he was in high spirits, looking forward to his new life.

It was the last time Reba ever saw her brother.

After Labor Day 1985, Reba thought she would hear from Everson about his arrival in Sacramento, what 1426 F Street was like or how he was getting along with Dorothea. Then more days passed without word. Knowing her brother was perhaps blinded to dangers by love, Reba called the Sacramento police, gave them Everson's new address and asked if they would go by and see if he was all right.

About September 17, police officers rang the doorbell at 1426 F Street and talked with Everson Gillmouth. He told them he was fine, there were no problems, they shouldn't have come out and bothered. He sounded peeved that his sister was checking up on him. He called Reba, complained about her worries and said the police had come by to see him. It was not a pleasant call.

It was the last time Reba heard Everson's voice.

She decided that if he wanted to be left alone, so be it.

Reba heard nothing more from Sacramento until October 14. She got her first letter from Puente. It was a sharpish note, annoyed that Reba had set the police on 1426 F Street. "Gill is staying at my house," Puente wrote. He was selling his carvings, too. He was angry with Reba, and "he doesn't want you to have the police out again." It ended, somewhat oddly, "Thinking of you."

A little over a week later, Reba got a second, much more chatty and cheery letter from Puente. It now sounded as though the two women had been friends for years. "Gill is busy with his carving, taking some down to Palm Springs to sell," Puente informed Reba. The bad news was that he had been "turned down by the Vets for assistance" and "his leg bothers him." They still planned on getting married in November.

The second letter was cozily signed, "Dorothea and Gill."

For a short time, Reba's vague suspicions about her brother and his new girlfriend ebbed.

Then, on November 2, 1985, Reba got a strange Mailgram. It was sent, purportedly, by Gillmouth. It said he was going to leave Dorothea. The wedding was off. He was planning on heading south.

Reba's fears flared up again. The wording, the tone, none of the Mailgram sounded like her brother had written it.

The Mailgram asked Reba not to try to stop him from taking the trip south. In his whole life, Everson had never asked her anything like that, nor had she ever tried to stop him from doing anything. But what could she do? Her brother had told her he didn't want to be checked up on, and the police had visited 1426 F Street and found everything in order.

Reba and her husband decided that Everson Gillmouth was obviously old enough to do as he pleased. It was interesting, though, that rather than call or write, Everson used a Mailgram, which bore no true sign he had written it.

There was a long, deep silence after that, and Reba worried about her brother.

Suddenly, in April 1986, she got a postcard from a woman named Irene. Irene wrote that she was Everson's new love. They had met during his travels. The postcard was chatty, like the letter Puente had sent. Irene told Reba, "We came to Sacramento to pick up the rest of Everson's things. He had a small stroke in January. I heard you had the police out." It was a peculiar reference, unless the postcard writer still felt nettled by Reba's concern for her brother.

She read on. Irene said that they had gone to the desert. "We're both health nuts," she gaily wrote, and Everson "has lost some weight." They also went to church every week. The card was signed, "Irene and Everson."

The whole thing—a new woman, the silence from Everson himself—was fishy, Reba thought. But she had no way of contacting her brother directly anymore. She hoped for the best and waited to hear from him.

Everson had actually gotten to 1426 F Street in mid-August 1985. He parked his camper and Ford pickup on the street until people complained, and then moved them a few blocks away.

His sole companion at 1426 F Street was Ricardo Odorica. The rest of the Odorica family lived in the south part of the city. Odorica was friendly and accommodating to Gillmouth, or Gill, as he called him. This man was about to marry Odorica's lady, the patroness of his family, the surrogate grandmother who so loved his wife and children.

Gill's excitement about meeting Dorothea for the first time mounted until September 9. He and Odorica drove to Fresno in his pickup. The three had a joyful, emotional reunion and drove back at once to Sacramento.

Gill and Dorothea set up housekeeping on the second floor at 1426 F. Odorica went on living on the first floor. After Gill had moved the pickup off the street, the two men took the Airstream camper to Odorica's sister's home in Lincoln for safekeeping. This was Dorothea's suggestion. She asked Ricardo if his sister had a place for the trailer while she and Gill ran a newspaper ad and sold it.

Everson Gillmouth was losing his worldly possessions to his future wife. Ricardo believed the gentleman had given the trailer to Dorothea as a gift. She herself had told him so.

Odorica liked Gill, who although much older than the lady, was courtly to her and dignified. He didn't see Gill very often, though, maybe once or twice a week. Odorica was working nights at the Clarion Hotel and sleeping during the day.

Gill seemed healthy for a man his age, even if he limped a little. He didn't complain about his health and the lady mothered him. In mid-December 1985, Odorica was preparing to make his annual Christmas trip to Mexico to see his father. One day, a little before he left, he saw Gill sitting in the front yard at 1426 F working on a wood carving. Gill, though, seemed in some pain, in his chest. Odorica had watched him take pills sometimes when he was having chest pains. But this time, when he told Gill he was going to the store, Gill didn't stop him, so the pains couldn't have been too bad.

In fact, the lady had once told him Gill was sick in bed, but that was the only time he reckoned Gill to be having physical difficulties of any importance.

Odorica left Sacramento, saying good bye to Gill and the lady, wishing them well. For some reason, the wedding seemed to be put off, November, then December, then no date. Gill looked tired, too.

Odorica got back on January 20, 1986. There was no one but the lady living at 1426 F Street. Where was Gill? Where had he gone? "He didn't like Sacramento," Puente told Odorica. "He went back to where he came from. He's gone back to Oregon."

The handyman, Ismael Florez, who had been doing paneling work around the house when Odorica left for Mexico, now had Gill's red Ford Pickup. "Gill sold it to him," Puente explained.

There was no further talk about Gill. He had left the lady. He no longer existed, as far as Odorica was concerned.

Shortly before Christmas 1985, right after Odorica had left the country and Gill and Puente lived alone at 1426 F Street, Jesus Meza stopped by to do a favor for his girlfriend.

Her name was Brenda Trujillo, and she was back in prison. When she was out, she lived at 1426 F off and on, was familiar with Puente, and left her belongings inside, too. Trujillo wanted Meza to pick up a box and some money.

Thin, dark-haired, a little twitchy, Meza was invited inside by Puente. They talked about Brenda, prison life, troubles.

Then white-haired, hard-faced Dorothea Puente told Meza she needed help. Meza, sitting in the upstairs living room with Puente, had noticed a pungent, unpleasant stink when he came inside. He didn't know what it was at first, but Puente's next words told him instantly.

"A man's died of a heart attack," Puente said calmly. "I don't know what to do with his body. I need help getting rid of it."

Meza was startled and disgusted. Puente said she'd pay him to take the body out, but he refused.

"Don't tell the police," Puente said, not quite begging and not quite ordering Meza.

"I won't. I won't," Meza promised, still shocked by the implication of this kindly-looking little old lady's words. A man was rotting somewhere nearby in the house.

As he left, in some haste, Meza recalled Puente's calm, her steely, bland conversation, her lack of concern about the things she was saying. As if having a dead man in the house was a garbage-disposal problem more than anything else.

Meza was determined it wasn't going to be his problem.

Ismael Florez, also dark-haired with a mustache, glum-looking most of the time, was drinking at the Rendezvous Club in downtown Sacramento, one night in September. A grand, almost regal-looking older woman swept in, ordered a drink. She sat with Florez. She needed someone to do work for her at 1426 F Street, she said.

He wanted to know what kind.

"General work, interior paneling, anything that needs to be fixed," she said.

Florez, who worked sometimes as a tile setter, knew basic carpentry, so he agreed. Over the next few months he nailed

Trial exhibit photos of victims Everson Gillmouth (left), James Gallop (bottom, left) and Betty Palmer.

Ruth Munroe with one of her grandchildren, about 1972. *(Photo courtesy of William Clausen)*

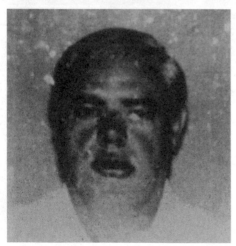

Trial exhibit photos of Alvaro "Bert" Montoya several years before his death

Trial exhibit photo of Vera Faye Martin, whose body was unearthed at 1426 F Street on November 14, 1988.

1426 F Street. *(Photo by Robert B. Templeman, Jr.)*

The Mirage bar, formerly Joe's Corner, where Dorothea Ouente cashed many of her tenants' checks. *(Photo by Robert B. Templeman, Jr.)*

Sacramento Police Homicide Detectives John Cabrera, left, and Terry Brown found the first body in 1988. *(Photo by Robert B. Templeman, Jr.)*

Mervin John McCauley, Puente's confidant, November 1988.

Gilmouth's coffin propped against the wall in the Monterey courtroom during Puente's 1993 trial.

One of the seven F Street victims, November 1988. Note the shallowness of the grave, similar to the other six graves.

Dorothea Montalvo Puente being arraigned in Sacramento Superior Court on nine counts of murder, fall 1990. One of her two defense attorneys, Kevin Clymo, is at left. *(Photo by Glen Korengold)*

Peter Vlautin, Puente's other defense attorney, during her trial.

away, sprucing up the paneling in the upstairs living room at the house. He was annoyed by Dorothea Puente's reluctance to pay him. She was always bargaining, negotiating, trying to whittle down his price, unwilling to actually give him much money for the work.

Finally it came time to settle up. "I'll pay you," Puente told Florez, "but I've got a truck I'd like to sell."

She took him outside and showed him a red Ford pickup. "It's my boyfriend's. He's away in L.A." Florez was interested in the truck, and two weeks later, in mid-December, he bought the truck from Puente for $800 and she insisted the low purchase price include Florez's wages for working around the house.

She was, he had learned, a very hard bargainer. And, although Florez didn't know it, a terrific survivor. She had gotten labor, $800, and disposed of an incriminating piece of evidence, the Ford pickup, all at the same time. What Florez also did not know was that the pickup's true owner, Everson Gillmouth, was dead inside 1426 F.

Florez had the run of the house in December when Puente was out, so he could do his work. She kept one or two rooms locked, but otherwise he was free to go anywhere. He saw nothing odd, and never came across the white-haired older man Odorica called Gill. Gillmouth was in one of the closed rooms, going nowhere.

In the latter part of December, after Meza had come and gone, Puente told Florez she needed a storage box. He'd have to build it. It was to be six feet by three feet. It had to have a top. She and Florez drove the Ford pickup to Lumberjack to get the wood and other material. Puente said she wanted to put old things inside, so the long, man-sized box had to be solid.

Florez worked in the living room, hammering away on the fresh smelling wood, taking a day to make it. Puente stopped by to inspect the work and was pleased. "Leave the top off," she told him when he left for the day.

In the next few days, Puente, probably hauled the newly built box into the kitchen. She could have lugged

Gillmouth's decaying corpse from its hiding place and struggled to get it into the box. Gillmouth was wrapped tightly in plastic and garbage bags so that he wouldn't flop around. When she had him in the box, she realized that something else was needed. Meza had noticed the smell a few days earlier. She found a handful of mothballs and a deodorant stick, and threw them onto Gillmouth's corpse. Then she hefted the wooden top onto the box and nailed it shut.

Florez came back, as she requested, three days later. "I'm ready to put this thing into storage," Puente told him. "Let's get this into the pickup."

She and Florez went outside and found a man doing construction work on the next-door house. He helped them lug the heavy box out of the kitchen, down the porch steps, and into the bed of the red Ford pickup. Gillmouth's truck had just become his hearse.

With Puente sitting beside him, Florez drove north and headed out onto Garden Highway along the Sacramento River. The early winter rains had turned the water muddy brown, rushed the current faster. "I'll tell you where to go," she said.

He followed the serpentine turns on the narrow levee road, going farther away from downtown Sacramento. "I've changed my mind," she said without fanfare. "There's no point in storing this stuff."

"What's inside anyway?" Florez asked.

"Just some junk."

Florez drove for another ten minutes. They had gone about twenty miles and passed into neighboring Sutter County. There were few houses nearby; the rural area was tree-shaded and chilly on the December morning. Something clicked for Puente. "This is fine," she said. "We can dump it here."

He parked, got a dolly out from the back of the truck, and with Puente's help, trundled the unwieldy box from the road, down toward the riverbank. The water moved by swiftly, and Puente told him to leave the box as close to the riverbank as possible. It looked like she believed the rising river, over the winter, would come up and carry the box of junk away.

They drove back to Sacramento.

Florez went on doing repair work around 1426 F Street through the rest of the month, mostly plumbing in a downstairs bathroom. He used the Ford pickup into 1986, then decided to sell it. He found a buyer, Richard Lopez, and sold it to him for $2300. It was annoying when Lopez, at his wife's insistence, went back to Florez and asked for a bill of sale showing that Florez actually owned the pickup.

Since he had never gotten anything from Puente, Florez took the bill of sale Lopez's wife had prepared, and returned to 1426 F Street. Puente, with some exasperation, filled in the bill of sale with the name Everson Gillmouth.

"It was mine to sell," she said. "He gave it to me."

A little before 8:00 A.M., Marvin Horstman, slightly paunchy, wearing glasses, and his wife, opened their small general store in Verona, in Sutter County. It was New Year's Day 1986, and they thought someone might want to come in early.

They had barely opened when one of the regulars, Roy, came rushing in excitedly, talking quickly about something he'd just found.

Horstman didn't quite understand what Roy was so worked up about. A body? A box? He and Roy drove two miles down toward the Sacramento River. It was cold, sharp, the new year coming in with an icy grip.

Roy led him from the levee road to the riverbank. Near an ancient oak tree was a large wooden box, only about twenty feet from the river. Horstman could immediately see that the box was clumsily constructed and the top coming apart. One board on the left was partly open. Roy urged him to look inside. Horstman peered down and got a shock. It looked like there was a plastic wrapped body inside. He got a

171

pair of pliers from the truck, and gingerly pulled the plastic wrapping back far enough to see that there was a man's rotting body in the box.

"We got to call the sheriff," Horstman said shakily.

The box and body were carefully removed by the Sutter County Sheriff's Department and taken to a mortuary in Yuba City. Dr. Frederick Hanf had the unpleasant duty of examining the remains.

Working in the somewhat primitive conditions of the mortuary, Dr. Hanf found that he first had to cut through several layers of black plastic garbage bags that had been put around the body. The man himself wore only Jockey shorts. Dr. Hanf noted the mothballs and deodorant on the body, some of the stranger attempts to hide the smell of decomposition he had ever seen. There was a very great decomposition, too, so great that Dr. Hanf couldn't rule out suffocation or strangulation because the dead man had a plastic garbage bag around his head. The neck had so decomposed he also could have been strangled with a rope or ligature of some kind.

There were no wounds, no cuts or bruises. The dead man, apparently in his late sixties or seventies, still had on a wristwatch. Lying in and around the body were dead fly pupae, so Dr. Hanf figured the man had been dead and in his makeshift coffin for weeks at least, long enough for flies to breed and die.

Opening up the body, he spotted arterial clogging—some bad, some minor—and decided that the state of the body would prevent making any judgment whether death had been natural or not. He took a sample of what remained of the blood, without any hope of finding much. The body had lain in the open, exposed to the elements, for too long.

There was no identification on the dead man. So Dr. Hanf finished his work, tagged the body, and it was locked away in the mortuary, in the custody of the Sutter County sheriff, as a John Doe.

* * *

Martin Marietta had been sending monthly pension checks, about $43 each time, for Everson Gillmouth, since 1985. The company had his change of address in late 1985 and sent checks where he requested. There was, though, a slip-up. Some of the checks got lost. In February 1986, the pension fund clerks got an irate letter from an unnamed person, demanding that Everson Gillmouth's checks be resumed. The goof was found, and the checks continued routinely, sent to 1426 F Street and whoever was annoyed the flow had been temporarily interrupted.

So ended the story of Everson Gillmouth, the wood-carver and hopeful suitor.

Frawley felt confident that the necessary connections to Gillmouth and Puente could be established. He also noticed the awful similarity to Ruth Munroe. Munroe was a healthy, happy, and forward-looking woman when she moved into 1426 F Street with Puente. Within weeks, she was dead.

Everson Gillmouth was also relatively healthy, according to his doctor who last saw him on August 2, 1985, medically stable and taking his blood pressure medication. He was happy, too. Within eight or so weeks of moving in with Dorothea Puente, Gillmouth was in a box by the river. People who survived quite well on their own seemed to die quickly near caring, motherly Puente.

And Frawley had another connection to ponder. Reba Nicklous had gotten a postcard from Irene, an unknown woman.

Irene Gregory was a victim from Puente's recent past, a name she would certainly remember.

So Frawley was left to figure out how many victims to charge Dorothea Puente with killing, and hope a cause of death might be found.

21

THE LAST FIVE WEEKS OF 1989 WERE VERY BUSY ONES FOR EVERY-one involved in the Puente investigation. There was fear, not very far beneath the surface, that so much circumstantial evidence had to be gathered, correctly presented, preserved, that Dorothea Puente might never be convicted of anything more serious than passing bad checks.

From the DA to the Social Security Administration, everyone learned that it is one thing to trap a monster and another to decide what to do with her.

Frawley kicked off an inquiry within Social Security in Washington and Sacramento to find out how many checks had been coming to Bert Montoya and the other identified Puente victims. By mid-December there were five victims with names, identified in part by the information in Puente's dining room and a matching comparison of missing social service clients. Besides Montoya, there were James Gallop, Ben Fink, Dorothy Miller, and Vera Faye Martin. All had been dead and buried no more than a year.

It was vital to find out how much money Puente had been receiving from the victims.

All of the social service groups—VOA, the county, St. Paul's Center, and the social workers themselves—were intensely questioned by the police, the DA, and their own staff. How long were you sending people to Puente? How many did you send? Did you have any suspicions about her? Why didn't you do anything if you suspected a problem?

The Sacramento police reacted sharply to the criticism of its handling of the case. Chief Kearns personally dressed down Cabrera and Terry Brown in his office, then had the two detectives transferred out of Homicide. Enloe and another detective were also transferred to less important assignments, a clear slap at them.

No one above the rank of lieutenant, much less Chief Kearns, was reprimanded.

Frawley had been kept busy sending out the numbered pages of reports and documents, in the dozens, then hundreds, that came to him. California automatically entitles the defense to "discovery" of all evidence against a charged defendant. The only documents Frawley held back from Vlautin and Clymo were my 1982 memos. He considered them internal DA office material. Like Cabrera's decision to fly down to Los Angeles with KCRA, the decision would snap back on Frawley later.

Puente made a second court appearance on December 1, her mouth pinched, looking irritated as her lawyers argued to Judge Gail Ohanesian. Frawley answered for the prosecution.

Vlautin wanted the DA to provide raw copies of the autopsy reports. Charging that the Sacramento coroner and DA were throwing a "veil of secrecy" over the information, Vlautin stammered a little and said the defense experts needed access to the unfiltered information.

Puente, meanwhile, signed a waiver request so she would not have to appear in court when these purely legal matters were being thrashed out. She disliked being hustled from RCCC, outside of the city, brought downtown, kept in the courthouse lockup, and missing her usual mealtimes.

Frawley knew, of course, why Vlautin was making his unprecedented request. Puente's defense was already shaping up. She would claim that all seven F Street victims had died of natural causes. The defense lawyers wanted outside doctors to scour the raw data for anything that would support that theory.

The judge listened and later agreed that the prosecution should provide greater than usual access to the autopsy results.

Outside the courtroom, holding what promised to be another in a series of press conferences, Clymo noddingly said Puente "feels safe and protected now. She's more secure, less afraid."

The two lawyers met with her often. "She's looking forward to her day in court," Vlautin said without embarrassment.

Puente, in fact, was very upset at the branch jail, angry that she was isolated, annoyed with her two appointed lawyers. She was anxious about her belongings at 1426 F Street and how the police were handling them. When Ismael Florez was arrested as an accomplice, then released because the statute of limitations had run out, Puente spoke out angrily within earshot of several other women prisoners.

She was bitterly resentful that Gillmouth and Florez had been linked so quickly by the police, and even more upset that Florez apparently was being given preferential treatment.

Her obscene tirades about Florez and Gillmouth were duly noted in the jail.

She was also worried about Frawley's announcement that new murder charges would be filed against her on January 18, 1989. It didn't help when some of her former neighbors, none with much good to say about her, went on "Geraldo" to talk about "murderers next door."

Sacramento's most famous killer produced a wealth of jokes and editorial commentary. Enterprising businessmen put together T-shirts, one showing a stylized Puente, leaning on a shovel with a hand clawing from the ground. I DIG SACRAMENTO read the caption. Phony menus from "Dorothea's Diner" featuring cannibalistic meals popped up all over the city. When the news broke that one victim was wearing a wristwatch, still running, local wits suggested the Timex company contact Puente for an endorsement.

The jokes and sight gags were a reflex by Sacramento, trying to hide its sense of shame and horror.

The best counterpoint was provided by the Roman Catholic bishop who said mass on November 28 for the seven F Street victims. It was a strained position for Francis Quinn, who found himself the only Catholic prelate in America who had praised and been photographed with a serial killer, then officiated at a mass for her victims.

In a partly filled cathedral downtown, only blocks from F Street, Bishop Quinn said, "We must not let the unusual, even bizarre circumstances cloud the fact that seven people have died."

He noted what would concern Frawley as a prosecutor. "Certainly if seven children had died, or young adults had died under similar mysterious circumstances, there would be an abiding sense of outrage. These victims were apparently older people, lonely and alone. They were hardly missed."

He ended solemnly, "Although their deaths have come in alarming circumstances, we are confident they have now found peace in the embrace of the eternal God."

Frawley's looming problem was that the victims were generally street people, shadows hard to pin down for the jurors in a trial. It would be hard to find witnesses as to when each victim had died. Or even to persuade the jury that the victims, who were society's castoffs in many ways, were still human beings, and none deserved the fate that had overtaken them with Dorothea Puente.

As if in answer to the bishop's prayer and Frawley's hope, the single most important discovery in the investigation occurred in early January.

22

TOXICOLOGISTS HAD DETERMINED THAT ALL SEVEN OF THE F Street victims—the five with names and two without, including the one headless, legless, handless victim buried in the front yard—had one, common drug in their bodies.

The bodies, so decomposed that accurate drug-level analysis was virtually impossible, contained a stew of medicines. Each person, Frawley learned, had been taking all kinds of medications. Some victims had a few medications in their organ tissues that had not been prescribed. This, though, did not surprise Frawley. Cabrera's search warrant report indicated that the kitchen, dining room, and Puente's bedroom at 1426 F Street had been packed with medicines.

But there was only one drug in all the victims.

Besides several different sedatives, Frawley found out from the state toxicologists that the victims had sedatives from the benzodiazepine family in their bodies. Frawley brightened at this news.

The benzodiazepines include the drug flurazepam, a central nervous system depressant that is marketed under the name Dalmane. It was the same drug Puente had stolen from Irene Gregory in 1982, and more significantly, it was empty Dalmane capsules that Cabrera had found in a drawer in Puente's bedroom.

Was this the cause of death? It was, Frawley knew, a start at pinning one down. He had already recognized that Puente's trial would be a massive presentation of almost completely circumstantial evidence. Every little link in the long chain around seven or eight or nine victims had to be tight.

So Frawley wondered whether Dalmane could be shown as the cause of death in the seven F Street bodies. "It would not be the thing I would use to kill someone," a California Department of Justice toxicologist said. "It takes so many of them [pills] to suppress the central nervous system to the point where you die."

The variable, of course, was alcohol. "You may have a drug that doesn't seem to be of a concentration high enough to cause death, but you may not know it was taken in combination with alcohol."

Puente's criminal history was marked by doping liquor or drinking with people who later lost consciousness. Frawley knew his major problem now was that the F Street bodies, and what was apparently Gillmouth's body, were so decomposed that any alcohol would be long gone.

Dr. Lackner publicly weighed in by stating that benzodiazepines with liquor were "today's Mickey Finn" and not especially lethal. "You're in general anesthesia until they wear off," which was what happened to Malcolm McKenzie and Dorothy Osborne.

But if his comments weren't particularly helpful to the prosecution, he did suggest how Dalmane and alcohol could be used to kill without leaving any marks. A helpless older person, while unconscious, said Dr. Lackner, could easily be asphyxiated. A pillow held over the face. A hand closing the mouth and nose. No struggle. No marks or bruises, no crushing of the hyoid bone in the throat, which would indicate manual strangulation.

The toxicologists assured Frawley they were working hard to isolate the benzodiazepine in the bodies. He could only hope it was flurazepam.

Which left a lot of open questions, too.

When did the victims take the Dalmane? Did it matter if they all had one drug if Frawley couldn't show they had taken it near the time they died?

And worse, with no specific cause of death, either physical or chemical, Frawley had a terrific obstacle to overcome in order to get Puente into the gas chamber.

Hastily on January 13, Puente was rushed into Judge Stroud's courtroom to plead not guilty to murdering Bert Montoya. Frawley had not yet filed any new charges, nor had he added the special circumstances which would make Puente eligible for the death penalty.

Judge Stroud had originally scheduled the appearance merely to litigate whether Puente should have some of her personal property back and if Vlautin and Clymo should be allowed into 1426 F Street. The judge, though, was worried.

After talking to Frawley and the defense lawyers, and seeing how every aspect of Puente's investigation was dissected for mistakes, Stroud was nervous about the waiver of personal appearance Puente had signed for him. Suppose a higher court looked back later and said he should have insisted that a defendant facing multiple murder charges be in court for every hearing?

Vlautin and Clymo reassured the judge. Puente really didn't want to be in court, an object of gawking and gossip, unless there were witnesses to be heard. They wouldn't raise any legal defect.

Puente herself owlishly peered around. She looked, as she had since getting back to Sacramento, rather irritated. She listened as the lawyers argued about getting her property back, including the $3,000 in her purse. Clymo told the court this money didn't come from dead victims or stolen SSI checks. Puente "won it with friends at Lake Tahoe" a few days before the police arrived.

They wrangled over furniture and rings Puente wanted returned, and Frawley agreed he wouldn't need them for his case so Puente could have them back. This obviously pleased Vlautin and Clymo. During their visits to Puente at RCCC she had been cranky, demanding her property. Her lawyers set the hearing to show her they would vigorously look out for her interests.

Puente's lawyers, like Frawley, had problems, too.

Back at his office, Frawley reviewed the videotape of Puente's November 11, 1988, interrogation by Cabrera. Her calm, which in retrospect was inhuman, would have a profound impact on a jury. I had seen about forty-five minutes of the tape on November 14 after we got back from the digging at 1426 F Street. Puente's unruffled expression, the blandness of a truly unaffected person, would strike home for a jury. She knew, at the very least, there were seven bodies in her yard. Yet she showed no human nervousness or anger about the police digging.

How could a jury of twelve ordinary people grasp a mind like that?

If Frawley and the police had difficulty mastering the huge volume of information in the case, so did Vlautin and Clymo. Amazingly, from January 1989 until well into her trial in March 1993, the defense attorneys didn't realize the interview with Cabrera had been videotaped. They had a summary of the interview, boldly headed that it had been videotaped, but neither Vlautin nor Clymo had seen the tape. Had they realized this omission earlier, they might not have been confident that Frawley had overwhelming proof problems without a definitive cause of death.

They also would not have been so blithe about saying that Puente might have buried people because she feared the authorities. She had called the police when Eugene Gamel died in front of 1426 F Street in 1987, apparently not afraid of authorities at that point.

The jury, Vlautin and Clymo belatedly realized, would see and hear Puente herself on the videotape, worried only about herself, thinking of her own situation. Lying over and over.

The last of the seven F Street bodies were finally identified in January. Betty May Palmer, in the front yard under the wooden St. Francis shrine, had been the hardest because her body had been mutilated apparently to impede identification. The final name added to remains in the yard was Leona Carpenter. Her bones had been dug up accidentally by Cabrera on November 11.

Finally they all had faces and names. The Sutter County Sheriff's Department announced that Everson Gillmouth had been positively identified as the body discovered beside the Sacramento River in 1986. He had been seventy-seven years old. The doubts about whether every Puente victim had been accounted for went on way past January 1989. Until late 1992, the Sacramento police were trying to match a missing man, a former F Street tenant, with a body found in the American River. His death was never resolved or credited to Puente.

Two days before Puente's lawyers appeared to argue, as she insisted, about her clothing and personal property, the body of Bert Montoya was removed from the antiseptic metal tray in cold storage at the county coroner's office and buried at St. Mary's Cemetery.

He had been a good Catholic. A priest asked God to take the soul of Montoya up "to the perfection and the company of the saints." Several members of his family, who had not seen him in years, stood at the gravesite in winter coats against the cold wind of the bright January day. It was his mother's birthday, although she was too old to fly to Sacramento.

Volunteers of America were present. Beth Valentine, who had long sought the fate of the missing Bert Montoya, sang "Amazing Grace" in a clear voice over his grave.

23

As the spring went on, Frawley's office filled with Puente materials. He soon crowded an entire bookcase with black notebooks of reports, and stacked boxes of evidence and papers anywhere else.

Puente had abundant sources of Dalmane, as it turned out. She used two doctors, unknown to each other, for multiple Dalmane prescriptions every month, in addition to the Dalmane she got from her court appointed psychiatrist, Dr. Doody. This last involvement put Doody on the spot.

Frawley wanted to examine Doody's records on Puente and check to see if the psychiatrist should have been aware he was overprescribing her a medication she could use, as she had in the past, for criminal purposes.

Doody went out to his storage locker only to discover that a police guard had already arrived. Frawley had sent the guard just in case Doody had any thoughts of removing the files from the storage locker. Everything ended up, as all of Puente's affairs seemed to, in court, with Dr. Doody fighting to protect the confidentiality of his files.

Doody had also treated Bert Montoya, at Puente's urging.

The judge ultimately let Frawley look at Dr. Doody's papers on Bert Montoya, who was dead and thus needed no privacy. But Puente's records remained sealed. Dr. Doody, grinning wanly, left the courtroom.

The Inspector-General of the Social Security Administration tabulated nearly $70,000 in tax-free income Puente had absorbed from her tenants in 1987 and 1988. She had spent the money, as she did in 1978, on her own whims and interests, which ranged from toys for the Odoricas to clothing and perfume for herself. Sometimes she gave a tenant a lavish gift, like a recliner chair for John Sharp and his bad back.

So Frawley had established useful evidence. Puente, on November 10, 1986, for example, got a thirty-day supply of Dalmane from one doctor and another thirty-day supply from Doody. She had the means to drug her tenants or kill them, and money was the fruit of either activity.

To underscore the results of this information for use at trial, two more F Street victims were buried in February, James Gallop and Leona Carpenter. Gallop's funeral, even though he was unmarried and had few friends and no known family, was attended by fifty people and leaders of ten Sacramento churches. A local mortuary donated Carpenter's funeral.

The city was publicly trying to say it was sorry for letting these shadow people fall into wicked hands.

Dorothea Puente herself, sometime in the spring, turned into an elusive vision. The mere possibility of her appearance in court drew crowds and reporters. Sometimes she disappointed them by not showing up, leaving Vlautin and Clymo the stage. Frawley declared on February 24 that he would be filing the long-awaited new charges against Puente in late March.

"The defendant must be present when that happens," he said.

Outside the courtroom, a lugubrious but defiant Clymo

dismissed the growing body of evidence against Puente. "Dorothea Puente didn't kill anyone," he said with a wave. "I have yet to see any physical evidence or any toxicological proof that would prompt me to change that opinion." It was all "guesses."

Frawley was uncomfortably aware of how much work the case needed, but by late March he had made up his mind to add Gillmouth, and after seven years, Ruth Munroe, to the official list of murders Dorothea Puente would have to answer for.

March 31, 1989 was a humid, dank day in Sacramento, clouds sailing over the city, the morning air biting.

In Department C, Judge Stroud waited until near the end of his morning calendar before having his most famous defendant brought in. Camera crews filled the jury box in the high-ceilinged courtroom. The audience section was packed tightly with the curious.

The judge called Puente's case. Frawley stood at the counsel table, Clymo went to the dock. Puente appeared in a pastel blue dress, waist length pearls, light makeup, her face still oddly tight from her cosmetic surgery. She whispered to Clymo in the quiet courtroom.

She spoke aloud only when Judge Stroud asked her if she would give up her right to a speedy preliminary hearing. Puente was soft, almost inaudible, when she agreed to September 12, 1989, for the hearing. A trial would follow, if the judge decided enough evidence had been presented on the charges against her.

Then Judge Stroud read the nine-count murder complaint to her. He stumbled once or twice, glanced at her, and ended with the recital of special circumstances in the commission of these murders that would, if found to be true, send her to her death.

The first seven counts were the 1988 F Street victims: Leona Carpenter, Bert Montoya, Ben Fink, Betty Palmer, Vera Martin, Dorothy Miller, James Gallop. Count Eight was Everson Gillmouth. Count Nine was Ruth Munroe.

Puente held on to the railing. She was lit up in the white camera lights, never looking at the audience or Cabrera and Terry Brown, sitting in the courtroom. They savored her discomfort.

On his client's behalf, Clymo entered nine pleas of not guilty.

Puente was taken back into the tank, the camera lights went out, the abrupt dimming leaving everyone with the feeling darkness had fallen over the courtroom.

Frawley went back across the street to his office. Clymo and Vlautin massaged the reporters in the hallway again.

The whole effort had taken only a few minutes, and the exercise of finally charging Dorothea Puente with so many murders, making her one of the most prolific female serial killers in American history, was curiously bureaucratic and lifeless.

Changes were coming in the DA's office, and while Puente had Vlautin and Clymo as her lawyers from the time she was back in Sacramento through the trial, she faced uncertainty about who would actually prosecute her.

Frawley was struggling with the complexity of the case. He felt, after Puente's arraignment, that he could get ahold of the facts and start additional inquiries that would be needed at trial.

But the DA suddenly resigned and the county Board of Supervisors appointed Steve White to take his place. White began casting around for someone to become his new chief deputy, the second-in-command in the office. White chose Frawley in June. It meant Frawley had to pass the Puente case, unformed and unfinished, to someone else immediately. Vlautin and Clymo would probably balk at postponing the preliminary hearing until the new prosecutor could master the nine-count murder case. Puente seemed certain to benefit, again, from the staff changes of her opponents, as she had when so many different federal parole agents were assigned to her.

Fortunately, a vigorous trial lawyer got her case and pressed ahead rapidly.

By the time George Williamson was named the new Puente prosecutor, flurazepam, marketed as Dalmane, had been definitively identified as the sole common drug in all seven F Street bodies. If he could properly interpret the significance of that information for a judge and jury, Williamson would go a long way toward convicting Puente.

Williamson was no stranger to the crimes of Dorothea Puente. I had consulted him about her victims in 1982, and like Frawley and O'Mara he once again found himself fighting to convict her.

He was taken off Major Narcotics and reassigned to Major Crimes to handle the case. Williamson was utterly without flamboyance. He dressed simply, worked hard, and gave the impression of compact, restless energy as he moved around the office or in court. He smoked constantly. At play he favored golf or skiing, just as Frawley liked marathon running and Vlautin and Clymo enjoyed sailing. Williamson, though, was harder on golf clubs and nearby shrubbery than the other lawyers were on their sports.

He was in his mid-forties when he got the Puente case. He had given up a career as an administrator at Kaiser Hospital to go to law school at night, then into the DA's office. His wife was also a deputy DA, and he had grown children. Williamson's single best asset was an ability to take bundles of facts, figures, and evidence and organize them into a coherent, relentless presentation that convinced as much by bulk as it did by logic. He was ideally suited to deal with the numerous victims and pieces of the Puente puzzle.

When he started looking at the mass of notebooks, boxes, and files in his new office, Williamson had some definite beliefs. He thought Frawley had woefully let the case drift. "The whole thing is a mess," he said. "There's no direction of the investigation from our side." He set about correcting that in early July, gathering medical records on the victims and more detail on when the victims had last been seen, and most importantly, nailing down from the state toxicologists just what the flurazepam evidence meant.

He needed a rational cause of death. He had it, but Williamson knew it needed a lot more development.

He also began the case believing Vlautin and Clymo were unscrupulous and mediocre. They had been overmatched by the intricacies of the case, and the international notoriety it had achieved dazzled, then clouded their judgment.

Williamson was short with reporters who tried to get him to comment on the case. One persisted over the phone, and he tersely replied, "Look, all I've got here is eight thousand pages of shit and it's my job to wade through it."

He refused to let a camera crew into his office even when the new DA Steve White personally escorted them.

He was bothered by how much catching up he had to do, that Puente's lawyers had a seven month advantage on him. One thing pleased him, as he checked over the evidence. Puente's conviction on 222 of the penal code in 1982 meant a jury would now hear she admitted drugging people to steal from them in the past.

An expected but still jarring statement came from the Sacramento County Coroner in July. The seven F Street bodies were so decomposed that no cause of death could be determined. Williamson had to make the most of the discovery of flurazepam in all of the victims.

His job was twofold and tough. He had to prove that Puente had criminal intent and acted as the criminal agent in the death of the seven F Street victims and the other two, and he had to prove these nine people died unnaturally in the first place.

Even as Williamson hurried to catch up, Puente's lawyers took every opportunity to wage a public relations campaign for her.

As soon as the coroner's decision was announced, Clymo told reporters, "There is no death penalty for unlawful burial. There is a big difference between people who have died of natural causes and people who have been murdered and are buried."

Puente, said her lawyers, was guilty only of stealing money, and being so terrified of going back to prison, that she buried her tenants as they died rather than report their deaths. From Everson Gillmouth onward, she was barred from having elderly people living with her, much less running a board-and-care business for them.

Vlautin was so confident that Williamson and the state of California had little proof Puente killed anyone that he declared she would walk away from the preliminary hearing. He claimed Williamson couldn't meet the first, easiest test of his case. "Considering the state of the evidence at this time," Vlautin said boldly, "we don't believe he would be able to do that."

Williamson, though, was pleasantly surprised when Puente's lawyers readily agreed to postpone the preliminary hearing. He surmised that they, too were having trouble staying current with all of the evidence and weren't anxious, despite what they said in public, to rush into court.

Some of the new evidence Williamson's investigation requests produced was bewildering and potentially damaging to his case. He learned that there were lead and mercury in the brain tissue of the victims. The amounts were sometimes eight times the fatal level for mercury, for example. It raised provocative questions. How did the mercury and lead get into the bodies? Before death or after? Did it come from the ground itself?

Williamson needed answers. Mercury or lead poisoning could account for some of the erratic behavior of Montoya or Ben Fink or other victims. A jury might speculate that Puente had nothing to do with poisoning anyone. It was accidental.

Another tantalizing bit of intelligence Williamson got was that Vlautin and Clymo had ordered two scale models built, costing about $15,000. One was a courtroom model of the street in front of 1426 F Street and the second was a cutaway model of 1426 itself. What could they possibly use these toys for? Williamson was scornful. He interpreted this to mean that the defense was scrambling. No defense theory could be demonstrated by the models. Since there was no precise date of death for any victim, nothing closer than days or weeks, where a witness was in the house was meaningless.

"They need something for the jury to play with," Williamson concluded happily.

The models also suggested that Puente might not testify at the preliminary hearing (which was normally not done anyway), or even later at the trial. Williamson's judgment was that she had never taken the stand in the past and now had so many questions to answer there were too many lies to explain.

It was, he believed, quite likely Puente would remain silent forever on what she had done behind the gingerbread-filagreed walls of 1426 F Street. If she had made that decision, either with or without her lawyers' agreement, Puente increased the chance a jury would find her guilty.

Jurors ache to hear the defendant's side of a story and, in the case of nine murders, would have a tough time acquitting Puente without hearing from her.

The one-year anniversary of Cabrera's discovery of a bone at 1426 F Street passed quietly in Sacramento.

24

BY DECEMBER 1989, GEORGE WILLIAMSON HAD A PLAN FOR presenting his mountain of evidence at the preliminary hearing. He also had the key to the cause of death for the seven F Street bodies.

When he first read the flurazepam discovery, Williamson's curiosity was piqued about how the drug actually worked in the human body. He wanted to know if flurazepam left a residue in the form of metabolites as it was broken down in the body. These metabolities would serve as a chemical trail showing that the parent drug had been taken. They might also provide an invaluable timetable for each victim. But Williamson faced a glaring problem: even though he could show that each F Street victim took Dalmane, he couldn't show when. Fortunately, the chemical breakdown of Dalmane would produce metabolites at a scientifically reliable rate. With luck, a pathologist could then testify about a narrow window when all seven victims had taken Dalmane.

The odds of seven people taking one common drug, which

caused stupor or death in combination with alcohol, very near each of their deaths, were astronomical. Williamson didn't think Puente could beat that.

Chain-smoking in his crowded office, Williamson outlined his strategy for the preliminary hearing like a general getting ready for battle.

"The case is divided into three parts," he said. "First, we have the early acts. That means Munroe and Gillmouth. I show them to the judge. Gillmouth, he's in good health, spends a little time with Puente, and he ends up in a box."

He said happily, "The next piece's a prosecutor's daydream." He would call me to the stand to identify Puente as having pled guilty to section 222. The judge now would know her history.

The second part of the presentation, he said, would be the seven F Street victims. He would put on many physicians to show that the victims were suffering from various ailments, but none had been immediately life-threatening. Moreover, all of the victims had been conscientious about seeing their doctors or calling them. These people had not been ignorant or indifferent to their own health.

Williamson hoped a massive showing of medical testimony would overcome his difficulty in proving death by criminal agency. If none of the victims were about to drop dead, someone must have intervened to cause their death.

Finally, he intended to put on a California Department of Justice pathologist to describe finding Dalmane in each of the seven bodies. He would testify to the effect of Dalmane in high dosages with alcohol. "My doc won't say Dalmane is the cause of death," Williamson said. So he had to imply and fill in the gaps other ways.

"I'm going to overwhelm the judge with evidence." Williamson ground out his cigarette, lit another, filling the office with smoke. "So much he won't be able to say no." Williamson was going to put on three or four times the amount of evidence normally heard at a preliminary hearing. In California, the prosecution's burden of proof to convince a judge that the case should be sent to Superior

Court for later trial is quite low. Williamson, knowing the deficiencies in his case, didn't want to take any chances Puente might go free.

He had another reason for dumping a lot of evidence on the hearing judge. "I'm going to smoke out Vlautin and Clymo, find out what they're planning for trial. I figure if I put on all my docs and my good evidence, they'll have to show me what their strategy's going to be later."

His last shower of evidence, he said, would be the financial records he would put before the judge. California income tax records, federal tax forms, SSI checks, General Assistance checks, California renter's credit checks—piles of documents—had been made out to each of the seven victims, but altered or signed by one person. Williamson's state handwriting expert was going to testify that Dorothea Puente had signed all of the checks.

He had gleaned a few other smaller, perplexing pieces of information lately. Betty Palmer's mutilated body had been the first victim buried at 1426 F Street. She had been killed after Gillmouth. But Williamson wondered why Puente mutilated Palmer and not Gillmouth? Palmer's mutilations obviously were intended to prevent her identification if she was ever discovered.

But Williamson's theory was simple. "I guess Puente didn't like chopping her head off," and left the next six victims intact.

It was one thing, Williamson knew from experience, to have a grand plan for putting on evidence, and another to actually follow through on it. Too many variables usually threw even the most elegant courtroom strategy into disarray.

And that, he knew, worked to Puente's advantage.

While Williamson and Puente's lawyers toiled over the upcoming preliminary hearing, the enormous drenching publicity surrounding her crimes caused politicians to take notice.

Locally, the Sacramento Police Department was besieged

with new calls for a civilian review board because it had bungled an important case. The Board of Supervisors and others thought various social service organizations needed closer guidance.

In the California Assembly, the Committee on Aging and Long Term Care held public hearings on how to prevent a future Puente from gaining control of vulnerable payees' benefit checks. The committee members nodded sagely when one witness said, "We give cash benefits to people who are incompetent and disabled and allow a payee system that gives motive and opportunity for criminals like Puente."

The committee chairman, a Democrat, used the hearing to attack the governor, a Republican, for vetoing budget items to monitor care for the elderly and disabled. Committee Republicans defended the governor, and Puente, the agent of the evil, was forgotten in the partisan criticism.

Farther east, in Washington, D.C., there were more hearings before House and Senate committees on aging. John Sharp, the thin, alert-eyed F Street tenant who told the police on November 7, 1988, that Puente was making him lie and that he had smelled Ben Fink's decomposing body in the "cursed" room near the kitchen, made a vivid picture as he recounted life at 1426 F. His testimony, in part, prompted Representative Claude Pepper and Senator John Heinz to urge that board-and-care residents have a bill of rights.

Amendments were speedily added to the Social Security Act to block a criminal like Puente from becoming a representative payee for dependents like Bert Montoya.

The major lesson of Puente's criminal life was never mentioned, much like the seldom seen woman herself. No new laws were needed. She was, by law, forbidden to be a Social Security payee. She was, by law, unable to run a board-and-care facility or associate with the elderly or vulnerable. She was in chronic violation of her federal parole, and until it was terminated in 1986, her California parole as well. Her Discharge Summary from state prison said, "Her prognosis for success in the community is good if she does not work with people who are dependent on her for their welfare."

Lost on the publicity-seeking legislators was the fact that too many people, ten agencies, twenty-five staffers, found it convenient to let Puente operate her business at 1426 F Street. It was not possible to pass laws prohibiting human weakness, stupidity, and greed.

All the law could do, in 1990, was try to put Dorothea Puente on trial for killing nine people.

Accomplishing that simple goal would be hard enough.

PART 5

Thou givest to the Guilty their calm mien
Which damns the crowd around the guillotine.

Charles Beaudelaire,
"Litany to Satan"

25

DOROTHEA PUENTE'S PRELIMINARY HEARING BEGAN ON APRIL 27, 1990, in the afternoon, following false starts when her lawyers objected to "extended media coverage" in the courtroom. Judge Gail Ohanesian eventually ruled that while sketch artists could be in the courtroom, no pool TV camera or still photographers would be allowed.

Puente didn't like the idea of being studied so implacably. She came in, dressed simply in a white skirt and blouse with black stitching, helped by three bailiffs. Her hair was tightly combed back. She sat down between Clymo and Vlautin. Clymo soothingly patted her on the back. She never looked behind her, nor did she even look up much at Judge Ohanesian. For the next seven weeks, Puente faded as if she were a mere spectator at her own hearing.

Williamson bustled over from his office, carrying an armful of black notebooks, smoking as he went. He was edgy as the case was about to start, worried that his witnesses were vulnerable, his voluminous circumstantial evidence insufficient to show Judge Ohanesian that Puente was an industrious killer. Williamson had flown north to Eureka with Clymo and two investigators to videotape the testimony of Julius Kelly, a former F Street boarder dying of a brain tumor. Kelly told the police in 1988 that Puente had given him some pills to take and told him Bert Montoya was on a bus going to Mexico after he disappeared.

While Clymo's clumsy questioning of the marginally competent old man in Eureka didn't impress Williamson at all, he was concerned that his whole case was like the videotape, a patchwork that could fall apart, bits and pieces of jailhouse information, scientific speculation, witnesses on TV.

He was also anxious about Judge Ohanesian. She had been on the bench only a short time and looked bewildered and hesitant. "She can't control the courtroom," Williamson fretted aloud. On the positive side, he believed he could push and prod her to rule his way because of her inexperience.

Curiously, Vlautin shared Williamson's misgivings about the judge, but also remained optimistic for his side. He too thought he could manipulate the new municipal court judge. They had gone to law school together.

Williamson also had another oddity on his mind as he brushed past the throng of disgruntled, excluded camera crews milling around Department H on the third floor of the courthouse. While researching how to get Puente's uncharged acts, like Eugene Gamel's mysterious death in 1987, into evidence Williamson came across the seminal 1960s case, *People v. Archerd*.

He had cited it before in court. Most prosecutors were very familiar with it because it laid down the rules for bringing uncharged acts by defendants before the court. But suddenly Williamson found something in the case that he had never seen before.

Archerd was on trial for using insulin to poison his victim. There were suspicious deaths in his past, but at the time, insulin overdose was undetectable as a cause of death.

In his current trial, the prosecutor wanted to introduce evidence of the earlier deaths, in 1948 in Riverside County. Key to the whole question was Archerd's accomplice, a woman identified only as "Dorothea," who had been helping him get money from his apparent victim. It was Dorothea who supplied the insulin.

"It's got to be her," Williamson said to the others in Major Crimes. The coincidence was too great.

He got the California Attorney General to dig through decades of old appellate transcripts and found the Archerd case. From the testimony of Dorothea Sheehan, otherwise unidentified and undescribed at Archerd's murder trial, Williamson learned that she had been a nurse at Kaiser Hospital in Fontana from 1939 through 1947. She married William Archerd in San Francisco on August 27, 1949, and the marriage was annulled in Nevada on May 14, 1956. She wasn't prosecuted, in return for her cooperation in Archerd's trial.

Williamson had a real, tantalizing puzzle. Puente had many aliases, had been vague and contradictory about her birth date and her whereabouts during the fifties, and it was plausible she was involved in a murder for profit by poison scheme.

As Puente's preliminary hearing started, Williamson needed to hear from the Los Angeles District Attorneys Office, which had prosecuted Archerd in 1967. Going through a warehouse full of old transcripts took time, and until the trial record was found, Williamson didn't know if Puente had been killing decades before anyone knew about it and the proof, the case in every law library, *People v. Archerd,* was right under everyone's nose.

Until he had some word from Los Angeles, Williamson kept this latest bizarre development from the defense.

Puente herself, just before the preliminary hearing, had been relaxing in her cell in the new county jail downtown. She had watched *Pet Sematary* with one of her jailers and enjoyed it.

* * *

I had been subpoenaed to testify against Puente, and I waited in the courthouse hallway with other witnesses and the large collection of curious people who couldn't find a place to sit in the packed courtroom.

Bill Clausen was waiting, too, with his wife. I hadn't seen him for years. We couldn't talk about the case because we were both going to testify. He said he was going to stay through the whole preliminary hearing and the trial, if he could. The long wait between Puente's murder of Ruth Munroe, her arrest in 1988, and finally getting to court, had taken their toll. Rosie, on hearing of the bodies being dug up at 1426 F Street in 1988, had attempted suicide according to Bill.

What troubled me most about this intense but reasonable-looking man and his wife, waiting patiently yet impatiently outside Department H, was that Bill had kept the 1982 *Bee* article announcing Puente's sentencing in his wallet. The clipping was yellowed, faded, much handled, obviously. He had kept it with him for eight years.

He had been waiting a very long time.

One of Williamson's first witnesses was a ratlike, nervous man, Donald Anthony, another Puente acquaintance, who was put on the witness stand to show Judge Ohanesian, as Malcolm McKenzie had shown Judge Canlis in 1982, that the meek old lady at the counsel table was not what she seemed.

Anthony, an ex-con, hesitantly told Williamson that Dorothea Puente had made him mail the letter purporting to be from Bert Montoya's relatives in Utah. The letter was postmarked in Reno.

Puente, said Anthony, directed him to leave Sacramento. He took a bus to Nevada to mail the letter and make it look genuine.

Did Puente give you any special instructions? Williamson asked sharply.

"She said wrap it in a paper towel so I don't have to get

any fingerprints on it," Anthony said. He glanced apprehensively at Puente, who didn't notice him.

And, Anthony said, Puente made him call Judy Moise and pretend to be Bert's brother-in-law. Puente reassured Anthony that Bert was in Mexico and having a fine time.

Williamson also had Anthony explain that in 1988 Puente had gotten him to dig for buried pipes in her backyard. He dug several shallow trenches, he said, looking for the pipes, but never found any. She was left with open trenches.

With his earliest witnesses, Williamson had stripped away Puente's mask. She had lied about a dead man, and gotten graves dug.

May 2 was a very good day for the prosecution. Williamson put on his pathologists and "fuzzed and shmoozed" in a cause of death for the seven victims based on the flurazepam metabolization.

He also managed to put on evidence that Dalmane would never be prescribed for any of the seven victims. "No doc is going to give you Dalmane in combination with what these people were already getting," he said, as court convened. He hoped Clymo and Vlautin missed the full importance of the testimony.

In a barely quarter-filled courtroom, much emptier than when the hearing started, Williamson called Dr. Robert Anthony, who sat with his reports in hand.

Anthony recounted the autopsies he conducted on Leona Carpenter and Ben Fink. Carpenter was eighty years old when she died and Williamson asked the pathologist to assume a state of facts, a hypothetical woman of that age, with a benign cyst in 1975, hypertension, alcoholism, a history of syphillis and anemia. Did such a woman have a medical history that would cause sudden, unexpected death or did she have chronic health problems?

"Chronic problems," Dr. Anthony answered quickly.

Then Williamson casually went into the heart of his case against Puente, the unnatural cause of death.

Dr. Anthony had done toxicological tests on Carpenter's

mostly skeletalized remains and found several drugs in her brain tissue, viscera, and dirt. The most important drug Anthony noted was flurazepam, or actually its metabolites. He also found codeine and Valium in Carpenter.

The flurazepam had broken down into two distinct metabolites, N-hydroxethylflurazepam of greatest interest. It had a very short half-life, the time it takes for the body to break down and eliminate half of the drug from the system. The half-life of flurazepam, or Dalmane, was one to one and a half hours, while N-hydroxethylflurazepam's was only a half hour.

The presence of the metabolite meant that Carpenter had taken Dalmane very shortly before her death.

"How long does Dalmane take to completely metabolize in the system?" Williamson asked, looking at his legal pad.

"Two to four hours, little of the parent drug is still present. It is totally metabolized in twenty-four hours."

Anthony was adamant that no reputable physician, without very close monitoring of a patient, would ever give an eighty-year-old woman both Dalmane and Valium. There was, he said emphatically, no medical benefit to giving two central nervous system depressants like Dalmane and Valium together.

Puente's reactions to this damning information were muted. She sipped water from a small paper cup, sat a little slumped. She seemed fairly indifferent to the testimony.

Williamson led Dr. Anthony through his autopsy of Ben Fink, body #88-3382, buried with a pad over his face, wrapped in clear plastic, then in blue plastic, and lastly a bedspread. He wore only boxer shorts and dark socks. He had a garbage bag wrapped around his lower left leg. A swastika and a skull were tattooed on the brown, shriveled flesh of his left shoulder. Above his right knee were tattooed the letters PSI, for Preston School of Industry, which he had attended as a teenager.

Like Carpenter and the other F Street victims, Fink's mild coronary artery disease wouldn't have caused sudden death.

Besides loxapine and amitriptyline, Fink's tissues yielded up flurazepam's two metabolites. Anthony was even more vigorous that no doctor would give a patient Dalmane, loxapine, and amitryptiline because it would "create a dangerous, very toxic situation."

Fink, too, had taken Dalmane within twenty-fours of his death.

Williamson's last victim for Dr. Anthony was the hideously mutilated Betty Palmer. She had been wearing a sleeveless white nightgown inside her makeshift shroud. Anthony described "tool-type marks at places on her spine." They were "cutting marks," but he could not determine whether they were made before or after death. He suspected that all of the mutilations were postmortem. She was not a candidate for sudden death, even at eighty, and her body also contained the short-lived N-hydroxethyl-flurazepam.

When it came time for him to turn Dr. Anthony over to Kevin Clymo for cross-examination, Williamson muttered distractedly at Clymo's slowness in court.

Could Dr. Anthony tell if the Dalmane had been given to these three victims or self-ingested? Clymo asked.

Dr. Anthony, with extreme puzzlement, answered there was no way he could determine that fact.

And since all three of these deaths were classified as of undetermined cause, Clymo went on, there is no way to eliminate any particular disease as fatal. Dr. Anthony nodded. He still looked puzzled.

"Well, you can't exclude sudden, unexpected death, either?"

"All deaths are sudden," Dr. Anthony said peevishly. "They might not be unexpected if I saw a disease process."

All three victims had various medical problems, and Dr. Anthony, as Williamson knew going in, wouldn't exclude any single ailment from conceivably causing death.

Dalmane, he also agreed, was an odd drug to kill with. There was no fatal dosage in the medical literature. It would require "hundreds or thousands" of pills to kill. But Clymo couldn't budge Anthony from his view that benzodiazepine and alcohol was a lethal cocktail.

For the visually stimulating image of the day, Clymo wound up his cross-examination by asking Dr. Anthony to imagine the amount of Dalmane alone needed to kill. "Dump a pile of powder out. Wouldn't that five hundred to a thousand capsule amount be about the size of a softball?"

"Probably," agreed Dr. Anthony.

Clymo leaned back in his chair. "Hard to hide that in a glass of water?" he asked.

Williamson objected, and Dr. Anthony never answered the question.

As court was adjourned, Puente was handcuffed, as she had been in the morning, the breaks, and at the end of the day. She complained that day that having handcuffs put on her while her hands were behind her back hurt her shoulders, so she was handcuffed from then on in the front, a little like she was praying coming into court.

Williamson felt very good going out of Department H. "How about that sleight of hand?" he said. He had gotten his cause of death, Dalmane with or without alcohol, before the judge without very much qualification and without Clymo or Vlautin raising a single objection to it.

26

As he had done for years in trial, Williamson got up at 4:00 A.M. to work on his next witnesses. It was dark outside his house, his family still asleep. They were used to his compulsive preparation.

The Puente case had started wearing down everyone. Clymo had put his head on the table in the courthouse cafeteria the day before and confessed he was exhausted. But the hearing had to go on. He was responsible for cross-examining the experts and medical personnel. The defense he and Vlautin had constructed to counter Williamson's flurazepam evidence was simple: the tissue samples from the victims were contaminated in the lab. Therefore, the pathologists' conclusions about Dalmane were meaningless.

Judge Ohanesian learned useful and useless information as the pathologists finished talking about Dorothy Miller, Montoya, James Gallop, and Vera Martin. Martin, for example, wore a wristwatch that was still running when she was unearthed, just as the jokers had suggested. She was sixty-four when she died, had TB, gallstones, and a bunion. She weighed only forty-four pounds when unearthed.

She was victim number six unearthed at F Street, the one I had seen lying near a board. It was pathetic to hear so many intimate details about Martin and the other victims, stripping them of all privacy in order to convict their killer.

Like the other victims, Martin's remains contained the short-lived flurazepam metabolites. All seven F Street victims had, by the estimates of the pathologists, taken or been unknowingly given, Dalmane within their last twenty-four hours of life.

But Vlautin and Clymo reserved their attack for James Beede, a forsenic toxicologist who prepared the specimens for analysis. Beede had submitted tissue samples from the seven victims to the state Department of Justice. Analysis of the first sample, from Ben Fink, showed cocaine, which was obviously a contaminant.

But Beede, neatly mustached, calm on the witness stand, never admitted making any mistake in preparing the samples. This gave Puente's defense lawyers a window from which to snipe at him. If he wouldn't admit an obvious mistake in the first sampling, he wouldn't admit contaminating all the samples he submitted in a second batch to be analyzed.

The defense allegation was that the second batch of tissue samples contained one sample, the first, with Dalmane in it. But Beede permitted that first tissue to mix with the next six and show a false positive residue of flurazepam. In other words, Puente's lawyers claimed only one victim had taken Dalmane.

Williamson pointed out, with exasperration, that the tissue samples still existed. Vlautin and Clymo could have them retested. But the defense didn't want to test again.

Puente listened without emotion to Beede's grisly description of how her former tenants were turned into tissue samples. She whispered to Clymo every so often, or the lawyers both patted her back, but otherwise she just sat.

Clymo's cross-examination of Beede made it clear that no one, much less a compassionate landlady, could listen to the details of the tissue preparation without showing revulsion or distress. That was not, though, the point he wanted to make.

"How did you actually get these samples?" Clymo asked slowly.

Beede said, "I scooped the samples into a four-ounce glass jar using a spatula. I added distilled water. I weighed the sample to get about twenty grams and then added enough water to make a total weight of one hundred grams."

He then poured the contents of the jars into a Waring blender.

"A regular kitchen blender?" Clymo asked in surprise.

"Regular blender. The homogenate is then poured into four-ounce jars."

Beede and Clymo, with Puente sitting by calmly, were discussing the liver and brains of Ben Fink, Vera Martin, Dorothy Miller, and the others.

But where was Dorothy Miller after she dropped from sight at 1426 F Street in the summer of 1988?

Miller, a slight, elfin woman who had served in the army, had acted as the messenger between the lower world of the tenants and Puente's living quarters on the second floor. She was viewed with amusement, a gossip.

She got into trouble with the law every so often, and when she vanished suddenly, Puente told the others, "Dorothy got arrested for shoplifting again. I'm not going to put up with it anymore. I threw her out," she said vehemently.

But on September 21, 1988, a woman calling herself Dorothy Miller came to the VA clinic on Broadway. Dr. Ruth Lawrence was working that day. It was unusual for a female veteran to come in, so Dr. Lawrence took note of it.

Dorothy Miller was stoutish, white-haired. She asked Dr. Lawrence for thyroid medicine and Dalmane. "I've had my thyroid removed," Miller told the doctor. Dr. Lawrence listened to her heart, checked her weight and eyesight quickly, and then prescribed the required thyroid medication. Dr. Lawrence believed Miller did need the medication: she could see the thyroid scar on the woman's throat.

Williamson put Dr. Lawrence on the witness stand and then asked if she recognized the person who claimed to be Dorothy Miller in court. "She's sitting there, dressed in white," the doctor said, pointing at Puente.

"Would you come down and take a look at her neck," Williamson asked.

Clymo and Vlautin quickly and loudly objected. Puente remained sitting stiffly as the doctor stepped off the witness stand and peered at her across the counsel table. There was a silence in the courtroom. "Would you have her raise her head?" Dr. Lawrence asked.

When Puente slowly lifted her head, Dr. Lawrence sighed. "There's a fine scar," she said, pointing at Puente's throat.

The key point was that Dorothy Miller was dead and buried in the yard at F Street when Puente brazenly impersonated her and tried to collect more Dalmane than even three other doctors were supplying to her.

Williamson wanted Judge Ohanesian to get a sense of how 1426 F Street functioned under Puente's control. Why did Dorothy Miller have to act as a go-between at all?

Simply put, Puente segregated the house into the people she ruled below her and her own apartment. She was a shepherd living above the herd.

Various witnesses talked about the house. Carol Durning, a former tenant in her thirties, bright and articulate, said that downstairs Puente ministered to the tenants, making them take their medicines, cleaning them, feeding the ones who couldn't eat. She also made persistent efforts to get control of their SSI benefits. She yelled at the tenants, even the very sick ones, about how much money they owed or when they were behind paying their rent. Sometimes Puente had violent temper tantrums and struck the old men or women.

When Durning lived at 1426 F Street there were four

other tenants, including James Gallop. He was old, sickly, had trouble seeing, and in mid-1987 he underwent brain surgery. He drank a lot and slept most of the time. Puente often gave Gallop medicine, telling Durning it was "for his pain." It quieted him.

Gallop was trouble for Puente. She told Durning he couldn't handle his money, and as long as she could be in charge of it, he could stay, but if she couldn't control Gallop's money, Puente said, "he'll have to find another place to live."

Sleeping on the dining room couch after his brain surgery, which removed a benign tumor, Gallop would be roused by Puente and told it was time to take a pill. "Have I taken it already?" he asked.

"No, it's time now," and Puente pushed a pill at him.

Gallop drank beer, up to a six-pack every day, and smoked as heavily after his operation, three packs a day, as he had before. His doctor had prescribed a weaker dosage of Dalmane than Puente's physicians supplied to her.

But Gallop complained often of pain and told Durning he thought he was going to die. He sounded like Ruth Munroe in her last days in 1982.

Puente yelled at Gallop several times because of his drinking and flew into a rage when he refused to sign over his SSI benefits to her. "He's not giving me the rent money," she yelled through the house. Puente, of course, collected and kept all rents.

Carol Durning also knew the thin, elderly Betty Palmer, who moved into 1426 in the middle of 1987 and was there only a month. Palmer, a spry, eccentric woman who formed imaginary romantic attachments to her doctors, grew suddenly ill once she got into 1426 F. More than once, Durning saw Puente give the old woman various pills. Then Durning came home from work one day and Betty Palmer was gone. Puente, who may have just finished cutting off the old woman's head, hands, and lower legs, told Durning, "Betty's daughter came and picked her up."

"Where did she go?"

Puente shook her head. She didn't know.

Gallop vanished, too, at the end of the summer 1987.

Williamson didn't try to hide any bias witnesses might have against Puente. He let the judge hear everything. Durning, for example, admitted being thrown out of 1426 F Street over money. She was evicted unceremoniously around midnight, after being slapped and cursed obscenely by Puente.

But Durning, like other former tenants, added a horrific coloration to the story of life at 1426 F. Though Puente did help certain tenants by feeding and cleaning for them, sometimes buying them shoes or clothing, she mistreated others, like Betty Palmer who was groaning constantly, and she kept them from seeing any outsiders, much less any doctors.

People who moved in with Puente left when she said they could leave. They were either thrown out or buried in the yard.

She wanted to control their lives absolutely.

Williamson, by the second week of the preliminary hearing, had sketched in the ability of the seven victims to take care of themselves on the street, soldiering through black eyes like Miller, broken legs like Fink, and sexual assaults.

These shadow people had made impressions on others, and that meant no one, no matter how ruthless, could erase them completely.

Puente listened, sipping water again, emotionless, as Marjorie Harper, a bartender at Henry's Lounge, talked about her and James Gallop. He was a regular at the bar, and Harper liked him. In 1986 he had started coming in, drinking beer, chatting. It was a bar, said Harper, frequented by elderly pensioners and thus one that attracted Puente. She had been coming since just after her 1978 federal conviction. The bartender liked Puente; she was a talkative customer. Her only defect, according to Marjorie Harper, was that she lied so often.

Puente struck up an acquaintance with Gallop at the bar,

as she had with so many other people in other bars, and he moved into 1426 F Street. Soon after that, and after having borrowed ten dollars from Harper, Gallop went into the hospital to have his brain tumor removed. Marjorie Harper was very touched when she got a phone call from him.

"He was calling from the hospital," she told the court, "and he was going to have surgery. He was afraid I'd think he'd skipped town still owing me money."

Gallop later came back to Henry's Lounge to see Harper. He was thinner, and his right eye drooped, but he was happy to see her. He came to the bar for the last time in April 1987 to cash a check.

Two weeks later, Puente strolled in for her usual round of drinks. Marjorie Harper asked where Gallop was.

Puente was indignant, then dismissive. "He left in the middle of the night," she said.

Harper didn't believe that for a minute. The man who had called her from a hospital room wouldn't just leave without saying good-bye. But she didn't ask Puente any more questions. Marjorie Harper had heard the stories about Puente's prison time, and about her temper.

Maybe James Gallop hadn't had time to call or come to see his old friend behind the bar.

But he had been keeping up his medical appointments until May. His doctors wanted him to stop smoking and drinking because he had emphysema, but otherwise he was in fair shape. He missed a number of appointments after May and Dr. David Pong, who had been treating him, found out that on July 27, 1987, word had come about Gallop.

A specialist treating Gallop told Dr. Pong that Gallop's landlord had just called. Gallop, said the landlord, was leaving for Los Angeles and wouldn't need the specialist's services any longer. But the missing Gallop seemed rather active.

In May 1987 a pharmacist about two blocks from 1426 F Street, filled a prescription for Dalmane for James Gallop. It was an odd prescription because the note indicated two refills were ordered, while the physician's record showed none. Someone, said the pharmacist, had jotted in enough refills for sixty more Dalmane pills.

Williamson then trundled in a large television and VCR, and the courtroom watched the dying Julius Kelly make a statement from his filthy, cluttered house in Eureka.

Kelly had moved into 1426 F Street in early 1988, living with Bert Montoya at one point. Because he was having trouble sleeping, Puente gave Kelly some pills, which she said were vitamins. When the police arrived in November, Kelly turned the pills in.

Williamson showed Kelly an SSI check for almost $10,000 that was made out to him in 1988. "I never got it," he said, looking at it in surprise. Williamson showed him the endorsement. "I never signed it, but there's my name."

Puente had gotten Kelly a new pair of glasses after his own were broken when someone punched him. She used James Gallop's ID to buy the glasses at medical discount. "I guess she wanted me to have the glasses." Kelly shrugged.

Puente knew Gallop would need neither his medical ID nor three bottles of Dalmane in his name.

As her lawyers tackled the witnesses, alternately sarcastic or laborious in their questioning, Dorothea Puente yawned, made a few notes, or stared straight ahead, not looking at the witness or the judge.

But she could not avoid hearing the testimony of the family survivors of her victims. Their testimony, layered on top of the medical and civilian witnesses, was the saddest, most devastating blow of all to Puente's case.

27

REBA NICKLOUS SAT AT A TABLE IN THE COURTHOUSE CAFETERIA. She was proudly showing Williamson and an uncomfortable Ricardo Odorica pictures of her brother. Then she dug in her purse and found pictures of Everson Gillmouth and one of his larger, complicated wood carvings, passing it around to the others. Odorica glanced at it, handed it back to her, unsmiling. A TV cameraman sneaked into the rear of the cafeteria and surreptitiously took shots of the little group at the table. Williamson had stashed Nicklous and Odorica in the cafeteria before they testified to hide them from reporters. The prosecutor smoked, tapped his hands on the table, waiting to go downstairs. Every so often, Odorica, who didn't talk much to Everson Gillmouth's formidable-looking sister, muttered half to himself, "I know many things about her," meaning Puente. He was terrified that their intertwined finances would make him a criminal.

Reba Nicklous, with obvious pride, took back the pictures of her brother and put them in her purse. She had not been listening to the worried little man to her left. She was thinking angrily about what she knew about Puente and what she'd say in court.

Before he called Reba Nicklous to the stand, Williamson brought in Robert Fink one morning, to talk about his dead brother.

Robert Fink was tall, dressed in jeans and a blue shirt, with a small mustache like his brother had worn, and a quiet, solemn appearance, like a nineteenth-century cowboy dumped into a twentieth-century atrocity. He set a tone the family members of Everson Gillmouth and Ruth Munroe, by and large, observed. It was one of stoical, untouchable sadness.

Everyone in the courtroom felt it. Judge Ohanesian sat back on the bench rather than leaning forward as she usually did, almost lost in the misery from the witness stand.

Robert Fink was younger than Ben by four years. He lived in nearby Rio Linda with his family.

Carefully, Williamson drew out everything about the two brothers and 1426 F Street. Robert visited his brother there about half a dozen times in 1987. He chatted with some of the tenants, including John Sharp.

To identify his brother for the judge, Robert brought along a Thanksgiving picture taken in 1986. It was, he said calmly and sadly, the last family gathering Ben went to "before he was killed."

Williamson didn't hide Ben's overriding problem, the one that alienated him from his family, most friends, made it hard for him to hold a job, and finally cast him up at 1426 F Street and into the grasp of Dorothea Puente. "He drank quite a bit," Robert said. "He just drank." Ben was a drinker who could start on day or days long benders and become unmanageable, feisty, and crude.

Robert last saw Ben in January or February 1987 when his brother needed clothes brought to him at 1426 F. Ben, as far as Robert knew, had no serious health problems and never complained of any physical ailments. One witness, in fact, had described how Ben helped unload the flatbed of a pickup of cement bags with Bert Montoya and Puente acting as supervisor. Even though he was wiry, Ben was strong and willing to pitch in.

As he had throughout the weeks of the hearing, Williamson never sat down. He leaned almost nonchalantly against the jury box, a legal pad in hand. He asked Robert Fink about Ben's views on doctors and medicines. "He didn't like to take medication." Robert Fink sighed, shoulders a little hunched. "He told me, 'I do enough drinking without taking any pills or anything.'" Robert had had trouble in 1987 obtaining medicine for Ben when he was using a hyperbaric chamber to help heal his legs, fractured badly when he was hit by a car. Ben simply refused to take the medicine.

What about the last visit to F Street, Williamson asked. What did you see there?

"I brought white golf shoes and some clothes," Robert said, his tone of voice resigned. He said he went to Ben's basement floor room, at the right of the house. Ben was in good spirits, and, with a small grin, Robert said, "He was pretty strong."

Williamson nodded. "Nothing further." He had told the judge enough. Ben Fink was in good health when last seen. Judge Ohanesian had already heard from John Sharp that in January 1988 one night Ben got rambunctiously, roaring drunk, disturbing the tenants, and apparently arousing Puente's hatred of alcoholics. She took him by the arm, guiding the cursing drunken man upward. "I'm going to take Ben upstairs and make him well," she told the other tenants with disguised irony. Everyone assumed she was helping him upstairs to her rooms.

That was the last time Ben Fink was ever seen until his body was unearthed from the yard. When he didn't show up the next day or the day after that, Puente repeatedly told the other tenants that Ben "had gone north."

Days later, the room beside the kitchen began stinking and Puente desperately tried rug shampoos, air fresheners. It was the "cursed room", she told everyone. It was the same room from which Cabrera had removed a stained carpet in November 1988. It was the room in which Ben Fink's decomposing body had rested before being shifted to its final grave in the yard.

Vlautin commenced the cross-examination of Robert Fink. He sat, papers around him, Puente to his right peering at them every so often, otherwise looking at the table. She seemed, as usual, unconcerned about the horrific testimony.

Vlautin's purpose was to make out, through the dead man's brother, that Ben Fink had been a sickly drunk.

It was true, Robert admitted, that he didn't want Ben living with his family as long as he was drinking. Ben used "foul language" when drunk, sometimes in front of Robert's teenage daughter. "I didn't feel it was right for her to be around this kind of thing." He told Ben to leave the house.

Vlautin stammered a little. What was Ben's behavior when he was drinking?

Robert Fink smiled slightly. "When Ben drank he thought he was Casanova, all the lovers in the world wrapped into one." He became expansive, big-hearted. When Ben got a five thousand dollar settlement from the car accident that broke his legs in 1980, he started drinking and saw "some guys coming down the street in torn Levi's and threw twenty-dollar bills at them."

The gesture amazed Robert.

"They need it more than I do," Ben said, going on with his drinking.

This sore point, of course, fascinated Vlautin. He pressed again and again at Ben Fink's alcoholism, as if to explain his disappearance and even, perhaps, Puente's lies about what had become of him. Vlautin asked Robert how long Ben drank. What was his pattern?

Sometimes, Robert said, "he drank for one day or for a week." Then in a rare flash of inner pain, he said, "I don't understand why Ben drank."

The inquiry turned specific. Did Robert recall anything about his last visit with Ben? It was, Robert sat back a little, about 2:00 P.M. on a warm day in February 1987. He saw Ben outside 1426 F Street. Ben had called and said he needed money. It was near the end of the month. "I never gave Ben more than twenty dollars and some food in a bag. I knew what he was going to do if I gave him more," Robert said. He stared briefly at Puente.

But on this visit, Ben had something else on his mind. He wanted his younger brother to hold $140 for him "because he didn't like living there" at 1426 F. He didn't trust the people.

"Someone is taking my money," Ben confided to Robert.

"Did he say who?" Vlautin asked sharply.

Robert Fink shook his head.

Did he ever say Dorothea Puente abused him?

No, he never did.

It dawned on the spectators and reporters, and probably on the judge, that through a painful cross-examination, Robert Fink, unlike so many other witnesses, never raised his voice or grew annoyed. He took Vlautin's probing and insinuations. He took it as he must have taken Ben's drinking. With resignation. Something to get past.

Ben called about a week later, Robert testified. He wanted the $140 back.

"So his concern about someone taking his money was gone," Vlautin immediately interjected.

Robert didn't know the answer.

Then, as it had for others, a sinister silence fell over Ben Fink. His family heard nothing from him. He stopped calling Robert's house. By Thanksgiving time, it was plain something was wrong. Robert's wife, who sympathized with her husband about Ben's good and bad sides, was worried. "It was kind of traditional," Robert said. "He'd come over and have dinner with us. He always phoned, he always came out. That's when I started getting worried," and notified the police that Ben Fink was missing.

But for Robert, there was no answer until November 1988, when the digging revealed his brother's fate.

Vlautin dug in himself. Did Robert know his brother had

been taking Dalmane for eleven years? Robert Fink grew suddenly stubborn. "All I know is Ben didn't like taking pills because he drank alcohol."

The interrogation went on, Vlautin trying to pull admissions from Robert that his dead brother had been a rowdy, unsocial, sick man. It went on until a tired Robert Fink said, summing up a lifetime's helplessness in the face of Ben's alcoholism, "I don't know whether he drank to pass out or to blot everything out."

Vlautin finished, and Robert Fink, with as much dignity as he entered the courtroom, left it. The stale tactics of Puente's lawyer lingered, as did the sadness.

Months before the hearing, Robert Fink had told reporters that Ben had been a restless, rough, rebellious man. Although he was Jewish, he defiantly had a swastika tattooed on his arm. But in his own way, he had been as exuberant about life as Ruth Munroe or Bert Montoya when he smoked a gift cigar.

One question hanging over the proceedings, besides how much the judge would let the public hear about Puente's 1982 crimes, was what she had been doing during those years in prison, from 1982 to 1985.

Williamson aimed to partly answer the question. He was nervous about it, talking to his witnesses in his office before court on Thursday, May 10. He was going to show the judge three women who had never met each other and only had Dorothea Puente in common, yet each one had been privy to guilty admissions from Puente in prison or in jail.

Williamson worried that his witnesses would be easy targets for Vlautin or Clymo. A prison snitch comes into court without much credibility and can rapidly lose it all.

Which would leave Williamson with holes in his case and Judge Ohanesian looking skeptically at him. She had, by the third week of the hearing, grown more sure on the bench.

May 10, 1990, turned into the worst day for Puente during her courtroom journey through trial.

The first prison witness was Joan Miller, who came into

court always oddly grinning from nervousness. She clutched a black purse on the witness stand.

Everyone was tense, even Puente, who breathed hard enough to tremble. Clymo became so agitated that Puente had to pat him on the back for a change, and Williamson, who rarely showed his tension, tossed a pen up and down into the air.

Miller sat nervously on the stand. Can you identify the woman you knew at Frontera in 1983? Williamson asked.

Miller pointed at Puente. "That's her." Miller was doing time for selling stock securities without a permit.

Miller had first met Puente near the end of 1983 when they were housed in the same part of the prison. She spoke with Puente during exercise periods and at night, nearly every day. They became good acquaintances, and Miller was impressed with Puente's wide experience. She told Miller she had been a restaurant owner, a physician, and a nurse who cared for the disabled and elderly. "She had done a number of things in her past," Miller said, and a few spectators repressed chuckles.

"She'd run some sort of care facility for the elderly, some sort of nursing home," Miller said in answer to Williamson's questions. Which was exactly what Puente planned to do as soon as she got out of prison. According to Miller, she intended to violate her parole from the start.

How would she get these people, the ones who'd live at the proposed nursing home, Williamson asked.

"They'd be referred by various county and social agencies," Miller reported Puente's thinking. She had already figured out, between 1983 and 1984, how the illegal business at 1426 F Street would operate. "It would be a money-making thing," Miller said.

Then Miller chilled the courtroom. "I got the impression she knew how to control people." Clymo raised a loud, angry objection to the "impression." So Williamson instantly asked Miller what Puente said. Specifically.

Miller glanced across at Puente, the half-smile frozen. "She said one way to control people she was going to use was over-the-counter medicines like Visine. You put it in their food."

Williamson showed nothing, keeping a poker face at the revelation that Puente had admitted a willingness to dope unknowing victims. No one in court had ever heard of Visine being toxic, but reporters hurriedly checked and found that the active ingredient in it, tetrahydrozoline, constricts blood vessels throughout the body. There was one fatality in California when Visine was injected.

Williamson ended, and Vlautin, shifting and wiggling irritably in his chair, began a sarcastic cross-examination of Miller. "Wasn't her plan to do her time and get out and make a living?" he demanded.

Miller nodded, then spoiled it all by saying that Puente formed the idea of getting "old, elderly, disabled, hard-to-care-for people" into some sort of nursing home she'd run.

"She wasn't going to do this for free, was she?" Vlautin asked waspishly.

Miller allowed that Puente definitely had no intention of running a board-and-care business for free. But why had Vlautin accepted the testimony that Puente intended to break parole the second she was out of prison by running such a business?

Vlautin's sole success was forcing an ever-smiling Miller to admit that Puente never used the words "rip-off" or "steal" in connection with her imagined business.

She only said, Miller persisted, "it was a way to make a lot of money in this kind of business" by billing the government for running a board-and-care facility.

Williamson's next jailhouse witness had bothered him all morning. He had finalized the deal to get her to testify only a little before court. She could, he knew, go completely sideways on him and undermine both Miller and the remaining jailhouse informant.

Just before lunch, Michelle Marie Crowl was brought into court. There was a moment of levity when Judge Ohanesian realized no one had remembered to bring Puente into court from the lockup. Puente had been so quiet, so unobtrusive and decorative, that even the judge could overlook her absence.

Crowl came in wearing a Sacramento County Jail T-shirt. She was uncuffed on the witness stand, her lawyer standing beside her in case any questions trespassed beyond her deal with Williamson.

She was young, attractive, with reddish hair. If a fragment of what she testified to was true, it was extraordinarily damaging to Puente.

Williamson, propping himself against the jury box railing, outlined the deal with Crowl. She was on parole for obtaining prescription drugs falsely. She had a parole violation pending that day, and Williamson would make "good faith efforts" to have the violation dropped by the Department of Corrections.

Crowl shifted uneasily on the witness stand. She didn't want to testify. She was not even satisfied when Williamson promised to relocate her in prison if she got threats because of her testimony. She had already gotten some threats from prison friends of Puente.

So Williamson plunged ahead, hoping to come out all right by the time Crowl stepped off the stand.

She had been housed, she said, with Dorothea Puente at the Rio Consumnes Correctional Center, Ramona section, starting in November 1988, shortly after Puente's capture.

The inmates at RCCC were in lockdown, which meant that they could not socialize, as Miller had with Puente years earlier. The RCCC women stayed in their cells except for very restricted periods. Crowl was separated from Puente's single cell by another cell. The cells shared a common high ceiling.

Crowl, led by Williamson, launched into the heart of her testimony. It was late November. She and the other inmates were watching the common TV placed in front of the cells. Puente grew very upset seeing the news coverage about Everson Gillmouth.

"She said he was the first body that was killed," Crowl

reported. He was put in a box by the river. "She was very close to him. He wanted to marry her. She said he grew very jealous when he found out she was close to others."

Did she say anything else about Mr. Gillmouth, Williamson asked.

Crowl nodded. "She said she killed him, and Mr. Florez was her helper." Puente was furious that Florez was "getting a deal" for turning on her.

Did she use the word "killed" or "died"? Williamson asked briskly.

"Killed," Crowl answered.

In the cell on the other side of Puente was a woman named Pauline Pinson. Crowl said Puente spoke to Pinson in a loud voice, easily heard between the cells. Crowl didn't have to rely on the acoustics of the area, either. She was a trusty for a while, and she brought hot water for coffee to the inmates so she sometimes talked directly to Puente about these matters.

Puente, Crowl said into the half-filled, very still courtroom, described the seven F Street victims as having been "killed." Puente was highly agitated by the TV news reports about the digging and the resultant discoveries. She loudly said that the people who came to her were on medication already.

Crowl swallowed. "She dispensed medication to them. Sometimes she said there was a little left over."

And what about the seven victims and their medication? Williamson wanted to know.

Puente, Crowl said clearly, admitted giving the seven victims "a little more."

But why kill these people? What was the point? Williamson went around the admissions again and again. Crowl nodded, saying Puente dismissed the seven victims as "already frail and elderly, some with heart conditions."

"She could get their Social Security checks," Crowl said. Puente, a little sheepishly, confessed that "she had gotten a little greedy" and killed the seven victims for money.

How was she able to kill these people so easily?

"She was Mom to them. She had established a rapport with them." Crowl cleared her throat. "They trusted her."

Ben Fink certainly had. So had Gallop and the others she gave pills to. And as for the exact mechanism of death, Crowl declared that Puente "gave the medication with alcohol; she'd slip some medication to them."

Did Mrs. Puente tell you why she did that? Williamson asked.

"To suppress their breathing," Crowl said, a little embarrassed. "I never heard that word until she used it."

Crowl grew defensive about overhearing the Puente-Pinson dialogues. Other inmates, she said, heard them, too, and she rattled off names. When Puente began loudly talking about Bert Montoya, everyone in the area heard her.

"Bert was retarded," Crowl repeated Puente's words. "He helped her around the house with the other people." Crowl was positive that Puente said she used Bert to bury the six other bodies. He went along "because he was very friendly to her."

Williamson recognized that even if Montoya helped bury a few victims, he hadn't been living at 1426 F Street long enough to bury James Gallop, for example. Still, the prosecution had privately always suspected that besides other helpers, Puente had used Bert as a gravedigger or hauler, getting the tightly wrapped cocoons from the house to the yard at night.

What lent credibility to Crowl's claims was that she had not approached the authorities. They had pursued her.

In February 1989, Crowl had been in the jail hospital with a pneumonia-like condition. Guarding her was a rookie deputy sheriff named Fromen. While they watched TV, Crowl mentioned the things she had overheard from Puente or talked to her about. Fromen, much to Crowl's dismay, said he had to report what she had just said.

Crowl, like most inmates, was terrified of being labeled a snitch. In fact, her remarks did cause trouble. Fromen's eventual report ended up in the hands of Puente's lawyers, and through them, Puente heard about it. Crowl had gone back to Frontera for several months and within days of arriving at the prison, she was threatened by Puente's friends.

Crowl grew upset on the witness stand. She told the investigator from the public defender's office that she didn't want to testify against Puente because of the threats. "I was going to recant my stories," Crowl firmly said.

Then she went to the PD's office and talked to Clymo. This face-to-face meeting so unsettled Clymo that he barely could contain his rage when Williamson turned Crowl over to him for cross-examination.

Throughout the hearing and the later trial Clymo showed anger or extreme agitation by slowing his questions to a crawl, coughing slightly, and rubbing the back of his head. When he tried to coherently cross-examine Crowl, all of these tics were on display.

He began early on by demanding of Crowl, didn't she lie "looking me right in the eye in my office?"

"I was being threatened," Crowl retorted. "I'd do whatever it takes to get out from under the threats."

Well, Clymo snapped, didn't you tell Fromen that Puente said the drug she used was Demerol and not Dalmane?

Crowl stuck to her earlier testimony. She had told Fromen and Detective Terry Brown the drug was Dalmane. They must have misheard.

The afternoon went on, with Clymo barely holding in his anger, Puente patting him on the back, and Williamson successfully making objections, which only increased Clymo's frustration. He could not make Crowl admit to being a deceitful, cowardly, self-serving person.

Did you take notes on any of these conversations with Puente or what you overheard? he barked at her.

Crowl shook her head. She had not recorded the admissions at all.

Clymo's real point was made when he asked Crowl if it wasn't true that the Ramona section had intercoms in it and officers listened in sometimes?

"Yes, they do," Crowl said. Her lawyer stood warily, obviously wondering if Clymo would explode.

Not only did the guards randomly listen in to what was going on, but they could wander in, unannounced. Clymo got Crowl to admit this, which left a major problem for the prosecution. If Puente was such a prison-wise con, would she openly blab about killing people not only within earshot of other inmates, but where guards could easily overhear her?

The answer, which neither Williamson nor Clymo pointed out, was that Puente was very worked up over the news reports. She felt she was being wronged, others were getting better deals, she was the injured party. As it had throughout her life, Puente's better judgment left her when she deeply desired something or when she felt victimized. She married foolishly or killed. Talking loudly was a small misstep by comparison.

With Crowl wilting a little, Clymo wound up by trying to paint her as an ingrate, if nothing else. Puente helped Crowl get candy or food from the jail commissary. It was, it turned out, only when Puente asked about Crowl's health, that they talked.

"Everybody talked about her case," Crowl said. Dorothea Puente was the most celebrated inmate at RCCC. Puente patted Clymo.

"She didn't like going to the rec room because people called her names there," Crowl said. A few spectators and more than one reporter grinned at the idea.

"Did Dorothea ever say she killed people with Dalmane?" Clymo sat forward suddenly in his chair.

"No," Crowl said. "She only dispensed Dalmane to people there," meaning 1426 F Street.

Crowl was cuffed again and taken away. Williamson felt he had gotten some untouchable testimony in front of the judge. A measure of that was Vlautin's instant fastening on every reporter, telling each that Crowl "just slithered off the stand." He was as worked up as Clymo, aware that Miller and Crowl had hurt Puente badly. He and Clymo took the time to walk several reporters through the contradictory statements Crowl had given to the defense investigator, trying to shape the day's news stories more favorably than the evidence in court.

The third and last jailhouse acquaintance of Puente didn't testify until several weeks later, but she completed the "confessions" Puente had made. Brenda Trujillo was easily the oddest of the trio who testified against Puente.

Williamson had agonized for weeks about even calling Trujillo to the stand. When he interviewed her in his office, he was appalled at how zany she was. "She's a wacko!" he exclaimed after one interview.

The dilemma, for him, was that Trujillo had known Puente intimately and offered information that, even if only partly accurate, was as damaging as either Crowl or Miller. Williamson reluctantly concluded he had to put Trujillo on the witness stand.

When she strolled slowly into court, from a rear corridor where Williamson had hidden her from reporters, Trujillo looked very unimpressive. She was fat, sluggish, dressed in a leatheroid skirt, and under the influence of methadone as a substitute for the heroin she had been addicted to for years.

It was a humid, stuffy afternoon, but Trujillo livened it up.

Williamson was as brusque with Trujillo as with any witness, maybe a little more to keep her awake. She kept licking her lips, glancing nastily at Puente, who for one of the few times in court, shook her head, folded her arms, and actually took an obvious interest in what a witness was saying.

Trujillo had met Puente in county jail in 1982. They then spent time together at Frontera. From 1986 to 1988 Trujillo lived with Puente at 1426 F Street, excluding the three times she returned to prison on parole violations.

When they were alone at 1426 F Street, Trujillo said Puente tutored her in the fine art of theft. Trujillo had small tattoos on her hands. Puente wanted them removed. "I should go to the hospital or get my parole officer to get them off so I wouldn't be so easily ID'd."

"Identified as what?" Williamson asked.

As a former convict. Puente had plans for me, Trujillo went on. "She wanted me to go into high class restaurants and drug people and take their money." How? "It was easy, she told me. All you had to do was drop a couple drops of Visine in their drinks."

Trujillo had never met Miller or Crowl, and when Trujillo told police about Puente's Visine scheme, Miller had not yet testified.

Where, Williamson asked, would Dorothea get her drugs?

One source was Dr. Doody. "He was her psychiatrist. She used to see him, and she could get any drug from him." Trujillo licked her lips as if recalling a menu. "Valium, codeine, Dalmane. All she had to do was pick up the phone."

Williamson especially wanted Trujillo to recount a very specific incident she witnessed involving Puente and her confidant, John McCauley.

It was in the mid-1980s, Trujillo said. "I seen her put tranquilizers into his drink, mix it, and give it to him." The two women went into the living room and talked, then Puente left and came back with McCauley's coat, going through the pockets and offering Trujillo some of the money she found.

Williamson wanted more detail. What exactly did Trujillo see Puente do to McCauley's drink?

"I was in the living room. I went into the kitchen. She was leaning over the table putting pink tranquilizers into a Bloody Mary drink." Trujillo watched Puente break open the capsules.

Cabrera had found empty capsules stashed in a bedroom drawer in 1988, and Puente had whipped up a similar sort of cocktail for Dorothy Osborne in 1982. This time Trujillo was impressed that Puente "put over seven capsules" into McCauley's Bloody Mary.

Williamson found he had to backtrack a little. In his office, Trujillo had told a somewhat different story. He asked her again about the drugging, and Trujillo picked up the incident. About an hour after Puente went through McCauley's coat, Trujillo followed her up to McCauley's bedroom and stood in the doorway. She saw Puente going through the unconscious McCauley's pants pockets, turning them inside out, looking for more money. It was all done with the same brisk, proprietary thoroughness Puente used on Malcolm McKenzie in 1982.

McCauley, when Williamson interviewed him, said he recalled several times Puente made a drink for him, he lost consciousness soon afterward, and came to missing money or valuables. Puente told him he had just passed out and forgotten where he put things or spent the money.

Puente used drugging as casually as other people flipped on the TV.

Clymo's cross-examination was stinging, contemptuous, and monotonous. He established, beyond all doubt, that Brenda Trujillo was a drug addict, convict, liar, and some-time hooker. She also, though, provided testimony remarkably consistent with what others said they had experienced around Dorothea Puente.

Trujillo had abundant bias against Puente. She blamed Puente for having her parole violated, snitching to her parole officer. Puente also falsely accused Trujillo of murder. "I think Dorothea just picked it out of a secret witness list" in a *Bee* article about unsolved crimes. Puente informed the police that Trujillo killed a man. "She was telling me about all the connections she had in the police department," Trujillo snapped, then faded out as she had before on the stand. "I forgot what I was going to say." Police dropped the investigation.

Clymo insisted Trujillo was so druggy she couldn't be properly cross-examined. He huffed about it, and Judge Ohanesian directed him to get along with things.

Trujillo, like Crowl, was depicted as an ingrate. Puente had obtained amenities for her in jail, like cigarettes. They talked often by phone after Puente was released, and "she told me not to be taking drugs," Trujillo said. Puente, as she had in the seventies, was mothering another "stepdaughter," although one more coarse than any before.

Another claim that Clymo's badgering questions slowly dragged from Trujillo was that Puente deliberately drugged her with methamphetamine, then called her parole officer, and had her parole violated so Puente could get rid of her.

But Clymo inexplicably managed to establish Trujillo's credibility more firmly by pressing her on the McCauley incident. He got her to recount that it took place in June or July. McCauley was sitting on his bed, watching TV, drinking a bottle of cheap white port, from "a green bottle," she remembered. McCauley wore plain jeans, a T-shirt, and the sun was out brightly.

Trujillo left the stand and returned the following morning, in approximately the same distant, sluggish condition. Clymo's only accomplishment was having Trujillo describe how Puente, who had her power of attorney while she was in prison in 1987, kept all of her benefit checks. "I used to ask her all the time if my money was there, and she never told me," Trujillo answered petulantly.

Puente did have an answer for many problems. When Trujillo, in prison, told Puente she had an appointment at the Social Security office in Sacramento, Puente offered to take care of it. "She told me she was going to send someone who fit my description over to Social Security," said Trujillo. Puente had done so herself when she impersonated the dead Dorothy Miller at the VA clinic.

Clymo sat back, waving his hand, asking Judge Ohanesian to strike all of Trujillo's direct testimony. It was so ambiguous, he said, about events between 1985 and 1987 that Puente couldn't defend herself.

Williamson, with alacrity, jumped in and reminded the hesitant judge that all Puente had to do was defend herself against charges, not mere accusations. The prosecution never charged Puente with drugging and robbing John McCauley.

Ohanesian worriedly ruled, after thinking about it for some time, that Williamson was correct. Trujillo's testimony, warts and all, would remain in the record.

Through these three women, Williamson presented the closest thing to a full statement from Dorothea Puente without hearing from the defendant herself.

And that no one ever did.

28

Two questions loomed over the Puente case for Williamson. How did she get hold of her victims' money? And what did she do with it?

Although motive is not part of the legal definition of the crime of murder, Williamson was certain he had to show Judge Ohanesian, and later a jury, just how Puente gained control of her victims' funds and how she then spent the money. Demonstrating these things made the terrible crimes comprehensible.

By the third and fourth weeks of the hearing, near the end of May, the clerk's desk in front of Judge Ohanesian's bench was piled high with evidence—papers, clothing, stacks of photos. Williamson next hauled in baskets of documents and traced Puente's financial scheming.

After Crowl and Miller had testified, Puente lapsed into a studied immobility. Her only indication of even paying attention to what happened in court was to change her wardrobe finally to a white dress with military-style epaulets and stylish black shoes.

Witnesses with dry voices and even drier records came into court from the California Franchise Tax Board and Social Security. All seven F Street victims got renter's assistance checks, many of which went to them after they were dead according to the testimony. Puente listed herself as "I am cousin to him" when she became Bert Montoya's representative payee in March 1988, soon after he arrived at 1426 F Street. No one at the Social Security office challenged the claim and Bert got $500 a month, which went directly to Puente.

Six of the victims simply had their checks sent to 1426 F Street and Puente seized them first. In the case of Dorothy Miller, Puente had Ricardo Odorica listed as her payee starting in November 1987.

Puente's defense lawyers noted that sixteen other people, including the victims, used 1426 F Street as an address for their checks. Puente didn't kill everyone, of course. What she did do, however, was take control of the tenant's finances, and if that tenant became a problem, like Betty Palmer or James Gallop, she disposed of them and continued to get the checks.

Strong willed tenants she either left alone or threw out, like Carol Durning. Only the mentally or physically feeble were killed.

On the hundreds of checks, various victims' names appeared. While in jail, Puente was required to make 530 handwriting samples, using her own name, other names, spelling them as the checks indicated. Vlautin bitterly denounced this procedure, declaring that Puente's handwriting would match the checks because she had been told exactly how to write.

It was, though, a very strange charge for Vlautin to make. Even Puente herself, flying back with Cabrera in November 1988, admitted stealing from the dead victims. The only plausible defense she had for murder was that she was a thief so afraid of discovery she buried people who died naturally rather than reveal their deaths.

Puente used Odorica's account at First Nationwide Savings as a repository for money she needed to conceal from her probation and parole officers. Agents located Social Security and veterans' pension fund checks from Miller, Palmer, Gallop, and Kelly in the account. The $9,980 check that surprised Julius Kelly in Eureka was endorsed: "payable to Ricardo Odorica."

Then, from this central account, Puente drew her laundered funds. In a one-month period in mid-1988, Puente was paid $4,000 from Odorica's account. Mysterious other sums flowed into the account, too. There were deposits of $10,000 and $1,200, and Odorica wrote a personal check to himself for $1,800.

No one who had met the tiny Odorica or the domineering Puente had any doubt who the driving influence was between the two. Puente had turned her adoring, almost supplicant landlord into an accomplice.

At the end of court one day, Williamson brought a panicky Odorica up to his office and angrily inveighed against Clymo, who had told the little man he would go to prison if he testified against Puente, that he might get immunity from Williamson for any state crimes, but he'd still be exposed to federal prosecution.

"When he's telling you stuff like you need a lawyer, he's wrong," Williamson lectured the fidgety, frightened little Odorica. "Look, he's going to say you're the biggest thief in the world, but you don't need a lawyer based on what you've told me. He's trying to scare you. You better be ready for it."

Nodding, obviously unconvinced, Odorica left the DA's office, steeling himself for his upcoming court appearance. Williamson fumed that "he's trying to intimidate my witness." It was a sign of the rancor between Williamson, Clymo, and Vlautin. It was also a sign that the Puente defense was hard put to do much more than try to keep bad evidence out of court.

The grand total of Puente's thefts for a thirteen-month period ending in November 1988 came to over $70,000. Had she actually been the one forging the checks?

Williamson's expert from the Department of Justice, a precise, pedantic man with an open briefcase beside him on the witness stand, offered a "range of conclusions" from certainty to probability. For example, Puente signed all seven of Betty Palmer's checks. Odorica endorsed one in June 1988, long after Palmer was dead and headless.

Twelve of Dorothy Miller's checks, from December 1987 to November 1988, were signed by Puente and endorsed with Miller's name. Likewise, thirteen checks for Vera Martin were endorsed by Puente or made payable to Fingerhut, a mail-order company. All of Bert Montoya's checks were signed with his name, by Puente.

Nine checks made out to James Gallop were forged by Puente. One was signed over to Odorica in June 1988, well after Gallop's death. Puente also endorsed thirteen checks made out to Ben Fink, for over $500 each. She forged Julius Kelly's name on his large check, too.

The handwriting expert peered at his report, studying the documents as Williamson handed them to him after they had been marked by the clerk. The expert said that the "Irene" postcard sent to Reba Nicklous had been written entirely by Puente.

Although the handwriting expert was questioned at great length by Vlautin, the fact remained that Dorothea Puente had signed, over years, all of the checks and phony documents that permitted her to spend the dead people's money. Or to conceal their deaths.

And what did she buy with the money?

Williamson called a shy, hesitant woman employee from Fingerhut. Did Dorothea Puente have an account with you? he asked.

"Yes, she did, from February 1986 until 1988," answered the woman. In other words, right after disposing of Everson Gillmouth and gaining control of his property, Puente opened up a mail-order account.

Fingerhut was ideal for Puente. It accepted any kind of

government check as payment for goods. And it sold clothing, luggage, TVs, tools, VCRs. Williamson showed the woman a check made out to James Gallop, now stamped with Fingerhut's name. "We cashed that check," the woman said.

When Williamson ended there, Vlautin asked the Fingerhut employee how much Mrs. Puente had spent. From February 1986 until 1988 she had bought $7,600 worth of merchandise. "Generally personal items," the woman said. Puente's shopping list included dresses, slacks, shoes, carpet, a nineteen-inch TV, pillows, bedspreads, a talking robot toy, broiler pans and cookware, and a sewing machine. These were all items she used herself, gave away to outsiders, or handed out to favored tenants. She used her Fingerhut account as an open-ended credit line for merchandise.

As the woman from Fingerhut testified, a few spectators in court took closer note of the white checked dress with epaulets Puente wore, wondering where she got it and who paid for it.

Puente ordered directly from Giorgio Beverly Hills the expensive perfumes and cosmetics she scattered over her bureau at 1426 F Street. The perfumes ran about $110 a bottle.

She went to other places for less common items than Fingerhut could provide. From Blair Corporation she bought $3,171 worth of clothing and jewelry, and she sent for $1,516 of personal items from the Mail Order Company in Arizona.

Her most shocking purchase was from Jackson & Perkins: the flowers and shrubs she used to decoratively trim and disguise the backyard gravesites at 1426 F Street. Her dead tenants paid $335 through her for that service.

And, as investigators determined, Puente kept a very strict accounting of who paid what, no matter whether they were living or dead. In a steno notebook ledger, Puente toted up the payments she got from each victim. "Jim 657," for example, referred to James Gallop's "contribution" of $416 SS and $241 SSI checks every month.

Puente's purchases were pathetically modest by many standards—household items, clothes. She indulged herself, of course, and used the money she stole to make herself a magnanimous gift-giver.

She was not entitled legally to any of the approximately $70,000 that she stole over two years. Some of it had gone into maintaining 1426 F Street and buying food for the tenants, but the way she spent the money did not matter to the law. It was all theft.

What did matter was that seven people had died for so little. Their deaths made it possible for Dorothea Puente to operate a modest boardinghouse, keep herself and her living tenants fed, and splurge on clothing, cosmetics, free rounds of drinks at bars, and gifts, as the whim moved her.

Ricardo Odorica finally took the witness stand on May 21, perching like a child just below the bench. He was as uneasy and fearful as he had been when Williamson read him the riot act. He kept looking nervously at Clymo.

As for "the lady" herself, when Williamson asked Odorica to identify her, he smiled and pointed at the counsel table, and Puente, for the first time, acknowledged a witness by nodding back at him.

While testifying largely about Everson Gillmouth's brief residence at 1426 F Street, Odorica inevitably found himself answering questions, in his halting English, about his financial connections to Puente.

Clymo, much to Williamson's annoyance, began by asking if Odorica knew he could be arrested for cashing the checks Puente gave him. "Did you express concerns to Mr. Williamson that you'd be arrested?" Clymo asked solicitously.

Odorica scrunched up his face. "He said if I was going to be honest, I didn't need a lawyer."

Clymo nodded, patting the back of his head. Did you know you could face federal charges for coming here today?

At that, Williamson's bottled-up anger erupted. He barked that Clymo was trying to "intimidate the witness into taking the Fifth Amendment" and thus end his testimony.

Ohanesian agreed swiftly, and Clymo, who had risen to his feet, flopped back in his chair. "I'm not prepared to cross-examine," he pouted, unless he could go over Odorica's financial links to Puente.

That area, in fact, would remain obscure until the trial years later. It was irrelevant at the preliminary hearing. It was clear Puente had had help from her landlord in operating the business at 1426 F Street.

When Odorica left the stand, he smiled and waved to her. She nodded regally back at him. Odorica was never charged with any crime.

By the end of Odorica's appearance, several mysteries had been solved. For instance, it had bothered police and prosecutors since 1988 why Everson Gillmouth was dumped by the river and Betty Palmer, the next victim in line, was so severely mutilated to hide her identity. By the end of May, it was plain Puente believed Gillmouth, from a small town in Oregon, had no contacts other than her in Sacramento. Palmer, though, had seen a half-dozen doctors and had acquaintances around town. A stranger could lie unmutilated on the riverbank while a tenant of 1426 F Street had to be disfigured to obscure a connection to Puente. Puente, according to Crowl, had been furious when police so quickly tied the body on the riverbank to Gillmouth and then to her. That was not her plan at all.

Williamson had also learned that the mercury and lead levels in the bodies were caused by ground metals leaching into the rotting tissues and had nothing to do with a cause of death.

To his surprise, he found out that the mysterious

"Dorothea" in the *Archerd* case was definitely not Puente. It was only another peculiar coincidence among many in the Puente case.

In the last week in May, Williamson prepared for the most confrontational part of the hearing, the explosive testimony I would give, and evidence Ruth Munroe's family and friends would offer about her murder years before 1426 F Street became notorious around the world.

29

I TOOK THE WITNESS STAND ON MAY 23, THE FIRST OF TWO appearances.

My testimony against Puente was preceded by days of acrimonious carping between Williamson and her lawyers. He had turned over to them the few pages Frawley had withheld, including my 1982 memos about Ruth Munroe. Vlautin and Clymo not very subtly suggested to Judge Ohanesian that the DA's office was engaged in some kind of cover-up and that they needed, at the very least, time to prepare for Munroe's witnesses.

So when Williamson and I walked to Department H, through the usual clutch of cameras and reporters, the tension level was higher than it had been since the start of the hearing a month earlier.

But I ended up waiting in the corridor until lunchtime, when Williamson hustled out of the courtroom, looking sour. "She can't make up her mind," he complained about the judge. Ohanesian didn't know if she could admit evidence of Puente's 1982 crimes. "I said, 'Judge, you've got all the stuff you've heard. This is a case about crimes for profit, and that's all the priors are," meaning the 1982 convictions.

That difficulty got sorted out after lunch, and I was called in at two-thirty.

The court clerk, a kindly woman with glasses, called me forward, told me to raise my right hand and answer the oath. I did. I sat down on the witness stand.

Looking from the brightly lit area around the bench toward the dimmer audience section of the courtroom was a disorienting experience. Judge Ohanesian, a few feet to my left and higher, seemed like a hovering black bird in her robes.

I was suddenly very tense. Whether or not Ruth Munroe's murder would ever come before a jury rested largely on my testimony.

Williamson, leaning against the jury box, asked me to identify Puente. I looked at her, from the front of the courtroom, as an accuser and witness, for the first time in eight years.

She stared at me, expressionless, her mouth set, her eyes opaque, black. Then she went back to idly picking at some papers on the counsel table.

Williamson showed me batches of documents, the 1982 convictions, asked me to identify them and to explain what I had prosecuted Puente for. As he did so, I kept reminding myself of what I used to tell every witness: tell the truth, keep it simple, answer in one word if possible, and think before answering if you need to. It's much harder doing those things than advising someone to do them.

Vlautin's cross-examination, this first appearance, was almost perfunctory. He wanted to know if I remembered what drug Puente used in 1982 or if I had seen the toxicology report on Dorothy Osborne. I didn't recall. Williamson grew excited, objecting to Vlautin's attempt to re-litigate the 1982 pleas.

Vlautin didn't go much further. When I got off the stand, I

realized the main bulk of his questions would come later. But for now Puente's 1982 convictions were finally being talked about in court. Judge Ohanesian, until that moment, had scrupulously tried to keep a mention of everything prior to 1986 out of the public record.

She had changed her mind. Puente's lawyers apparently would be free to attack the 1982 plea bargain and perhaps get Ruth Munroe's murder thrown out entirely.

Between my first and second appearances, Williamson put on Ruth Munroe's family, and the awful image of Munroe lying helplessly paralyzed in bed on April 27, 1982. Everyone in court was moved except Puente, who rested one cheek against her hand.

Williamson was nearly finished with his case. He ended by calling a pharmacist who filled fourteen prescriptions for Puente for Dalmane, written by Dr. Doody. There were nine refills, and the total number of pills Puente collected was about five hundred. At her later trial, the prosecution calculated she had direct access to about a thousand Dalmane capsules between 1986 and 1988. It was a lot of Dalmane.

Several days earlier, as part of his Munroe evidence, Williamson put on Bernice Stone, a tough, gray-haired toxicologist, to explain the significance of the drugs found in Munroe.

Gruffly, Stone said the Miltown was at its prescribed, therapeutic dosage. But, Stone said, the Tylenol and codeine were at "toxic lethal levels."

"Would these amounts cause sudden death?" Williamson asked. As one would expect if Munroe had taken the overdose all at once to commit suicide.

"Tylenol isn't known to cause rapid death," Stone said. Nor was codeine. Death would come "in a couple of hours," even with all the acetaminophen and codeine Munroe had in her body.

Clymo, of course, liked the idea of a sudden suicidal ingestion of drugs by Munroe. He could not explain her fastidiousness in removing the lethal drugs from her bedroom, taking Miltown to calm down, or leaving no suicide note.

While Stone agreed it might take about forty Tylenol pills to reach the levels of drug in Munroe's blood, "I can't really talk about the time of ingestion," she said bluntly. No one, of course, commits a slow motion suicide, swallowing a few pills at a time over hours.

Stone believed "the drugs were all administered at once," which helped the defense.

Vlautin took over as the codeine expert. Getting Stone to borrow a calculator from the court clerk, he had her fuss through computations that would mean Munroe had taken fifty codeine tablets at sixty-milligram strength or one hundred tablets at the usual thirty-milligram dosage. It sounded like the sickly Munroe had managed to gulp a huge number of pills.

Vlautin was leading to the fatty liver damage observed in Munroe's liver at autopsy on April 28, 1982. He believed Stone would agree that the liver damage was consistent with Munroe being a chronic Tylenol abuser.

Williamson lowered his head in surprise. A few moments earlier, Vlautin had successfully prevented him from asking Stone about drug effects in the body. Now Vlautin was trying to do exactly the same thing.

Based on the amount of codeine and Tylenol in the liver sample, Stone said, "I would expect them to live more than a couple of hours," meaning anyone who took so much. But death would come quickly after that.

Vlautin nodded, apparently believing he had just established that Munroe's damaged liver meant she had taken the overdose and died soon afterward.

He had opened himself up to a wholly different interpretation.

Williamson practically leaped into redirect examination, asking toxicologist Stone about the harmful effects of Tylenol. "Isn't necrosis of the liver well documented in the profession's literature?"

Both Vlautin and Clymo objected loudly. Stone was only an expert on drug analysis, not the effects of drugs. Judge Ohanesian, then Williamson, tartly reminded the defense lawyers that they themselves had turned Bernice Stone into an expert on physiological effects of drugs.

Stone listened grumpily. She agreed with Williamson that the liver destruction in Ruth Munroe was thoroughly documented in cases of chronic Tylenol abuse. And, Stone said, Munroe's liver damage was consistent with a massive overdose of Tylenol.

Williamson's questions came rapid-fire, nonstop, ending with, "Wouldn't three days of massive Tylenol overdose cause the liver damage we see here?"

"Yes, it could," the toxicologist answered. Over three days of constantly high doses—introduced in crème de menthe cocktails for example—Munroe's liver would show the fatty damage from Tylenol observed at autopsy.

The prosecution had in Ruth Munroe not only the sole victim with an established cause of death but also one whose death was completely consistent with the pattern of stupefaction over several days leading to death, which friends and family had seen.

Williamson ended his side of the preliminary hearing with a bang.

When he finished several days later, he moved one hundred eight exhibits into evidence and rested.

How Clymo and Vlautin intended to present a defense remained a mystery over the three-day Memorial Day weekend that followed. In a preliminary hearing, as in a trial, the defense is under no legal obligation to put on any evidence or witnesses. It can simply argue that the prosecution has failed to establish the necessary elements of the crimes charged against the defendant.

But Puente's lawyers wanted to affirmatively get some of their side out in public, test it before a judge, possibly have one or more murders dismissed.

They planned to attack Puente's 1982 pleas as uninformed, therefore involuntary. Since Puente had already served her prison time, the only purpose in rehashing all the 1982 crimes was to prevent a jury from ever hearing about them.

Part of this strategy meant arguing that Ruth Munroe had been part of the 1982 plea bargain and that the DA's office had known of her murder prior to Puente's sentencing.

This meant I had to testify again, and so did Puente's 1982 lawyer, Dennis Porter. Puente's crimes meant that the past reached out for everyone connected to her— prosecutors, cops, DAs, families. Everything came back.

If Judge Ohanesian believed the DA's office had covered up knowledge of Munroe's murder prior to sentencing in 1982, she would dismiss the charge, and it would be barred forever from going to a jury.

There was, as the defense started up, Vlautin leading off, an unpleasant, charged tension in Ohanesian's courtroom. Williamson, beside the jury box, seethed at what he knew was going to happen.

Vlautin began Puente's defense by calling the bartender at the Zebra Club in January 1982 and asking him if Malcolm McKenzie looked drunk when he left the bar with Puente.

"He wasn't really bad," said the bartender.

It was a small way of saying, Vlautin hoped, that McKenzie had passed out on his own when they got to his apartment. But what the bartender said in court now wasn't quite what he had told police eight years before.

All Williamson had to do was blandly but crisply ask the bartender if his memory of what he saw was sharper on January 16, 1982, or that day, May 29, 1990?

It was fresher on the earlier date, the witness answered.

The defense moved on to witnesses who attacked the credibility of Brenda Trujillo. Their testimony was repetitious, though, since she had admitted so many flaws herself.

Vlautin went on swiftly to Pauline Pinson, Puente's friendly next-door cell mate at RCCC. Pinson came into court looking startlingly tan and trim, with carefully styled brown hair and wearing a white county-jail T-shirt and black jeans. One reporter wrote that she looked "amazingly good for a forty-one-year-old ex-junkie with a prison record that would shame a Mafia don." Like Crowl, Pinson was in custody, so she was uncuffed on the witness stand.

Williamson watched her closely. He had been tracking her down for weeks, but she fled from the DA's office whenever he was about to question her.

He decided to let the defense have its way. He believed Pinson's truculent, con-wise attitude would sour Judge Ohanesian all by itself.

Pinson, it turned out, was another in Puente's long string of rehab projects with younger women. Puente "was always asking, are you all right? Are you feeling better?" from her adjacent cell in Ramona when Pinson was sick, withdrawing from from heroin and cocaine.

Puente at that point in court started to dab at her eyes, and asked Clymo for a tissue.

Pinson briskly, almost belligerently, said that she and Puente did not talk much at all when they were locked down in their cells and that they never discussed Puente's case or her custody status, contrary to what Crowl said. All Puente ever did was express a "longing for western novels." She claimed to have written two.

No matter how coldly, callously, or contemptuously the guards treated her, Pinson said Dorothea Puente never got angry or even raised her voice.

Vlautin asked about watching TV. Well, Pinson smugly said, we never looked at any news stories. "We used to get into watching movies on TV," Pinson said. Puente especially liked *Lonesome Dove.*

And as Crowl had acknowledged, Pinson snappishly told Vlautin that the guards listened in on conversations through the intercom, and if there was any loud talking after 10:00 P.M. a deputy sheriff would order everyone to shut up. Crowl couldn't have overheard talking that didn't take place.

Finally Vlautin asked Pinson, who looked pleased with her appearance in court, what she thought of Michelle Crowl.

Pinson said acidly, "She's a manipulating, conniving liar, and she's used Dorothea's case to get out of jail."

Williamson stepped away from the jury box and toward Pinson, then asked her what she thought about Dorothea Puente.

"I consider her my friend. She helped me out just as another human being." Pinson had given Puente a Saint Jude prayer as a thank-you.

While Williamson tried to show obvious holes in Pinson's testimony, all he really established was that she hated Crowl and felt very close to Puente.

Was she lying or was Crowl? Were they both lying partly or completely, which was possible, too? Judge Ohanesian had to sort it out, and Williamson only hoped she had heard enough about Puente to do it correctly.

On behalf of Dorothea Puente, Vlautin rested the defense as to the last eight counts of the complaint soon afterward. He was going to concentrate the majority of the defense on throwing out the Ruth Munroe murder.

Munroe's murder, in a strange way, had become pivotal for the prosecution and defense. It gave the prosecution a definite cause of death and a victim who was not shadowy or sick or forgotten.

For Puente's defense, Munroe's 1982 murder would telegraph to a trial jury that she had been a killer long before November 1988 and destroy any defense that her frail tenants simply died of natural causes.

So Vlautin and Clymo had to make Ruth Munroe vanish. They wanted my help to do so.

30

I WAS NOT LOOKING FORWARD TO SITTING ON THE WITNESS stand, facing that white-faced, bitter woman at the counsel table.

But on June 14, after the defense had fortified itself with a break and sought out any potential problems in the new material Williamson handed over from 1982, Vlautin called me to the witness stand.

This second time I decided to really look around. I saw that Judge Ohanesian made her trial notes on a pad, not in the bulky legal-looking logbooks that most judges use. Her bench was neat, almost like the desk of a proper grade schooler.

Puente again rarely looked at me. She kept her eyes downcast, peering through her glasses with a tiny squint, as she read Clymo's notes. Sometimes she scratched out a note herself, using the stubby pencils provided by the jail. From my vantage point I could see that Clymo's socks had sagged down around his ankles.

I had on my only suit. I wanted to look formal for the occasion.

Vlautin stood up at the counsel table, nervously buttoning the middle button of his coat. He started his questions.

We had met in his office across from the courthouse three days earlier. Since I had known him for a decade, I didn't mind talking to him out of court.

He showed me the old memos, talked about the sequence of Puente's 1982 cases. He was scornful of Dennis Porter. "We'll have to do an incompetency-of-counsel hearing on him sometime," he said. Porter had talked to Puente only three times before she entered the guilty pleas. He had made no notes. He had obviously been winging a major case in 1982.

What I didn't know as Vlautin and I sat casually in his office that morning was that he had Porter's 1982 files. He knew what I had told Porter and what I had given Porter to help him persuade Puente to plead guilty.

Vlautin was certain I would never see those files. It is extremely rare for a defense attorney's case files to be exposed in a preliminary hearing or trial. Vlautin could say almost anything about the 1982 plea bargain without worrying that Puente's original lawyer's files would contradict him.

Vlautin and I talked for a long time about Esther Busby and Detective Schwartz. It was plain that Puente's defense would claim that Ruth Munroe, and not Busby, was the possible homicide covered by the plea bargain.

We strolled out later, talking about another serial-murder trial Vlautin was working on. Clymo, he said, was out buying a sailboat.

It was hot in Sacramento on June 14, a promise of a sweltering summer to come. The heat seemed to find ways into the courtroom, making the atmosphere heavy and stifling. The reporters and sketch artists and curiosity-seekers were back in force.

As I started testifying, Williamson fidgeted. He was straining to get at whatever Puente had told Porter, and if

Vlautin asked me what I had told Porter, Williamson believed the door would be open. He could get at any admissions of murder Puente might have made to her lawyer in 1982.

Vlautin probed and sidestepped, asking questions about why the plea transcript was silent about which crimes the DA wouldn't prosecute. The name Esther Busby doesn't appear anywhere in that transcript, does it? I said it didn't.

No murder at all had been discussed in Judge Warren's court.

Vlautin had set the stage for Porter. He turned me over to Williamson.

Williamson's questions were sharp. He introduced my August 1982 memos into evidence. He showed me the yellowed *Bee* clipping Bill Clausen had preserved all these years.

After dispelling the possibility of ambiguity about what I did to inform the police and John O'Mara about the Clausen family's suspicions, Williamson characteristically wound up cleanly: "The only potential homicide you knew, or that she could be involved in, concerned a person known to you as Esther Busby, is that right?"

"Yes," I said.

"And you communicated that to her lawyer, Mr. Porter?"

"Yes."

Williamson pointed at me. "At no time did you ever mention the name Ruth Munroe or any incident concerning Ruth Munroe during the plea negotiations and/or plea bargain in this case, is that true?"

When I said, "That's true," Williamson nodded.

"I have no further questions."

Vlautin had a great deal more, though, and he and Williamson got into long, heated objections that the judge tried to keep in bounds. The festering animosity between Williamson and Puente's lawyers was about to spill out over Ruth Munroe's murder.

Vlautin's major thrust was that the Clausens, when interviewed by the Sacramento police in December 1988, had given a different chronology of when they talked to me in 1982. In fact, none of the Clausens, when they all trooped back to the witness stand after me, said anything different from my testimony. Bill, especially, was furious that Clymo, who took over the cross-examination, would suggest that he was trying to lie or cover up facts.

Clymo finally resorted to showing how much Bill hated Puente to discredit his testimony. He asked Bill about an interview with a defense investigator, "Did you tell him, 'If that bitch hits the streets, she's dead, get out of here, you're history'?"

"Close," Bill said, staring angrily at Clymo.

Williamson, a moment later, asked Bill exactly what he said. "I told the guy, 'Hey, if she hits the streets, she'll die,'" Bill replied.

The hearing grew more angry after Bill Clausen left the stand. Vlautin put a pudgier, nervous Dennis Porter on the stand. For a moment I sympathized with his discomfort. Testifying in a major murder trial is unpleasant. Having asked questions of witnesses for years doesn't leaven the experience any. I sweated through my suit.

But my sympathy for Porter evaporated the instant he implicitly said I had committed perjury when I testified.

Vlautin was asking him about the 1982 plea bargain. "Did the district attorney tell you the name of the person who was supposedly killed by Dorothea Puente?"

Porter nodded, swallowed, hunched forward. "The district attorney told me the name in the phone conversation."

What name? Vlautin asked.

"Ruth Munroe," Porter said flatly.

It was jolting to hear that. Suddenly Judge Ohanesian not only had to rule on whether Ruth Munroe's murder could go to a jury but whether I had fabricated evidence in 1982 and committed perjury a few hours earlier in her courtroom.

Vlautin pressed onward, "Did District Attorney Bill Wood ever discuss with you a person by the name of Esther Busby?"

"No," Porter said equally flatly.

Porter went on to say that the first time in his life he ever heard the name Esther Busby was on June 13, 1990, from Vlautin.

Williamson immediately went on the attack. "Where is that file?" he demanded of Porter, referring to the file on the plea negotiations.

"Mr. Vlautin has it," Porter said.

Is the name Ruth Munroe noted anywhere in that thorough, well-documented file?

"No," Porter admitted. "Ruth Munroe's name did not show when I looked at that file."

Since he acknowledged reviewing the 1982 files before testifying, Porter made it possible for Williamson to demand to see the file. The Puente lawyers objected vociferously.

Judge Ohanesian squinted. "I think he's entitled to it." She gestured at Williamson.

Eventually Vlautin gave Williamson two of Porter's four files. Williamson distrusted Vlautin so much that when the defense lawyer asked for the file back, the prosecutor said, "I'll hang on to this one." He sincerely believed Vlautin and Clymo would alter or destroy any file they got back.

The judge gave Williamson the other two files, and he secretly marked a page in one with a paper clip. When Clymo asked Judge Ohanesian to review Porter's files to see if Puente could still claim a right to keep them secret, Williamson handed her the marked one, too.

Court broke while the judge went back into chambers. The reporters were delighted with the theatrics and drama. Puente sat as quietly as ever, letting Clymo rub her back.

Finally Judge Ohanesian returned. My anxiety was growing. I had never seen Porter's files, and I had no idea what was in them. He could have written anything.

It developed, as Williamson went on a slash-and-burn cross-examination, that Ruth Munroe's name did not appear in any file.

The whole scene became ludicrous when Vlautin tried to take back several of Porter's old files. Williamson, looking grim, yanked the files away, and the two men briefly grappled across the counsel table, tugging the files back and forth between them until Williamson, more compact and solid than Vlautin, pulled the files free.

Through this whole spectacle, Ohanesian said nothing, and Puente faintly shook her head, as if commenting on how silly this all must look.

The caustic testimony went on, Clymo objecting, Williamson snapping back, and Porter repeating again and again that he had never heard of Esther Busby until the day before.

Then Judge Ohanesian half embarrassedly mumbled, "The problem I'm having with this is that there was a mention of Esther Busby." It was in the file Williamson had flagged with a paper clip so the judge would be sure to stop there.

Innocently Williamson asked, "If the court would help me and show me what you're talking about, I'd sure like to know if there is something in this file about Esther Busby."

The judge obligingly pointed out a page in Porter's file. It was Schwartz's one-page police summary that I had given to Porter the day after Puente agreed to plead guilty.

When an irate Williamson thrust the file at him, Porter said stubbornly, "It's in the file. I'm saying I don't recall seeing it."

For all intents and purposes, the defense attorneys' effort to dump Ruth Munroe's murder ended at that moment. It was plain to Judge Ohanesian that Esther Busby's name had been raised before Puente pled guilty in 1982.

It also meant, by extension, that I was not a perjurer or a fabricator of evidence. A plot like that in the DA's office would have required O'Mara's cooperation, since he had the Munroe murder investigated, and Frawley's as well, since he supervised Puente's crime report filings. It was not something I could pull off on my own.

The one galling thing was that Puente, conscienceless and murderous, had been given the pleasure of seeing people she hated—the Clausens, Porter, me—twisting on the witness stand.

But a decision on Puente was coming on fast. The preliminary hearing rushed to its conclusion.

After seven weeks, seventy-one witnesses, many exhibits, Williamson had accomplished his goal of smoking out Puente's defense. In front of a jury, he now knew, Puente's lawyers would argue that there had been one suicide and eight heart attacks while she lived at 1426 F Street. She dumped one beside the river and buried the others because she was afraid of going back to prison. She stole the money simply because it was available.

If he got his case past this preliminary hearing, Williamson would be ready for trial.

31

By 9:30 ON THE SULTRY MORNING OF TUESDAY, JUNE 19, 1990, TV news trucks ringed the front of the courthouse, generators rumbling, reporters staking out places on the broad concrete plaza from which to do live coverage. Judge Ohanesian was scheduled to hear the final arguments in the preliminary hearing and to rule on whether or not the Munroe murder charge should be dismissed.

Curious spectators walked by the reporters, chatting among themselves. The corridor outside Department H was solidly packed with camera crews, reporters, spectators—a motley, almost theatergoing crowd.

Williamson, his ever-present black notebooks under one arm, tossed away his last cigarette before rushing into the courthouse, running through the last comments he would make to the judge.

Clymo and Vlautin sauntered into the courtroom a little before 10:00 A.M., smiling and waving slightly.

Puente was brought into court and settled between her two lawyers. The murmuring audience subsided only when

Judge Ohanesian came in, her eyes dowcast, avoiding the sketch artists who were staring at her. She mounted the three small steps to the bench, sat down, and called for Peter Vlautin to make his last arguments in Puente's defense.

Vlautin stood up at the counsel table, one hand in his pocket, a trifle self-conscious suddenly. He cleared his throat. Clymo sat with his arm draped casually across the back of Puente's chair.

In the audience, tightly holding his wife's hand, Bill Clausen listened intently to every word.

Vlautin began by declaring that the Munroe murder charge should be thrown out. The DA's office had lied about it in 1982 and lied again during the preliminary hearing. The DAs were only "trying to extricate themselves from further embarrassment" by pursuing it.

He proposed two choices for Judge Ohanesian. She could compel specific performance of the 1982 plea bargain, which "encompassed" Ruth Munroe, or allow Puente's defense to re-litigate all four of the 1982 cases for which Puente had served time in prison. He sat down.

Williamson stood up and argued curtly, summarizing the evidence the judge had heard.

Ohanesian nodded quickly. "I am persuaded," she ruled, "the Clausens did not contact the DA's office until after August 1982." The effect of that decision was that "I am satisfied that Ruth Munroe was not part of the plea bargain."

The judge had utterly rejected Puente's legal claims.

Bill Clausen clutched his wife's hand harder and said, "All *right!*" loud enough for the courtroom to hear him.

Vlautin rallied to argue about the remaining eight counts. Leona Carpenter had overdosed on Dalmane in 1986, he said. She had a history of poor health. Miller was sick. Montoya schizophrenic and suicidal. Fink an alcoholic. Gallop had heart trouble and a brain tumor. Vera Martin had hardening of the arteries. Palmer collected sleeping pills and had heart trouble. Gillmouth, too, had heart trouble.

The DA, said Vlautin, had only shown that "nine people died and Dorothea Puente didn't report their deaths."

He ridiculed the testimony of Miller, Crowl, and Trujillo as inherently unbelievable and said they only proved "how far the DA is reaching in an attempt to make his case."

Vlautin finished, and the judge called on Williamson. He said he had submitted all his arguments in writing and would add nothing.

The reporters and spectators bristled as if they'd been denied half of a prizefight.

But Williamson did carry out a threat made a few days earlier: he charged the Puente defense lawyers had knowingly put on evidence, through Dennis Porter, they knew to be false. It was about the most serious charge a lawyer could make against another lawyer.

Both Clymo and Vlautin spluttered, rising to their own defense. They didn't know what Dennis Porter knew. How could they? Porter had spent a lot of time on the witness stand saying he didn't remember events. Besides, they said defensively, Frawley had held back vital information.

After the lawyers sank down into silence, Judge Ohanesian shook her head. Emotions had run high throughout the hearing. "This has been a very lengthy, complicated case," she said. Mistakes were to be expected.

Then, reading carefully and slowly, Judge Ohanesian glanced from time to time at the stiffly propped-up Puente and announced there was "ample circumstantial evidence to believe that all of the deaths charged against the defendant were the result of criminal means."

The two defense lawyers sighed slightly in the very still courtroom. Puente, said the judge, "had the opportunity and motive to kill for financial gain, and had the knowledge to accomplish it by using drugs."

Puente, the keen practitioner of appearance, must have known the cameras and artists would study her slightest reaction as a clue to her inner thoughts. So she became absolutely immobile, as if she had stopped breathing. She tried to become invisible.

Judge Ohanesian, with the son of one of Puente's victims listening in long-delayed relief, read off the names of nine murdered people. Puente would have to answer to a jury for each of these crimes.

Williamson broke in, asking the court to retain control of all of the exhibits, rather than having them go back to him and the defense. He still believed Clymo and Vlautin would alter any evidence they had in their hands.

The mundane business was disposed of. The judge set Puente's arraignment date in Superior Court for July 10, 1990. Puente would stay in jail, no bail permitted.

Clymo and Vlautin went on patting and whispering to her as she was handcuffed, led out.

Their client now faced the gas chamber.

The courtroom emptied explosively, reporters and cameras jamming the doorway, Williamson, like a linebacker, bulling his way silently through them, avoiding their shouted questions, a bobbing gang of cameramen and lights trotting futilely after him.

As he got to the restricted access stairwell, one enterprising reporter threw his microphone at Williamson's legs to slow him down. Without breaking stride, Williamson hopped over the microphone and vanished through the stairwell door.

Clymo and Vlautin were not so reticent. They held forth for the mass of reporters surrounding them. Clymo said blithely, "You saw the best of what the prosecution has. I don't think anyone can convict on the quantity and quality of the evidence presented."

Vlautin was even more combative. "The battle has just begun," he announced. "There are lots of unanswered questions, and this wasn't the forum to ask them."

As a last, cynical comment, the two defense lawyers expressed hope that despite all of this publicity, Puente's trial could stay in Sacramento. Since they had worked for months to inflame and prolong the media's interest in the case, this wasn't taken seriously by anyone covering the case. Puente's defense intended to get her trial moved out of Sacramento to someplace they thought more favorable as soon as possible.

The flock of reporters wheeled like birds, running full tilt down the corridor to where I stood, near Department H. I said I thought Puente would be convicted and Ruth Munroe's murder would help send her to the gas chamber.

But what I said and what Puente's lawyers said didn't really matter at all. Most of Ruth Munroe's children and one grandchild had been present during parts of the preliminary hearing. But on the day Judge Ohanesian ruled, only Bill Clausen and his wife could be in court. He was melancholy, happy, excited. "Puente's finally held up as my mom's killer," he said.

Later that day, to a reporter from the *Bee,* he summed up in one sentence how monstrous Puente's crimes were. On the verge of tears, Bill said, "My mom meant the world to me."

Williamson, relaxing thirty minutes later in his office, smoking, said aloud, "What's the point of hanging around when you know what's going to happen?" explaining his exit from the courthouse.

Other deputy DAs stopped by to congratulate him, joke, hear his war stories about how he handled the Puente case.

He felt very good about the hearing. "We got everything we came in for and they got nothing."

And Puente returned to the courthouse lockup. She changed back into her jail jumpsuit, gave up her fashionable dress and shoes, the modest jewelry she'd worn. Her female guards were cheery around her, after so many months of being together. Puente said nothing.

She was then taken back to her solitary cell in the main jail. Below her cell, the bustle of downtown Sacramento went on, people hearing the flash news of the judge's ruling, others indifferent to the whole thing.

Alone in her cell, Puente faced the knowledge that if she

was convicted on just two of the nine murders, and the jury found the special circumstances true, she would die in the San Quentin gas chamber. Or spend the rest of her life in prison.

It was a long way from forging a check for shoes in 1948.

PART 6

"It is of the first importance," he said, "not to allow your judgment to be biased by personal qualities. . . . The emotional qualities are antagonistic to clear reasoning. I assure you that the most winning woman I ever knew was hanged for poisoning three little children for their insurance money."

Sir Arthur Conan Doyle,
The Sign of the Four

32

THE MONTEREY PENINSULA OF CALIFORNIA IS HELD BY MIST AND fog during a great deal of the year. The mornings, especially in the winter and early spring, are often gray and clammy, and when the sun breaks through, it is feeble. There are days of great clarity and brightness, but the rocky landscape remains obscure and chill.

Seen from the air, while approaching the well-to-do city of Monterey, the dark green water of the bay is dotted with pleasure boats and white marinas. The city clings against the wooded, hilly land. It was a strange setting for the trial of the most notorious female killer in California's history. It was about as different from the declining, crowded blocks of Alkali Flat as anywhere in the state.

On Tuesday, February 9, 1993, Dorothea Puente was awakened early at the Monterey County Adult Detention Facility, the dun-colored, angular walls visible from her cell. It was a big day. Her trial was going to begin.

She ate quietly, not very much. She dressed simply in a

flower-print blouse and skirt, wearing a black sweater over it against the winter's pervading damp.

By 7:00 A.M. she was in a small van, under guard, being driven twenty miles from the jail to the small courthouse in Monterey. A municipal courtroom had been dedicated exclusively to her trial for the last four months. Through the van's windows she saw a brown, foggy landscape, small cities, tall eucalyptus along the road. She had come four hours south by car from Sacramento, into the heart of John Steinbeck's Cannery Row.

Puente was somber on February 9. At the start of picking a jury laboriously in this strange new setting, she had been upbeat, smiling. Clymo had told reporters, "She's very happy today, happier than she's been in a long time."

Vlautin added, "Her spirits are high. She's very anxious to get things going, to get her side of the story across."

Now, in February, gently bouncing along the road to the courthouse, Puente faced a jury of eight men and four women who would decide her fate.

In recent weeks, her worries and the sedentary life in the jail, sitting for boring hours in court as the jurors were painstakingly chosen, one at a time over four months, had taken their toll. She was fatter and whiter than she had been in Sacramento at the preliminary hearing. Her artificially tightened face had no way to fill out so the taut skin over her cheeks gave her a stark, harried look. She looked much older than her sixty-four years.

The usual crowd of reporters waited outside the small modern white courthouse when the jail van rolled up. Puente got out. She had had a lot of teeth pulled, the neglect of years catching up. Then her thyroid medicine went out of balance, and she had unpleasant mood swings. As she stepped from the van, walking between two Monterey County deputy sheriffs, head lowered, into the courthouse, aware of but ignoring the reporters shouting at her, the camera lights swinging over her, Puente was chilled by the cold, pulling her sweater tighter for warmth.

The courtroom was medium-sized, usually given over to drunk driving and petty theft cases; there is not much crime in Monterey. The spectator seats were hard benches, like church pews, the jury box ample and roomy. At the counsel table were high-backed Naugahyde chairs, making the attorneys and Puente look like executives at a board meeting. The judge sat on a slightly lower bench than in Sacramento. Since the judge was a tall, broad man, he looked like he was shoehorned into the confines of the bench.

To the prosecutor's right sat the jury. Vlautin was to his left, then Puente, then Clymo at the other end of the long counsel table. In California, jurors in death penalty trials are questioned by the judge and lawyers separately and alone. Each juror finally seated had been interviewed in the jury box for as long as a day, isolated, answering questions about their feelings on the death penalty, if they could spare the six to eight months needed for the trial, if they had decided Dorothea Puente's guilt or innocence before any evidence was heard in court.

By the time this process exhausted itself, the eight men and four women were joined by six alternate jurors in case one of the others couldn't deliberate for some reason. Three large pools of potential jurors, three hundred in each, had been drawn from around Monterey County.

During jury selection, Clymo and Vlautin had the benefit of a jury-selection expert sitting with them. The expert examined the jurors, reviewed the long questionnaire each had filled out about personal habits, jobs, residences, and advised the defense lawyers whether to keep or excuse the juror. The expert, of course, billed Sacramento County for the service.

John O'Mara, who had replaced Williamson on the case, rejected only obviously biased jurors.

In California that meant the prosecution could not out of hand reject jurors who had strong reservations about the death penalty. As long as a juror said he or she could impose the death penalty in at least one situation, that juror could not be excused without using up a challenge. The prosecutor risked running out of challenges and letting the defense shape the jury to its liking.

One juror, Gary Frost of Seaside, was a computer technician at Fort Ord. He was in his early forties and sometimes came to court in biker belts and psychedelic T-shirts. He didn't think the death penalty stopped any crime, but wrote on his questionnaire that "obviously smarter people than myself have enacted this punishment."

Another juror thought "all loss of life is regrettable." Still another, Gregory Miller of King City said capital punishment is "not a pretty thing to think about," but agreed with what the DA hoped would be the jury's dominant view: "the law is the law."

All of the jurors and alternates were employed. Jesus Sanchez, sitting in the far left upper corner of the jury box, was juror number one. He was in his early thirties, an equipment troubleshooter for J. M. Smucker Company, with two children. Puente's crimes aroused "shock, intrigue, curiosity" in him. He did not realize at the outset what a major role he would play in the trial.

A forty-nine-year-old bank teller was also on the panel, as was a salesman for Gallo wines. Juror Stephen Hinds had served in Vietnam, had been married for twenty years, and worked in Salinas as a mechanic. The oldest juror was Marjorie Simpson, sixty-five, a divorcée and manager at the California Lettuce Producers' Co-Op.

The others were a mailman, another former soldier, a free-lance, just married editor, and Michael Esplin, forty-two, blond and upright. He became foreman and rode herd on an unruly jury. A part-time student at Hartnell College, he had four children and served as a Boy Scout leader and church deacon.

It was a generally young jury, generally inexperienced. But by any measure, they were twelve ordinary people, who had lived mercifully ordinary lives, yet would soon be called on to judge the unimaginable and extraordinary.

* * *

Puente sat, eyes forward, avoiding looking at the court clerk or the court reporter. She studiously kept her eyes off the jury, never making contact. The jurors studied her, though, until it became obvious after several weeks that they would see nothing from the iceberg facade she presented in public. They gave up paying attention to her. As she had in the preliminary hearing, Puente turned into a fixture at her own trial.

That first morning, as court settled in, the jurors put away the paperback books, newspapers, the notes they had made to kill time. They rose when the bailiff announced the judge, and the whole mobbed little courtroom—reporters from London and Paris, around California and the United States, a few curious Monterey residents—sat down again, and the tall, husky prosecutor, with his neatly clipped mustache and dark suit, stood in front of them.

Puente wiped her mouth with a Kleenex. She reached for a coffee mug on the counsel table and took a drink.

Clymo and Vlautin took notes as the prosecutor, John O'Mara, began his opening statement to the jury.

With the exception of her own lawyers, nothing about Puente's case was the same as at the end of the preliminary hearing in 1990.

Besides a wholly new location, the judge in the case was new. His name was Michael Virga. He was in his early sixties, dark-haired, soft-spoken but authoritative on the bench. He played baseball as a young man and had family connections deep into Sacramento: one brother was a prominent defense lawyer; a son had recently been elected to the bench himself.

Big Mike, as he was known downtown, had just finished presiding over another serial-murder trial in which both Vlautin and O'Mara were the lawyers. He knew every attorney in the city and more than he would like to think about had appeared before him over the years. Appointed to the bench by California governor Ronald Reagan in 1970, Virga had resigned in 1984 and joined a Sacramento law firm. He believed, he said, that he had turned hardened, grown tired of crimes as a judge for fourteen years.

But private practice wasn't the answer, either. By 1987 he had been reappointed to the Superior Court and stayed happily there ever since. "No judge can look for perfection in people," he said before the Puente trial decamped to Monterey. "You got to try and find out what makes them tick."

He would never manage that feat in Puente's case. His only other thought was that after so many years on the bench, "It gets to the point where nothing surprises you."

John O'Mara, standing in front of the jury, large blowups of 1426 F Street beside him, the raw pictures of open graves, bound and wrapped bodies, shown for the first time to the jury, had ended up, ironically, prosecuting Puente after so many years of knowing about her. He had investigated one murder of hers in 1982, advised Williamson in 1990, and now was about to begin his opening statement in her trial.

It was not the course he would have chosen.

But events intervened. A new administration had come into the California Attorney General's Office in the fall of 1990. Out went all the senior lawyers, and a search started for seasoned prosecutors to take their places.

On the short list, from the start, to head the Criminal Division was George Williamson. His handling of Puente's preliminary hearing had been noted favorably. He was everything the new Attorney General wanted—smart, tough, fair, and a veteran courtroom lawyer.

By January 1991, the AG had made Williamson an offer he couldn't ignore, even if administration wasn't his primary interest. Williamson would get a salary boost, prestige, and become the third highest law enforcement official in California. He accepted the job.

On a flight back to Sacramento after he had been working in the AG's office for a few months, Williamson and I talked about the upcoming Puente trial. He didn't want to watch any of it. He never checked on how another lawyer put on one of his cases.

He had only one regret in taking his high paying, important new job. "The only bad part is I had to give up Puente," he said.

O'Mara had worked very hard getting ready for the opening statement, his road map of where he intended to take the jurors. He had thousands of exhibits he wanted to show them, hundreds of witnesses.

He began forthrightly. The jury would have to get past the fact that no expert would come in and simply state a cause of death for the seven F Street victims. It will be, he told the attentive jurors, the totality of the circumstances about the victims that proves these people did not die naturally. They were bound up, carried from the house, and buried. There was a conscious, deliberate plan at work.

He described each victim, going back to Ruth Munroe, and their relationship to Puente. But O'Mara grew emotional when he talked about the "shadow people" Puente killed, touching on the same theme Bishop Quinn had sounded in 1988. These people had lives, hopes, and activities. No one had the right to take any of those things from them.

It was, for two days, a powerful, emotional recital. Puente passed notes as O'Mara spoke, expressing her annoyance at things the prosecutor said about her.

For all of this public confidence and the mass of information he commanded, O'Mara was harried, overworked, and felt nearly overwhelmed by the enormous volume of material in the case. He had been working literally day and night ever since coming to Monterey.

Peter Vlautin was still arguing Puente's case. Clymo had quit the public defender's office. Once in private practice, however, he was reappointed to Puente's case, billing Sacramento County a new hourly rate.

Clymo rocked a little in his chair in the courtroom, listening to what O'Mara said, sometimes faintly smiling. O'Mara had a slightly different theory of Puente's actions than did Williamson. O'Mara agreed that Puente already had control over her victims' money. She didn't kill to get the money. She killed, O'Mara believed, only those tenants who became sick or troublesome, like Betty Palmer and Ben Fink.

As far as how she did it, O'Mara thought Puente smothered the drugged or dying victims or held their noses and mouths shut. Either that or she gave them so much alcohol and Dalmane that they stopped breathing.

The defense theory was approximately the same as it had been. Acting as spokesman for himself and Vlautin, Clymo talked to a reporter from the *Los Angeles Times* on February 9.

"She didn't do it," Clymo told the reporter. "They've got it all wrong." Munroe committed suicide, he argued. The eight others had heart attacks.

"There are no eyewitnesses that say Dorothea buried bodies there," he said, referring to 1426 F Street. "There is no allegation there were accomplices involved. It requires a huge leap of nothing but pure faith."

Clymo tried to mislead the reporter about what Puente did when someone died at 1426 F. He said she notified the police when Ruth Munroe died, but she didn't inform authorities about the other deaths from 1985-1988 because she was on parole. "One of the conditions of her parole was that she not be in working contact with elderly or disabled folks," Clymo helpfully explained.

He omitted telling the reporter that Puente called the police in 1987 when Eugene Gamel apparently committed suicide in front of 1426 F Street and she talked at length with officers.

As Clymo listened in court to O'Mara's damaging account of how Puente spent the money she stole, he was shaping up his own opening statement.

O'Mara ended his two-day statement by calling Puente a manipulative and greedy killer. She bought herself a $2,500 face-lift, $1,700 worth of dental implants, $200 tickets to the legislature's year-end party, $482 for perfume in four months in 1988. He sharply called out to the jury that on July 14, 1988, Puente bought $361.60 worth of "shoes for Leona," according to the billing. Leona Carpenter, O'Mara said, pointing at the stoical Puente, had been dead and buried in the yard for months. Dorothea Puente was vain and high-living. And a stone-cold killer.

Clymo and Vlautin had an entirely different picture of their grandmotherly client for the jury to hear.

On Thursday, Clymo stood up, hands in his pockets, lunging toward the jurors every so often, making a folksy, repetitive opening statement. The costly scale models of 1426 F and the 1400 block were wheeled out into the courtroom.

Clymo admitted that Puente was vain. He nodded gently at her. But she was also a fearful old woman who only did what anyone in her place would have done.

Then Clymo made one of the most unintentionally grotesque comments in the whole case. Grinning at the jury, as if at a small character flaw, he said "Dorothea Puente has a touch of larceny in her heart." But this slight greed "doesn't make her an evil serial killer."

When seventy-seven-year-old Everson Gillmouth died on her, she hid his body because she didn't want to face going back to prison. She knew, Clymo admitted again, that she wasn't supposed to have old people living near her.

O'Mara, unlike Williamson, had decided to keep Puente's time in prison away from the jury. Rather than clutter up his case and expose Miller or Crowl to cross-examination, O'Mara had no intention of discussing Puente's 1982 convictions or where she was from 1982 to 1985. O'Mara intended to put on a much more focused, narrow case than Williamson. O'Mara, after all, didn't have to smoke out the defense theory. He knew it already.

Then Clymo did something O'Mara hadn't expected. He made a point of Puente being an ex-con. "Mr. O'Mara has kept something from you about Dorothea," Clymo said with a rueful grin. "But we're not going to keep anything from you." He told the jury about Puente's incarceration.

Why did he do that? The only explanation is that Puente's defense assumed O'Mara would shove a prison record at the jury.

Clymo's remaining statement harped on Puente's benevolence. Using huge, grainy photos of the front yard, the St. Francis shrine, the backyard, he said Puente had opened her heart "to the down-and-out, the derelicts, the dregs of society who really didn't have anyplace else to go."

Clymo came toward the jury. "She provided food, a warm, clean place to stay, laundry services, clothes, and furnished areas."

But all did not go perfectly. Some of the older tenants sickened and died. "It's hard to imagine that Dorothea could throw these people over a shoulder and plant them in the yard." Clymo made a gesture as if toting a sack. "But it's a reasonable inference to draw that she was connected to the burial of those bodies."

He had forgotten the comments he made to the *Times* on February 9 ridiculing the idea she was linked to burying anybody.

Then, in bizarre statements and an unctuous manner, Clymo tried to woo the jurors for Puente. He held up the large, grainy St. Francis shrine photo, so it looked like a deep-space surveillance picture. Puente tenderly cared for the people at 1426 F Street, Clymo said. She gave them loving attention, but some, sadly, did die naturally.

Her attention didn't end with their death, though. Pointing at the St. Francis shrine, Clymo spoke of "these forgotten people, people nobody cared about. But it looks to me like she remembered them, remembered them in her own way."

Clymo wrapped up briskly from there. Ruth Munroe, he said, killed herself with a massive Tylenol and codeine overdose. Her medical records disclosed that, far from being allergic to codeine, she "actually liked it." Clymo sat down.

O'Mara, who had been taking copious notes, glanced up, surprised. The defense opening statement made no sense. If the jury never heard any evidence, Puente's lawyers could have said the things Clymo had just said, but the witnesses and exhibits would blow it all apart.

Sitting in seat number one in the jury box, Jesus Sanchez, quiet, serious, had listened with intense attention. He was already thinking about Puente.

33

A WEEK BEFORE THE TRIAL STARTED, JUDGE VIRGA INVITED O'Mara and the two defense lawyers to dinner at his vacation home in nearby Santa Cruz. Even though he had recently finished another serial murder case with O'Mara and Vlautin, he wanted to establish the ground rules for good behavior in the trial, and he hoped that a convivial evening might make what promised to be a very long, contentious trial go more smoothly.

If that was his hope, the dinner was a failure.

O'Mara, although outwardly friendly, distrusted Vlautin and Clymo as much as Williamson had. He disregarded Clymo's coy suggestions that Puente might testify during the guilt phase of the trial. She would never take the stand, O'Mara believed. The defense would be waged by proxy.

So, a week before the trial began, O'Mara had decided that the defense was resigned to Puente getting convicted of multiple murder, something more than two of the nine murder charges. He thought Clymo and Vlautin would concentrate on trying to spare Puente from the gas chamber during the penalty phase of the trial. Clymo's weirdly inconsistent, almost foolish opening statement had emphasized Puente's kindness toward her tenants, which would be a mitigating factor as far as her penalty was concerned, but it would do nothing to dispute her guilt.

O'Mara's job, as the trial commenced, was to paint Puente as accurately, thus as blackly, as the mountain of circumstantial evidence permitted.

Why had it taken so long to get Puente into trial? Her preliminary hearing had been over for two years before jury selection even got started in her trial.

California is remarkably relaxed about speedy trials, especially those that are complex or involve the death penalty. Every time Puente's lawyers wanted a continuance of the trial, or O'Mara requested one, the court granted it.

Her lawyers filed dozens of motions before and just up to trial date, seeking to limit or twist the evidence the jury would hear. Some motions were routine, intended to exclude any statements Puente had made, exclude autopsy or gravesite photos as prejudicially gruesome, exclude mention of any prior bad acts, like drugging John McCauley.

Then Clymo and Vlautin dumped a series of unique motions on Judge Virga. They wanted two juries, more preliminary hearings on uncharged offenses, another stab at throwing out Ruth Munroe's murder count.

Virga declined to drop the Munroe count. A Superior Court judge and the Third District Court of Appeal also disagreed with the defense. Short of going to the California Supreme Court, Puente's lawyers had lost every single legal question they put to lower courts.

Except one. It was the costliest, most exhausting, and perhaps silliest of all, but Clymo and Vlautin did succeed in moving Puente's trial out of Sacramento.

The motion to change the venue, or site, of Dorothea Puente's trial was heard in a Sacramento municipal courtroom in February 1992 in front of a visiting judge from Lake County, one of the smallest counties in the state.

O'Mara hoped that a judge from such a small county

"would think about cases he's heard, where everybody knows everybody and you can still do the trial." He displayed the style he would use in the trial itself: rarely objecting, forcefully questioning a witness, trying to cut down on delays.

The small courtroom was claustrophobic, with two camera crews squeezed into the jury box, reporters scattered around, and outsized blowups of newspaper articles and pictures stacked near the bench like a giant's toys.

Clymo and Vlautin put on the standard defense experts who could be counted on to say a trial should move somewhere else. A psychologist, who had looked at dozens of news videotapes and read a thousand news stories, told the visiting judge the press had conducted a "circus" and sensationalized the story.

The effect was to "embed" in every Sacramentan's mind an image of Puente in her "trademark" red overcoat with her white hair and glasses. She could never get a fair trial in Sacramento. Puente herself wasn't in court, disliking to show herself when witnesses weren't present and she absolutely didn't have to be around.

The psychologist—who, O'Mara wryly conceded, "thinks I'm the devil incarnate"—was snappish during cross-examination. She said again that the "demand structure" of a trial, the "forces at work on us in court"—a robed judge, a flag, oath-taking—made it impossible for people to treat a case other than rigidly and formally. Puente would be prejudiced by a "demand structure" that assumed, because she was on trial, that she was guilty.

O'Mara never budged her from any statement.

The other defense witness was a tiny, bearded statistician who proudly described coining the term "minimization" to denote how jurors tend to minimize their own prejudices during jury selection. In other words, jurors didn't know their own minds, but he did. They were biased against Puente no matter what they said to the contrary.

The clocks had stopped in the courthouse during the hearing and no one talked about the real world of real people or real evidence. It was all abstraction and theory and polls.

O'Mara's hopes came to nothing. The visiting judge fell on the side of caution and ordered Puente's trial moved elsewhere.

If the decision to move the trial disappointed O'Mara and the DA's office because of the added time and inconvenience, it horrified Sacramento officials. It would be an enormous burden on the county.

The judge's ruling prompted the County Executive to take the unprecedented step in August 1992 of writing to him, urging strongly that he reconsider.

Vlautin learned of the letter and wrote a stern reply to the judge and the County Executive. "Kevin and I are both aware of the fiscal situation the county is in," he wrote, but they insisted the order be upheld and the trial moved.

A complex series of events was set into motion. Each of the lawyers in Puente's trial was allocated a $1,600 monthly allowance for food and lodging. More money was set aside for office rent, telephone service, and transportation for witnesses. Judge Virga would bring his own clerk to Monterey.

Budgets for the Sacramento Sheriff's Department, the DA, and others were cannibalized to get the money. Shuttles for witnesses were arranged. By February 1993, Puente's defense had submitted to the county a bill of about $400,000 for her trial. More bills followed. Her trial ended up costing close to $2 million.

Hoping to head off this kind of disastrously expensive trial, the DA's office offered Puente a plea bargain.

In July and August 1992, O'Mara and DA Steve White crafted a proposal that began by offering Puente a guarantee of life in prison without parole. She would escape the gas chamber. Neither she nor her lawyers paid much attention to the offer.

By mid-November, with jury selection under way in Monterey, a new, more generous offer was made. Puente, said the DA's office, could plead guilty to five counts of first degree murder and four counts of second degree murder. There would be no special circumstances. The terms would run consecutively, but she would still be eligible for parole.

Vlautin called the offer "more encouraging," but again he, Clymo, and Puente let it lapse. Puente had the flu just before Thanksgiving and was irritable. Besides, she and her lawyers had calculated her chances of getting the death penalty were slim. And even if she did, would California really execute a kindly little old lady? If she was sentenced to life in prison without parole, after ten or so years she could petition to be released on good behavior and advancing age. Puente did not believe she would die in the prison equivalent of an old folks' home.

She and her lawyers thought she might beat some of the murder charges anyway. So why bargain at all?

Puente's trial, in distant Monterey County, was a bitter pill the taxpayers of Sacramento would have to swallow.

Puente, gambling on the trial outcome, was reportedly annoyed at the answers some potential jurors gave on their court questionnaires. One juror bluntly wrote, "Gas her." Another suggestion read, "Let her swing."

For both sides, this trial would be long, brutal, and uncertain.

34

CLYMO ESTIMATED THE TRIAL WOULD TAKE FROM TEN MONTHS TO a year and would involve five hundred witnesses. O'Mara laughed at the claim.

The estimate wasn't far off, though.

The stresses and strains the long trial would put on everyone were obvious at the beginning. At a softball game with his wife and eleven-year-old son in mid-October 1992, O'Mara teasingly said he would be away for a year. He was startled when his son blurted out solemnly, "I don't think you should do any more of these out-of-county change-of-venue cases or whatever you call them. They're too disruptive."

Puente's trial would separate families for weeks at a time.

Puente herself, having no family at hand, didn't worry about long separations. She was, until the trial shifted to Monterey, the star of the Sacramento county jail, where, as they had in 1982, the inmates treated her well, confided in her. She in turn took the vulnerable under her wing, educating them on the ways of prison. One guard was disgusted watching the other inmates "kowtow" to Puente.

She was, as her trial began, the most celebrated prisoner in Sacramento, and famous throughout the state. One book had been published about her case, two more were in preparation, a TV movie was ready to start shooting when the trial ended. One movie, a black comedy called *Evil Spirits,* starring Karen Black and Arte Johnson had come out on videocassette.

But, as it had from the outset, a pall hung over everything about Puente. Bad things happened to many people near her. This was epitomized by evidence for her trial, stored in the Sacramento Police Department's property warehouse in a separate corner, like the woman herself, set apart from routine crimes. A white freezer chest contained tissue and other samples. Thick dust coated it. Someone had written "Dorothea Puente's" in the dust and hung a hand lettered sign on the freezer latch: "Don't Open Unless You Have to. You'll Be Sorry."

Like everyone forced to put on her trial.

O'Mara began calling witnesses after his opening statement. For weeks he had fretted about the order of evidence. He decided to leave Ruth Munroe for later, and begin with his strongest, most emotional evidence, the disappearance and death of Bert Montoya.

Back came all the social workers, the doctors, everyone who had contact with Montoya. The defense lawyers had each witness point out where he or she stood or lived in the house apparently in order to justify the bulky models of 1426 F in the courtroom.

O'Mara had noticed that the model, however detailed, was inaccurate. James Gallop's grave had been mixed up with Ben Fink's. The prosecutor decided to wait to spring his discovery.

The moment came when Detective Cabrera came to the stand in April. Cabrera, nattily dressed as usual, had ridden up and down and up again in the police department. He had been reinstated to Homicide by the time he testified.

Going through the events of November 11–14, 1988, Cabrera used the 1426 F model as Clymo pointed things out. O'Mara helpfully suggested tipping the model upward so the jury could see it very clearly. Vlautin took one side, O'Mara the other. Cabrera went on speaking, then blurted out that the graves were all confused. The jury, as O'Mara hoped, broke into laughter.

By the end of the trial's first six weeks, the jury looked cohesive, chummy. The jurors felt comfortable enough in court to lean over and chat with O'Mara or one of the defense lawyers when they walked by. Judge Virga finally warned the jurors he didn't condone talking to the lawyers in or out of court.

Still, the jurors looked relaxed, socially easy together. They talked and laughed among themselves.

It was, if true, a bad thing for Puente to have such a confident jury. She required a jury filled with confusion and doubt in order to avoid conviction.

But one juror, Sanchez, rarely mixed in. He stayed aloof from the others, seldom smiling, seldom talking to them. He simply came into court, listened to the testimony, and kept his own thoughts.

O'Mara methodically worked his way through the victims. He put on twice as many witnesses as Williamson, to decisively end any doubt or speculation about what a doctor thought of Vera Martin's health, or how Betty Palmer's orthopedic problems were being treated.

But, otherwise, the Puente trial was anticlimactic. While the jury was hearing the evidence for the first time, all of the information required to convict Puente had been public since her preliminary hearing in 1990.

Reba Nicklous appeared again, as did the neighbors around 1426 F Street and the bartender at Joe's Corner.

O'Mara felt good enough about the way his evidence was coming into court that he joked to an unsmiling Clymo. The Centers for Disease Control in Atlanta should be notified about 1426 F, O'Mara cracked. "We've got the Bermuda Triangle of Death in Sacramento."

Clymo turned away. He didn't find the idea funny.

O'Mara's more detailed presentation meant that while the jury didn't hear from witnesses like Crowl and Miller, they did learn from a former F Street tenant that Betty Palmer "looked as close to death as anyone I've ever seen." Palmer, said the tenant, "belonged in a hospital," which was precisely where Puente did not want her to be. Palmer moaned all the time the witness said. Then she vanished. Puente had said the woman's daughter took her away.

Like most of Puente's lies, this one was subject to instant alteration. Did anyone ever come looking for Betty Palmer? O'Mara asked the witness.

The former tenant nodded. A woman came knocking at the front door when Puente was out. The woman wanted to find her mother, Betty Palmer. When later confronted with this contradiction, Puente unhesitatingly said, "Actually, I've taken her to another nursing home, but we don't want her daughter to find her."

Puente, O'Mara demonstrated, told a lot of lies about everyone, including herself. In mid-1988, she told a security guard at Woolworth's that she had just had brain surgery. She had a bandage on, the guard testified. Puente claimed to have brain cancer and said she was undergoing chemotherapy. None of it was true. She had just had a face-lift.

The only brain surgery at 1426 F Street had been done on James Gallop the year before, and he was recovering until the moment Puente killed him.

O'Mara showed, as the days went on, that Puente's day-to-day existence consisted of one lie about another lie told to buttress yet another lie.

* * *

O'Mara kept a close eye on how Clymo and Vlautin acted in court.

He was now utterly convinced they had essentially given up hope of getting Puente acquitted of the murder charges. Most days the two defense lawyers didn't even bother to bring over the actual reports and documents relating to whichever witness was about to testify. Instead, they worked from computer summaries, which left them at the mercy of a witness's memory and willingness to co-operate. O'Mara often successfully objected that a page reference made by Clymo or Vlautin was wrong or that the quotes they tossed at a witness were incomplete or incorrect. Without the actual report, the defense lawyers frequently let the cross-examination point drop. If they were dead serious about saving Puente from conviction, they would have troubled to bring the necessary files to court.

They were saving their fire for the penalty phase, O'Mara believed. That helped explain the odd directions Clymo took. When Dr. Anthony appeared, Clymo asked the pathologist at length about the postmortem mutilations to Palmer's body. Weren't these consistent, Clymo asked, with an attempt to hide the person's identity?

Anthony agreed he had seen extremities removed for that purpose.

The prosecutor sat back in bewilderment, wondering why the defense wanted to focus the jury on something as calculated and deliberate as cutting up a dead body to conceal its identity. It didn't change the fact that Puente still had a body buried in her front yard, and she was charged with murder even if no one ever figured out who the victim was.

It was all, O'Mara concluded, confusing. The defense lawyers seemed to have a murky idea of how to protect Puente.

On at least one occasion this murkiness aided O'Mara and hurt Puente badly.

When Brenda Trujillo took the stand in early May, she

was as droopy and sluggish as she had been in 1990. Vlautin had adopted a more theatrical courtroom style, sometimes raising his voice, flapping his arms. This awakened Trujillo and led her to make a terrible admission.

Vlautin sharply asked Trujillo, "Dorothea Puente never told you she killed people, did she?"

"Yes. She did," Trujillo replied with vigor, then cast a cold glance at Puente, whose head was lowered.

"She told you she killed these people?" Vlautin repeated, too startled to keep from driving the point home.

"Yes," said Trujillo. "She told me herself that she had killed people and they were buried in her yard."

Vlautin recovered somewhat by emphasizing that Trujillo never informed the police Puente killed anyone. She told Cabrera and Brown people were "dying" at 1426 F Street.

However impeachable her own past was, Trujillo struck a sympathetic chord with the jury when she talked about James Gallop.

Back in prison in 1988, Trujillo said, she had asked Puente about Gallop. Puente said, "He died. I asked if she knew where he was buried because I wanted to go there. She said no, she had his body cremated because he had no family." Gallop, who had impressed bartender Marjorie Harper, also had touched Trujillo. She began crying on the witness stand thinking of him.

Trujillo also knew about Everson Gillmouth. Puente told her he had died of a heart attack. "She said she couldn't afford to call the ambulance because he was dead and she didn't want to go back to prison. She wanted to know if I knew anybody who could get rid of the body. She would pay four thousand dollars. I told her I would ask around."

Trujillo eventually got her sometime boyfriend, Jesus Meza, to call at 1426 F Street, but Meza turned the job down.

Trujillo's tears were not the first in the trial, and they were not the last. O'Mara soon called the Clausens to the stand to tell the jury about Ruth Munroe's cruel death.

Before he did so, O'Mara had to make Munroe's children face their own suspicions of suicide a decade earlier. Otherwise, Clymo and Vlautin would rip apart the inconsistencies of claims that the family never thought Munroe killed herself.

35

O'MARA GATHERED RUTH MUNROE'S CHILDREN IN A MOTEL room the night before he would start calling them to the stand.

He was blunt, unsentimental, and harsh. If any of them persisted in claiming they never even suspected Ruth killed herself in 1982, the defense lawyers would make it look as if they were being untruthful in everything else.

It was a tough meeting. A decade after Ruth's death, Bill, Rosie, and Allan did not want to admit having been mistaken about their mother's death. But they finally agreed with O'Mara. It was better for the jury to hear they had been wrong on April 28, 1982, than for the Clausens to lie or try to shade the old memories.

What O'Mara was actually telling them was this: Trust me. Just take the stand, let everything come out, and I'll show the jury how to handle it.

Late in May, O'Mara called Rosie into court after Bill had appeared and had told a hushed courtroom about his mother's last night, the horrific tear falling down her paralyzed face. Rosie also began crying as she told the jury about those last days.

The tears were everywhere in the last weeks of the trial.

O'Mara put Ricardo Odorica on the stand, no more happy about appearing in court again than he had been three years before. Grudgingly, Odorica admitted he put a $293 check made out to Dorothy Miller into his own MasterCard account. He had, he said, become Miller's payee at Puente's request.

O'Mara had a large pile of financial records and bank statements on the counsel table and the clerk's desk. The courtroom overflowed with papers, bits of clothing, blown-up photos, and the upright wooden coffin that had contained Everson Gillmouth propped up to the left of the bench, like a sentry box.

O'Mara was nowhere near as gentle with Odorica as Williamson. He definitely wanted the jury to see how Puente had gotten away with murder using Odorica as a financial helper.

At one point O'Mara flourished records at Odorica showing that Puente's landlord managed to pay off two credit card bills of over $1,500 each in 1987 and 1988 on a monthly salary of only $1,000.

"Where did you get the money to meet those obligations?" O'Mara demanded.

"Sometimes I borrow money from my nieces." Odorica nervously peered at Puente.

He also admitted cashing checks, at Puente's behest, that were made out to one or more of the dead tenants. What happened to *that* money? O'Mara asked curtly.

"I gave it to her." Odorica pointed at Puente.

The next day, Odorica startled Puente and everyone else. As the jury was leaving for lunch, Odorica strolled off the witness stand, past the bailiffs near Puente, around the counsel table, whispered into Puente's ear and then tenderly kissed her on the cheek. He had lost none of his affection for his "lady."

Warned by the embarrassed bailiffs to stay away from the

in-custody defendant, Odorica came back after lunch for a tough cross-examination. "My children called her the grandmother they never had," he said, his voice thickening, his eyes filling with tears. "When my children come home from school, they run to her. My daughters dream of her. In our hearts, emotionally, she is still part of our family."

As he spoke, Puente, watching with one finger against her right cheek, started wiping her own eyes. Clymo comforted her.

Odorica's testimony highlighted Puente's financial thefts for the jury, and his bold show of affection for her showed how lax security was in the Monterey courtroom. On several occasions, Puente was left alone just before a break ended or before the morning session was about to start. The judge was out, the bailiffs gone, none of the lawyers around. She was as much of a flight risk in 1993 as in 1982 or 1988, but the Monterey deputy sheriffs seemed to believe five years in custody had slowed her up and anyway, there was nowhere she could go outside of the courtroom.

One troubling incident had been kept from the jury. A bailiff who guarded Puente, apparently a healthy, sound man, had been absent for the last weeks of O'Mara's case. The bailiff had gone home, sickened, and died. It all happened in a very short time.

The death of someone the jury had come to know, so swiftly and unexpectedly, had the unfortunate effect of underlining Clymo and Vlautin's central defense theory.

A perfectly healthy looking person could quickly die without much warning.

O'Mara did not mention the bailiff's death, nor did the judge.

Not long after the Clausens testified, O'Mara completed his case-in-chief and rested on June 7, 1993. He had called 136 witnesses and introduced over 3,000 exhibits, mostly financial records.

His last witness was Dr. Anthony, the pathologist who believed all seven F Street victims had taken or been given Dalmane within twenty-fours of their death.

Clymo's more exact cross-examination at trial, versus the preliminary hearing, centered on Anthony's agreement that putrefaction of tissues could very well upset his timetable. No studies had been done on how decaying tissue alters the chemical composition of flurazepam.

When Dr. Anthony walked out of the courtroom, O'Mara rested.

It was now Clymo and Vlautin's turn to persuade the jury. They promised to begin their case on June 15 and end it by June 24. O'Mara instantly knew that meant Puente wouldn't testify. He could consume days on cross-examination alone and such a short defense case wouldn't permit it.

Puente, sitting quietly between her lawyers, sometimes pulling her sweater tightly even in the comfortably warm courtroom, had her own definite ideas about how the jury should view her defense.

Even if she wasn't going to testify, she intended to make her feelings public.

She sat composedly as O'Mara ended. She would, as she had before, bide her time.

Midafternoon, June 25, 1993, and Dorothea Puente sat almost alone in the courtroom. In front of her, piled against the bench and around the clerk's desk, were the charts and exhibits O'Mara had introduced, the enlarged photos of the dead, the crime scene. Gillmouth's makeshift coffin stood to the left against the wall.

The court was going to reconvene soon. The judge was still in his chambers, the jury in the corridor, the attorneys absent. Only a single bailiff and an investigator from the Sacramento public defender's office, along with a reporter from the *Sacramento Bee,* were in court.

Puente's lawyers were about to return and rest their short and very limited defense on her behalf.

Puente began talking to herself, then directed her agitated words to the bailiff or the investigator. The reporter could also hear her. Her voice stayed calm.

"I've never killed anyone," she said. "I've said so since the day I was arrested."

The bailiff nodded, surprised, and suggested she remain quiet.

Puente's voice rose; she turned a little in her chair. "The *Bee* has not been very kind to me. The *Bee* and Channel 3. That's two I'd never give an interview to." KCRA's coverage of her trial had stirred her ire. Her face was tight, her voice tough. Mike Boyd, who had been with her on the flight back to Sacramento five years earlier, had covered most of the trial for KCRA.

Puente went on talking bitterly. The bailiff again gently suggested she stop talking. The public defender's investigator, knowing Clymo and Vlautin would be furious she was speaking without them present, did nothing. He was afraid she would become angry if he tried to silence her. He had no idea what she might say in spite.

Puente said, "If I get the death penalty, I'll make damn sure they don't get to be there. All this shit they've been writing about me."

It was the first time, even if in an almost empty courtroom, that the voice so many tenants had quailed at finally was heard. This was the wronged, irate, furious woman who was heard yelling over the telephone when Bert Montoya fearfully called the post office, the slapping, shouting, punching landlady who ran her domain with fear much of the time.

Finally, when the bailiff tried a last time to quiet her, Puente said angrily about the reporter, "I know he's sitting there," making no attempt to look behind her. "That's why I said it. It's pretty bad when you have to make a living off someone else's misery."

O'Mara had accused her of doing exactly that herself.

Yet Puente believed, as she had throughout her life, that only she deserved sympathy and attention. Only she was the victim.

She talked about what would happen if she was sentenced

to death, and seemed pleased that she could exclude unsympathetic news organizations. "It's all right," she said to the bailiff. "When you're going to be executed, you get to choose who your witnesses are going to be."

She wanted to craft her audience herself; she wanted to control even her own death.

The court came into session, and Puente went back on her best behavior.

Her outburst may not have been unplanned. O'Mara thought she timed it. "She didn't want to testify, but she wanted to get this stuff out, her own statement. She waited until she had a reporter who had to write it down."

Puente was also perhaps unhappy with the brief defense she had just been given.

As promised, Clymo had opened Puente's defense ten days earlier. A large portion of it was devoted to five witnesses who attacked the credibility of Brenda Trujillo. A casual observer, seeing how much time was expended on demolishing Trujillo, would have concluded she was the whole prosecution case, and not just one of dozens of other witnesses.

One witness, brought in from prison, had known Trujillo since childhood. "Brenda told me she lied about what she said, and I didn't think it was right." He started crying, like so many others.

O'Mara did not cross-examine many of these witnesses. He had nothing to gain and did not wish to prolong their time in front of the jury. Let the defense put them on and get them out quickly, he thought.

He jotted endless notes in black notebooks.

Sometimes O'Mara tried for a laugh from the jury. Clymo called Lloyd Lambert, who had run a board-and-care home in 1972. Lambert had known Montoya and said he drank "anytime he could get a bottle."

But Lambert was in court mostly to illustrate the hardships of running a facility for the sick, drunk, and mentally ill. He talked about the strict procedures he used for everything, like locking the mailbox so tenants wouldn't take their checks and run out, holding money for tenants, cashing their checks after they signed them.

Clymo was confident Lambert's ways sounded very much like Puente's habits at 1426 F Street. In fact, Clymo asked, didn't someone die on you?

Lambert nodded. A tenant had died unexpectedly. "He was an alcoholic. He got some pills and drank too much. He swallowed his tongue and choked to death."

Clymo nodded, then looked to the jury. This was what had happened to the seven F Street victims, he seemed to say.

O'Mara stood up, straight-faced. Did you notify the police when this man died on you? he asked Lambert.

Lambert quickly said, "Oh, yes."

O'Mara paused theatrically, knowing the jury and everyone else had jumped to the next logical question. When the jurors began grinning, he asked Lambert, "Did you ever think about burying him in the backyard?"

Judge Virga broke in over the jury's laughter and told the witness not to answer.

However, Clymo did put on two significant witnesses.

On June 17, Dean Fesler, the first husband of Ruth Munroe's daughter, Rosie, took the stand. He was in court only a short time and was not cross-examined by O'Mara, but he gave the jury a very different picture of Ruth Munroe from the one presented earlier in the trial.

Fesler looked somewhat odd, in a brown silk-type suit with a flowered shirt. He knew Ruth, he said, from 1975 until he divorced Rosie in 1978. Ruth, he said, struck him as a whining, hypochondriacal woman. She always had at hand a cardboard box filled with drug samples from Gemco's pharmacy.

"She was a chronic complainer," Fesler related to Clymo. "Each time she ate something or got in the sun, she would have aches and pains." Her remedy was "to reach into her box and take a pill."

Fesler made no secret of the fact that he disliked the whole family. "I basically cut myself off from that Clausen clan," he said.

The most substantive witness in the last days of the trial was Dr. Randall Baselt, who appeared to dispute Dr. Anthony's critical estimate of when the seven F Street victims took flurazepam.

Clymo lovingly enumerated Baselt's qualifications: he had been a forensic and clinical toxicologist for twenty-seven years, an expert witness in over a thousand court proceedings.

Baselt spoke easily to the jurors, without using much scientific jargon. He said the basic problem with the twenty-four-hour estimate of flurazepam ingestion was that it was drawn from liver and brain tissue samples so decomposed and dehydrated they were often less than half their normal size.

The metabolite and flurazepam residues found in the samples, Baselt said, were hard to extrapolate into any reliable estimate for a time of ingestion. "We are much less familiar with brain and liver samples, and even less familiar with decomposed tissue." The same was true, he said, of the blood samples used for analysis. "I can't imagine anyone being comfortable making any kind of determination using the low levels found here."

Clymo leaned forward, hands sometimes clasped. This was just what he wanted to hear.

Baselt's apparently dogmatic certainty that the metabolite residues couldn't be validly interpreted faded under a long and minute cross-examination. He was one defense witness O'Mara was prepared to keep on the stand for as much time as it took to fully explore his thinking. The metabolite evidence meant too much to the prosecution case to let Dr. Baselt walk away.

Baselt began modifying his earlier declarations. He apparently knew that O'Mara had been given a mass of technical literature on half-life estimates in drug residues from Dr. Anthony. What he didn't know was how little O'Mara understood of the highly specialized material.

By the final hours of the examination, O'Mara felt Dr. Baselt had waffled enough. The prosecutor bluntly asked if there was some period before death he felt comfortable agreeing was reasonable for the victims to have ingested Dalmane.

"What are we talking about?" O'Mara asked. "A day, a couple of days, a week, a month? Would you be comfortable saying a couple of days,—seventy-two hours?"

At that, Dr. Baselt nodded. "I would be comfortable with seventy-two hours."

O'Mara was happy. Even the defense's premier expert was willing to say the victims had all ingested Dalmane, the only drug common to them all, no less than seventy-two hours before death. It was not much of a jump from that to O'Mara's insistence to the jury that the victims took Dalmane within twenty-four hours of death.

Either way, the odds that seven people, dying over a period of a year, all got Dalmane into their systems so soon before they died, were too high for Puente to beat.

On the day Puente vented her feelings publicly, Clymo and Vlautin rested their case. The jury was excused for the night. Closing arguments for both sides would begin after the July Fourth holiday.

Reporters clustering into court, hoping Puente might testify, pressed her lawyers about the decision to keep her off the stand. "We didn't feel it was necessary," Vlautin asserted. "The prosecution didn't prove its case."

Clymo was emphatic. "The jury heard her deny killing anyone many months ago." He was referring to the videotaped interview with Cabrera on November 11, 1988, which was played in court. "They saw what she had to say. They listened to her at that time. And I believe they were moved by that. The effect of that was real."

He raised his eyebrows. "What else do they need to know, given the state of the evidence?"

The reporters weren't happy with Puente's silence and being deprived of the drama of O'Mara questioning her.

Clymo said that O'Mara would have hounded and harassed Puente. "I believe it would be an attack on her beyond anything that would be in good faith."

"They don't need to see Puente badgered for three or four days," Vlautin added indignantly.

He and Clymo hoped to answer the multitude of questions about their client's actions during closing arguments.

And one juror, as the holiday weekend began, had been affected by Puente's performance in court and on tape. Jesus Sanchez, a thoughtful and quiet man, was moved. How he expressed his feelings during the jury's deliberations amazed everyone and made California history.

John O'Mara, on behalf of the people, would have first shot at Puente in the closing arguments.

36

MOST DAYS O'MARA USED THE SECURITY ELEVATOR BEHIND THE courtroom to ride to the basement to get a Coke from the machine there. Most days he rode down with Puente and her guards during the morning and afternoon breaks. She was kept in the basement holding cell when court was in recess.

O'Mara was surprised that she would chat pleasantly with him in the elevator. She never said anything of substance about the trial, but commented on the length of a session, how the day was going generally, almost a neighborly chat. O'Mara never said anything beyond bare civilities.

He was perplexed by Puente's girlish behavior, coy and innocent. Juxtaposed with that girlishness was the horrible evidence they both had just seen in the courtroom. She seemed unfazed by it.

In his closing argument, O'Mara knew he had to convey this central mystery of the trial to the jury: there was a jarring contrast between how Puente looked and sounded and what she had done.

The prosecution's closing argument to the jury went on for four days. O'Mara hadn't intended to go on so long, but the vast number of financial records required it. He gave the jurors booklets of easy-to-read dates and names to follow as he talked. For Everson Gillmouth, he had outlined the whole melancholy journey from Oregon to the riverbank in bold black print.

O'Mara was frankly tired. The trial had gone on for a long time, and he had had very few visitors—his wife twice, a fellow DA. He rarely got away for weekends. He had lost over fifteen pounds, mostly because he felt it was hardly worth the effort to eat when he got home to the rented cottage after ten or eleven at night.

Forgoing his usual courtroom style, O'Mara roused himself to roam restlessly in front of the jury box, declaiming and arguing. He was passionate about the victims and their killer.

Puente listened, one hand lightly touching her right cheek, sometimes wiping her eyes or whispering to Vlautin.

She was, the prosecutor sternly announced to the jurors, "a cold and calculating killer." Her white hair, mild features, and glasses disguised the "reality that was experienced" by those who lived and died near her.

She demonstrated "some kind of callousness," O'Mara went on, by cutting up the body of Betty Palmer after death or dumping her putative fiancé "along the Sacramento River" to lie unmourned and unidentified for three years.

He pleaded with the jury to "recognize the humanity of the victims," these "shadow people" who had died at 1426 F Street.

Puente, in a blue sweater with the sleeves pushed up on her fleshy white arms, raised papers in front of her face if she thought one of the cameramen allowed in for the arguments was going to take her picture. The courtroom, after being almost empty for weeks at a time, was crowded again, tight and uncomfortably warm.

O'Mara meticulously dismantled the defense claims. Puente *had* called authorities in 1987 when Eugene Gamel died. She was not afraid of the police on July 31, 1987, when Gamel was dead in front of the house. But she didn't call anyone when James Gallop died, apparently on July 21, inside 1426 F Street.

Puente controlled what happened in the house, who lived and who died, and when their deaths were announced.

Scornfully, O'Mara waved papers at the jury. Puente didn't flee to Los Angeles to get some rest from the noise, lights, and chaos outside the house in 1988. "If all she wanted was a rest, she could have gone to the Clarion and gotten a room. She had three thousand dollars in her purse."

When he got to Ruth Munroe's murder, O'Mara was subdued. It was, he said candidly, "the most troubling" because "the system did a terrible job investigating."

It was the closest he came, in public or in private, to admitting a shared failure to properly check the Clausen family's suspicions in August 1982.

But, he said, "when you look at the total picture, the information we have proves that Ruth Munroe was poisoned, and the only other person in that house was Dorothea Puente."

He came back again and again to his basic point: "Follow the money. When you find money, you'll find Dorothea Puente. She followed the money." So too, he said, must the jury.

On the third day of his dramatic argument, O'Mara strongly hit on the juxtaposition of appearances, the outward lie and the inner truth. He used Puente's home as his example. The house at 1426 F Street, he said, "was a visual and logical contradiction. We have this quaint Victorian house with beautiful, lush gardens beside it, a wrought-iron fence, brick pillars, decorations on the front door. And we see the primary occupant of that house, Dorothea Puente."

O'Mara almost lunged at the jurors. It did not "compute," seeing the inviting, pleasant house, and knowing what went on inside it. Nor did Puente's grandmotherly outer appearance square with her inner anger, cruelty, and coldness.

Then, on the last day, O'Mara summed up the five-year-long belief of the prosecution that Puente went ahead and killed people whose money she already controlled. Why? "She wanted to live in a style she could not afford. She wanted to present herself as a woman of substance, of power. To do this she needed their money." She also needed to be free.

"What good is all the money in the world," O'Mara said, staring into the jurors' faces, then pointing at Puente, "if you're changing sheets all day and taking care of a bunch of sick people?"

She got rid of the sickest, unruliest, most abandoned tenants.

O'Mara said to the jurors, at last, that the Puente trial was "the mother of all circumstantial evidence cases. Use your logic. Look at the totality of the evidence." He quoted from Henry David Thoreau, " 'Some circumstantial evidence is very strong, as when you find a trout in the milk.' "

He paused. "The trout is in the milk."

Judge Virga would later instruct the jurors that it is black-letter, or basic, law in California that circumstantial evidence is just as valuable as direct or eyewitness evidence. The jury would have to string facts and inferences together to reach a verdict.

O'Mara sat down, drained. The judge adjourned after setting Clymo's closing argument for Puente for July 12.

O'Mara avoided looking at Puente, when he got into the elevator that day. She had just heard him condemn her in the roughest language, and he was asking for her life.

Puente smiled at him as the elevator doors closed. "Well, speak of the devil," she said genially.

With Vlautin sitting beside Puente at the counsel table, fussing and making notes, Clymo began a three-and-a-half-day closing argument.

He rejected the fervent and dunning quality of O'Mara's presentation, preferring to stroll in front of the jurors with charts, speak slowly, repeat thoughts many times, sometimes sipping from a cup of water he carried, as if the whole thing were casual.

He led off by trivializing the 1988 discoveries at F Street. "They dug and they found a body. Then they found another." Clymo raised his arms. "They found a graveyard. That's all." The jury could draw no more sinister inference than that.

Dorothea Puente, he said, is like all of us. "She's a little bit of good. A little bit of bad. And sometimes the mix is not always in balance."

Clymo strenuously denied that she was the wicked monster O'Mara depicted. She was, Clymo agreed, a thief. No more. He felt so sure of this fact, he said, that he could look her in the face and call her a thief.

He turned from the jury, walked a few steps, stood in front of Puente, who regarded him with the same fish-eyed coldness with which she viewed all witnesses, and he said loudly, "Dorothea Montalvo, you're a thief!"

He looked back at the jurors. "But that doesn't make her a killer. Separate the two."

At best, it was an awkward piece of theatrics. Clymo's remaining days of argument were rambling, but he did remind the jurors they must not lump all nine murders together and must consider each charge individually. "It is truly a tough case," he said. "It will take a courageous jury to evaluate all the facts objectively."

But Clymo violated two inviolable rules of trial lawyers. First, never tell the jury something false. Second, never hide something the jurors know or will find out.

He egregiously did both of those things when he tried again to portray the burial of the seven victims and the dumping of Gillmouth as acts of respect and kindness. He recalled for the jury that each body was "wrapped up, layer after layer. Sometimes ten, twelve, fourteen layers of wrapping stitched together."

He came close to the bland-faced jurors. "Didn't these wrappings show some crude form of trying to provide a measure of dignity to these people?"

The jury knew that, aside from Clymo's statements, there was no certain evidence that Puente wrapped anyone. O'Mara argued she did, but there was no witness to any of it. Moreover, the jurors knew that some of the victims—Fink, Palmer, and Gallop, for example—were not merely heavily wrapped but bunched into the fetal position. They were easier to handle in that compact form.

And, of course, the jurors knew of Puente's attempts to hide the stench of decay, both in Fink's case and in Gillmouth's. Sprinkling mothballs on Gillmouth wasn't an effort to provide any kind of dignity.

Clymo's best arguments, and the ones that spurred him to drama, raised voice, eyebrows, gestures, dealt with the health of eight of the victims. He used detailed charts to list the ailments each person had and the numerous drugs found in the bodies. "What are the odds," he asked incredulously, "that I could make up the medical history of Leona Carpenter? What are the odds I could make up the medical history of James Gallop?"

He touched his chest. "I can't prove these people died of natural causes. But, it's not my job to prove to you that this woman is not guilty. It is up to the prosecutor to prove she is. And he hasn't done that."

In closing, Clymo neatly turned O'Mara's Thoreau quotation back on him. Citing an 1860 diary entry Thoreau made, Clymo told the jurors about the writer coming upon a rabbit that had been killed and eaten in the woods. Because of paw prints nearby, a fox was thought the culprit. However, as Thoreau looked at the matter closely, he realized that a predatory bird had killed the rabbit and the fox had merely come upon the bird devouring its kill. Clymo read triumphantly, "'Though the circumstantial evidence against the fox was strong, I was mistaken.'" He slowly read the next words of Thoreau: "'Any jury would have convicted him.'"

It was the jury's duty, Clymo said, to find Dorothea Puente not guilty of every crime if the evidence was susceptible of two reasonable interpretations, one pointing to guilt, the other away from it. The law demanded the jury adopt "the interpretation which points to Mrs. Puente's innocence." He stared into the jurors' eyes. "Hold the prosecutor to his burden." He sat down, and the occupants of the courtroom exhaled.

Although O'Mara made a rebuttal argument that Clymo was tricking the jurors, by late Tuesday, it was over.

The issue before the Puente jury was whether her actions over ten years were subject to two reasonable interpretations or only one.

Before the jurors could deliberate, Judge Virga sonorously read from a thick packet of instructions, giving them the law they must apply to the facts.

In the important and awkward way California defines "reasonable doubt," he directed the jury that O'Mara's burden of proof amounted to overcoming more than simple guesswork. "It is not a mere possible doubt," Judge Virga read to the attentive jury, "because everything relating to human affairs, and depending on moral evidence, is open to some possible or imaginary doubt. It is that state of the case which, after the entire consideration and comparison of all the evidence, leaves the minds of the jurors in the condition that they cannot say they feel an abiding conviction, to a moral certainty, of the truth of the charge."

The reading went on until after 11:00 A.M. on July 15. The jurors got fifty-seven possible verdict forms: murder in the first degree, murder in the second degree, and manslaughter for each of the nine victims. The rest of the forms dealt with the special circumstances that could send Puente either to the gas chamber or to prison for life without parole.

The bailiff, after he was sworn by the clerk, marched the solemn jurors out. Puente was taken downstairs to the basement holding cell, and the judge and lawyers agreed that no one needed to come back to court until a verdict was reached, unless some jury request could not be resolved over the phone.

The jurors found themselves in a room at one end of the courthouse, a wide view of Monterey Bay before them through broad windows. The most easily carried trial exhibits were brought in. The crude coffin Ismael Florez had made for Everson Gillmouth remained upended against a courtroom wall, too fragile to move and too big. One by one, the rest of the exhibits came into the jury room and were placed on the long table among photos, charts, maps, and drawings of gravesites and crime scenes.

The jurors elected Michael Esplin their foreman and broke for lunch.

They came back at 1:30 and quickly requested a rereading of the testimony from the police officer and the coroner's assistant about going to 1426 F Street on April 28, 1982, and finding Ruth Munroe.

O'Mara, Clymo, and Vlautin all thought this might mean very long, slow deliberations. The jurors were starting at the top with count one. O'Mara was resigned to the jury hanging up or acquitting Puente of Munroe's murder. Vlautin, when he left the courthouse on Thursday afternoon, gave a thumbs-up sign of victory.

But none of the lawyers had any idea how much trouble the jury was in.

37

FOR THE FIRST SEVERAL DAYS, THE JURORS CAME AND WENT QUIET-ly from the courtroom, going to lunch, going home. The lawyers were not present, nor was Puente. It had been agreed she would be brought to Monterey at noon each day, and any verdict would be announced in the afternoon.

But behind the closed doors of the jury room, the tension was terrific.

After going through the evidence bit by bit, recalling Clymo's words about saving "the death penalty for the worst of the worst," and realizing Puente fit that description completely, eleven of the jurors were ready to convict her.

But Jesus Sanchez—or Jesse, as the others called him—wouldn't agree to anything. "Let's send it back to the judge and let somebody else decide," he told the others.

They took turns trying to persuade him.

They went over each count, each witness, the checks and drugs, the things Puente had said. But Sanchez shook his head. "I don't have enough information to make a decision," he said over and over.

Esplin asked Sanchez to explain what he meant. Why couldn't he find Puente guilty of killing Vera Martin, for example?

Sitting with a set, stubborn expression, Sanchez said to the foreman, "I don't have enough information."

"What do you need?"

"I need more."

When Esplin or one of the other jurors asked what facts he wished to hear or have laid out again, Sanchez became quiet. He wouldn't talk at all.

Rapidly the atmosphere in the jury room turned sharp and hostile as frustration grew. Jesse was intelligent, and he obviously had heard and seen everything the others had, but he simply would not tell them why he refused to reach any verdict.

Haunting the jurors were the obscenely horrific photos of Puente's victims scattered around the room.

O'Mara stayed around his rented cottage in Carmel. He bought a lot of newspapers and caught up on what was happening in the rest of the world. He hadn't kept up during the trial.

He did a little work on what he assumed would be the upcoming penalty phase of the trial. Since all of the 1982 victims were now dead, O'Mara could only put on Malcolm McKenzie's preliminary hearing testimony. It would be a ten-minute case for the prosecution.

Clymo and Vlautin worked in their rented offices about two miles from the courthouse. They were heartened each day the jury stayed out. Apparently the jurors weren't sold on Puente's responsibility. Unlike O'Mara, Puente's lawyers went to see her when she was in the courthouse holding cell. She was not happy at being taken from jail every day, but like her lawyers, she was cautiously pleased the jury was staying out so long.

In their cluttered, notebook-littered office, Clymo kept a suit and tie on a hanger. He wanted to be ready to change quickly from casual clothes before he rushed to court.

A week came and went. The jury wanted to hear about Bert Montoya's last public sighting and Ben Fink's disappearance.

Judge Virga was assigned a two-week civil case by the Monterey court so he would have something to do.

The Puente jury adjourned on July 28 without any sign of progress. They were given a four-day recess to take care of personal or business affairs that had accumulated during the trial.

When they returned on August 2, everyone hoped that four days of being near family, home, and office would cause something to happen.

It did. As the dog days of August began and heat pressed down all over California, the Puente jurors shocked everyone.

A little past 3:00 P.M., after a seemingly normal workday, Esplin, on behalf of the jury, sent a note to Judge Virga. "Deadlocked on all nine counts. We would like further instruction," he wrote.

Judge Virga immediately summoned the lawyers, and the reporters waiting listlessly around the courthouse scrambled breathlessly to get the news on the air.

Clymo was the first lawyer into the courthouse. He went down to Puente's cell and broke the news to her. She wept, leaning on him. Then she stopped crying, blew her nose and smiled broadly, very happy that all seemed to be going her way.

Clymo couldn't quite believe it himself. His heart pounded uncomfortably, and he had trouble calmly going into court, back to the judge's chambers.

A somber Judge Virga told O'Mara and Vlautin when they arrived that he was puzzled by the jury's declaration. He wasn't going to do anything hasty, as the defense lawyers wished. They both urged him to declare a mistrial. Too much time and money had gone into the trial, the judge said. He would proceed slowly and carefully.

The jury was brought in. They were stone-faced, unhappy,

but no one knew what was wrong. Judge Virga told them to return Tuesday morning, August 3, and he would tell them the choices open to him and to them.

Puente, in a blue and white dress, looking very old and frail suddenly, put her head on Clymo's shoulder. Clymo put his arm around her, almost mother and son.

O'Mara's disappointment and worry were enormous. He was aware of things the judge could do to prolong deliberations, but if the jury was hopelessly deadlocked, the whole trial was a waste. He would have to start over. Another year or more.

Clymo and Vlautin held another press conference. "I'm going to have a sleepless night," Vlautin said, a little out of breath. The jury was very courageous. "We'll be saying a prayer for them."

Whether he meant himself and Clymo or Dorothea Puente was unclear.

The news shocked and disgusted Sacramento. It had been a hot day, triple-digit late-summer weather, and through the hot night, camera trucks prowled around 1426 F Street again, seeking out friends and neighbors of Puente for comment. In the five years since the first body was found, many people had left, but some bravely stood up for her, a few condemned her, and all wondered why the jury was so confused.

At 1426 F Street, the backyard was strewn with children's toys. A swing and ragged clumps of hardy grass had appeared on top of the hard, dry dirt. New tenants, a family, lived in the house, and they didn't want to talk to anyone. The TV trucks and reporters set up their cameras on the sidewalk and pointed them up unblinkingly at the unchanged facade of the Victorian mansion.

After a sleepless night for almost everyone involved in the trial, the Puente case reconvened the next morning.

To a crowded, silent courtroom, Judge Virga read out gentle, persuasive additional instructions for the jurors.

Hunched forward, a little nervous, he was a large man in a black robe, looking batlike.

He suggested, not directing or ordering, that the jurors might want to start deliberating all over again. They might try using "role reversal." Switch sides and argue for conviction if you are against it, the judge said.

If he sounded meek and even apologetic, Virga was iron hard on one point. He would not let the jury simply throw up its hands and go home without coming to a decision. He would use every available legal tool to keep them deliberating.

Puente sipped water. A grave-looking O'Mara rocked gently in his chair. The judge told the jurors to return at 4:00 P.M. on Wednesday and report any progress. He would decide what further steps might be needed at that point.

O'Mara called Sacramento as soon as court was out. He relayed the situation, and said he assumed that the case would be retried if the jury couldn't budge by the next day. The fourth floor of the DA's office looked like any average day after O'Mara's call, but everyone was uncertain, anxious that the most expensive trial in Sacramento history end soon with verdicts.

For the family members of Puente's victims, the waiting was hard. Bill Clausen said the jurors in Monterey owed them all a decision at long last. "We're not going to give up," he said that night, with bitterness. He would never get over what had happened to his mother.

As Tuesday ended and Wednesday's deadline approached, a bureau chief in the Sacramento DA's office thought out loud. "This is the kind of case that affects people," meaning O'Mara if he lost, but all of the families, too. "It's the kind of case that changes people's lives."

When the jurors settled into their high-backed, cushiony chairs Wednesday afternoon, Esplin, glancing at his fellow jurors, said "There's been quite a lot of progress." Others nodded. Sanchez did not.

O'Mara was relieved that things seemed to have gone back to normal among the jurors. They filed out, ready to return on Thursday for an ordinary day of deliberations. Clymo and Vlautin comforted Puente in her cell with the thought that the longer the jury stayed out now, after expressing doubts about convicting, the less likely she would ever be convicted.

"I don't believe, in my heart, that this jury is looking for reasons to convict Dorothea Puente," Clymo said to the battery of reporters and cameras outside the courthouse a little later.

Vlautin also was encouraged. "They seem to be jovial and very happy, and that's a good sign."

It might have been a good sign for Puente, but it was agony for everyone else.

The jurors were, in fact, anything but happy. They could look out on the placid waters of the bay and at the Santa Cruz Mountains, but the jury room remained in turmoil.

Sanchez was adamant. He would do no more than listen to the arguments and painstaking examinations of each piece of evidence from the other jurors.

Stephen Hinds tried arguing with Sanchez. He was mystified and angry that the other man couldn't decipher the information about Puente as the other jurors had. His stubbornness also rankled several jurors. They felt they were being held hostage by him. Still, he simply wouldn't argue back to them. He was like a stone wall.

One by one, the other jurors took turns explaining the evidence against Puente on particular counts. Here, they'd say, is what happened to Bert Montoya. Look how she lied about him, look at how he vanished, look how she used him. Or Ben Fink. What about taking him upstairs? What about the Dalmane in all the bodies?

Nothing worked. The jurors beat themselves against Sanchez futilely. All he would say was, "Somebody else should decide. It should go back to the judge."

Even a strong earthquake on August 11, rattling the

courthouse around three-thirty, shaking pictures, even Gillmouth's coffin in the courtroom, didn't disturb Jesse Sanchez's fixed position.

The weeks rolled on.

One courthouse observer thought Puente's step was becoming lighter as she was brought in each day. She plainly thought the jury was hopelessly deadlocked.

Judge Virga finished his civil case and got a verdict for the defense. He waited in his chambers for the Puente jury.

Several times the judge had to recess jury deliberations when a juror got sick. Seating an alternate would mean starting the deliberations all over, and no one liked that prospect.

People looked at the calendar bemusedly. If the Puente jury stayed out until August 25, it would become the longest-deliberating murder trial jury in California history. After that, it would be making history every day.

Meanwhile, in the jury room, things had reached a boiling point.

After pitching facts and evidence at Sanchez, the other jurors were startled and pleased when he relented and agreed to vote for a first degree murder conviction against Puente.

Several days later, however, Sanchez dug in again. Then, on August 25, a little before noon, Esplin sent out a note asking the judge to explain whether a motive in one count could be applied to others and what constituted poisoning. Everyone came back into court—a tense, divided jury, the lawyers, and Puente. It was closed to the press and public for fifty minutes. Then the jury went out again.

They returned Thursday morning, August 26, for a last instruction from Judge Virga. Excitement had started building around the courthouse, the reporters multiplying, the spectators packing in.

The jurors returned to deliberate. They used the new instructions to argue with Sanchez. Finally Sanchez agreed to another first degree murder conviction, then a second degree as well. A juror suggested another victim whose death warranted conviction, and Sanchez balked again. "No more. That's all," he said.

They debated again, but it was obvious Jesse Sanchez had crossed a final line. "Look, every time I agree to something, you want more," he lectured the others, "and I'm telling you right now, you're not getting more."

He stared at Hinds and the other jurors seated at the table. He meant it.

Esplin signed the three verdict forms and the additional form for a finding of special circumstances of multiple murder.

It was a little before noon on Thursday, a record-breaking date. Esplin sent a note to the judge.

Judge Virga read Esplin's note and directed everyone into court at 4:00 P.M.

It was a mild day in Monterey, hot in Sacramento. KCRA began continuous live coverage of the trial just before four, and a camera in the courtroom prepared to televise the proceedings.

Puente was brought in, dressed starkly in dark clothes, without jewelry, and took her seat between Vlautin and Clymo, her face set and lined, her mouth turned down. Clymo took a deep breath as the judge entered. O'Mara sat forward in his seat, a pad ready to note down what the jury said.

The jurors took their seats, and Judge Virga began questioning Esplin. He had glanced at the verdict forms and could see that some counts had not been decided.

"Would further deliberations on any of these counts be useful? Do you think it would help?" the judge asked Esplin.

"No, sir," Esplin answered.

Puente remained immobile, only her eyes drifting to the right, then back to the judge. She had just heard the jury foreman say they were deadlocked on six of the nine counts against her. Perhaps, she thought, the jury was going to acquit on the others.

Judge Virga, looking stolid, but speaking so carefully and

moving so deliberately that he betrayed an unusual nervousness, directed the foreman to pass the verdict package to the clerk through the bailiff. The clerk handed the large manila envelope to Virga.

Peering over his glasses slightly, Virga asked Esplin if it was intended that six forms remain blank. It was, he was told.

"All right, then," the judge said, straightening the papers on his cluttered bench. "I will declare mistrials as to Count One, relating to Ruth Munroe; Count Two, relating to the death of Everson Gillmouth; Count Three, relating to the death of Alvaro Montoya; Count Six, relating to the death of James Gallop; Count Eight, relating to the death of Vera Faye Martin; and Count Nine, relating to Betty Palmer."

He told his clerk to read the verdicts just as he handed them to her. O'Mara had mentally sorted out the verdicts: Leona Carpenter, Dorothy Miller, and Benjamin Fink had been decided.

Facing the counsel table and the silent, humid press of people, the Sacramento County clerk read clearly, "In the Superior Court of California, in and for the County of Monterey," the case name, the *People versus Dorothea Montalvo Puente,* "we, the jury in the above-entitled cause, find the defendant not guilty of murder in the first degree of Leona Carpenter." There was a gasp through the courtroom.

Puente's right hand flashed into Vlautin's, and he raised it partway above the table, the two of them clutching each other. O'Mara glowered silently, staring ahead. Puente slumped down, and a tiny smile broke the crust of her impenetrable features.

The clerk read on, "We, the jury in the above-entitled cause, find the defendant Dorothea Montalvo Puente guilty of murder in the second degree of Leona Carpenter."

Vlautin's left hand slid from his client's, and he went on jotting down the verdicts. Puente drooped subtly. Her breath, which barely moved her, seemed to pause.

She watched the clerk, like everyone else in court.

Count 5: "After the title of court and cause. Verdict. We,

the jury in the above-entitled cause, find the defendant Dorothea Montalvo Puente guilty of murder in the first degree of Dorothy Miller."

The last verdict. The jury found Puente guilty of murder in the first degree of Benjamin Fink.

O'Mara leaned back in his chair, his expression fixed after years of hearing good and bad verdicts, his legs crossed. The last form was read. "We, the jury in the above-entitled cause, find the allegation of special circumstances to be true."

It was 4:26 P.M. on Thursday, late summer, years after the bodies had been unearthed. There was no ground shaking or applause in the courtroom, and from Puente's blank, frozen look, it would have been impossible to guess that anything significant had happened. But something had. A jury, after reviewing months of evidence, had said she deserved some form of ultimate punishment, death or life in prison forever, for her crimes.

O'Mara showed no triumph or relief, although he felt both. Vlautin's mouth became a dot as he studied the damning reckoning in his notes. Clymo thoughtfully rubbed his chin and stared upward, as if pondering what had gone wrong.

The jury had completely rejected the long-held defense theory of Puente's conduct. Both of her lawyers, at that instant, realized that she had come within one vote of being convicted of much more than three murders.

The judge took up tedious but vital housekeeping chores. The jury was polled on each verdict; each juror was asked in open court if that was his or her verdict. Sanchez four times answered that it was. Hinds stared at Puente and answered firmly. Esplin said those were his verdicts.

Puente glanced sideways, only her eyes moving, trapped. Judge Virga toyed with his gold pen as the clerk put the question to each juror. Reporters from several TV stations jumped up to notify their viewers.

O'Mara's mind raced through the meaning of the verdicts. Why Carpenter, Miller, and Fink? How could the jury have hung up, even by eleven to one, on Bert Montoya? Or Ruth Munroe? Or how could they have failed to convict Puente for killing Betty Palmer?

All he could think of was that the verdicts were compromises. Fink was easy; Puente was last seen with him. Miller had Dalmane in her, which she was never prescribed, and Puente had impersonated her. Carpenter was sick, and Puente kept her inside 1426 F Street, away from medical attention. But she did similar things to the others.

His thoughts were interrupted at 4:35 when Judge Virga sternly instructed the jury about the upcoming penalty phase. It was scheduled to begin September 21 and run until October 8. "Don't go back to your place of employment," the judge commanded. "If that causes a problem for your employers, let me know. Don't go to parties or restaurants." He warned them not to talk about the verdicts even to their wives, husbands, or children. This was a most sensitive time, and he didn't want the trial verdicts thrown out because of a careless comment outside of court from a juror.

Puente had folded her arms and crossed her legs, one black pump tapping up and down slowly, as if she was impatient to get out of court now that the verdicts were in. O'Mara suspected that she wouldn't be on her party manners for much longer. She had lost, and she knew it and didn't care if the jury heard her displeasure.

Judge Virga had the jury leave the courtroom by the rear doors to avoid the encampment of cameras and reporters on the courthouse steps.

Shortly before five, it was all over. Puente rose and was gently taken in hand by bailiffs and led out the back of the courtroom. O'Mara did not join her on that trip to the basement. He left quietly, going to his temporary office in the Monterey County DA's office just down the corridor from the courtroom. He changed from his dark suit to a baseball cap and T-shirt.

Vlautin and Clymo went with Puente to the elevator, and as soon as she was out of public view, she began to cry, sobbing and shaking. Her lawyers took her hand, patted her, gave her Kleenex. She was unable to understand how the jury could have done this to her—except for all the lies O'Mara had thrown up. Shocked themselves, Clymo and Vlautin pledged to fight for her life in the penalty phase. The battle was not over, they told her.

Still, as Dorothea Puente was taken to her cell and then to the van for the lonely drive back to Salinas, she could not compose herself. The jurors had been tricking her with their weeks of silence. They had turned around and believed the lies told in court.

Outside the courthouse, as their client was driven away, Vlautin and Clymo moved with brisk, somber speed to get away from the reporters and cameras darting around them. Clymo, face ashen, said, "I'm very disappointed. I feel very low right now." He was asked what he intended to do.

"Beg this jury not to kill that woman," he replied.

Vlautin, briefcase in hand, strode as if to outrun the reporters. It was an abrupt change from his usual dawdling among them. "She rolled the dice but came up short," he said tersely. "Dorothea is very upset. But the jury worked very hard and we're going to urge them to vote for life without parole."

The reporters caught up with O'Mara a half hour later as he tried to sneak out a back door. He said, "I'm happy, I'm relieved"—his only comments publicly throughout the trial. He got into his car to hurry back to Sacramento. He was going to take a three-week vacation with his family.

But, driving from Monterey, O'Mara faced the hurdle that lay ahead: one juror was going to make a death sentence for Puente hard to get.

Other people involved with the case swiftly heard about the verdicts. George Williamson had just gotten back to his sixth-floor office in the attorney general's building in Sacramento. He was tired, a little breathless from a hot drive from Fairfield where he was doing a murder retrial. He enjoyed trials more than administration.

I told him the verdicts.

"I always thought Munroe was one of the strongest counts, then Montoya, then Gillmouth," he said in puzzlement. We talked about the lone holdout on the jury.

Williamson sighed. These verdicts were "ones you can live with," he said. "There's no question about re-trial on the hung counts. They won't be. You get the murders and the specials and that's it."

No matter what happened next, Williamson was satisfied Puente would stay in prison. "Hey, sometimes you got to be happy the thing just doesn't go down the crapper."

I told him how Puente took the jury's decisions, with that unearthly calm.

The news didn't surprise him. "Of course she didn't move a muscle," Williamson said bluntly. "She's just a stone-cold killer."

At the Sacramento Police Department almost all of the detectives and the people on the second floor had wedged into an office to watch the live TV coverage as the verdicts were read.

John Cabrera stayed at his desk in an adjacent office. He had two murder cases in front of him. He could hear the TV, the voices next door. He was so deadened he found himself cutting up his files instead of carefully snipping the bits he wanted.

He did not want to be with other people. He wasn't sure how to sort out the welter of emotions he felt—anger, relief, worry—as the verdicts came in on the case that had changed his career and life.

Cabrera heard shouts and cheers, and suddenly his cramped office in the Homicide Bureau was filled with detectives congratulating him. After the years of criticism, humiliation, and hard work, he didn't know how to take this vindication.

When he went home a little later, tired, drained, he was pleased that detectives kept calling, even from around the country, to congratulate him. It felt good at last, he realized.

But like Williamson and O'Mara, Cabrera couldn't understand how the jury had picked its three victims from the nine. He had been positive they would convict Puente of killing Montoya. Only a lone nut on the jury could explain the verdicts, Cabrera thought.

If his reaction to the verdicts and his own public exoneration was bittersweet, he was clear about Puente. "She's just a bad seed," he told people that night. "We should just smoke her. She's a killing machine. We just stopped her. If we hadn't caught her, she'd have gone on killing. With the first one, she got the taste of blood in her mouth."

That night Cabrera loathed Puente's lawyers. "Imagine how they feel," he said. "They left that courtroom just like whipped dogs with their tails between their legs."

At the DA's office, Tim Frawley watched the TV with Steve White until the cameras came in, and White, sitting behind his large brown desk, flanked by flags, defended the cost of going after Puente. What else could we do, he asked? We had to take her to trial.

Frawley was unhappy that Puente hadn't been officially marked with all of the victims, but he knew that everything the law permitted as punishment could be done to her now. There had been cheering and applause in the fourth-floor administration offices as soon as the first shock of hearing a not guilty verdict ended.

Frawley also realized, as White talked to the cameras, that the county would never permit Puente to be retried on the six deadlocked counts. It was a one-time roll of the dice for the prosecution as much as for Puente.

He was glad it was over.

For the families of the victims, anger mingled with relief, too. Vera Martin's son told a reporter, "I'd like to be the one that drops the pellets in the gas chamber."

Bill Clausen, after seeing the TV coverage and talking with his brothers and sister, was defiant. "I'll keep pushing until they agree to try her again. No way does this finalize my mom's case."

It was an especially bitter blow to learn that Ruth Munroe had come so close to justice after so long and missed it by one juror.

Judy Moise was likewise mystified by the verdicts. She echoed Williamson and Cabrera's comments about Bert Montoya. "All the evidence pointed to foul play," she said in bewilderment. "I can't explain it."

No one, finally, could pull apart the jury's verdicts. People like Bill Clausen and Moise, who had encountered genuine evil, were saddened and chastened when they realized how little recompense was truly available to them.

On Friday I went to 1426 F Street, as I had in November 1988. It was near the century mark in Sacramento, the day after the verdicts, a dusty heated glaze over downtown, around Alkali Flat. The women wore halter tops; the kids were bare-chested on the sidewalk around the Victorian house, under the heavy old trees.

What did I feel, after a decade of talking to Puente's victims, reading about her crimes, seeing bodies coming from the ground?

Numb. On that hot day I was numb. A monster like Dorothea Puente marked anyone who got close to her.

Part of the disorientation I felt was that 1426 F didn't look the same on a hot day. A new family lived in it, the front yard where Betty Palmer had rested was a ragged vegetable garden, the driveway under which others had lain was strewn with car parts and two cars parked end to end. People still slowed down as they drove by, pointing at the house, but it was only a dusty, fading Victorian with peeling paint five years later. It was a ghost in the noonday sun.

The real 1426 F Street, like the real Puente, lay in the past. It was draped with Thanksgiving decorations, and little Santa Claus heads on the fence, the gardens rich, thick, fertile. It was a paradox presided over by a grandmotherly woman in glasses with neat white hair who killed again and again without passion or remorse.

I wished I had never heard of her. No one likes to be reminded of how much evil can reside in the human heart.

Starting in September, far from the scene of her crimes and the suffering she caused, Dorothea Puente would beg a jury for her life. Standing outside 1426 F Street that hot day, I knew what my answer would have been to her plea.

But someone else had different ideas. Jesse Sanchez had approached Judge Virga. He told the judge he was concerned about the verdicts and "what occurred during deliberations." Virga stopped him. He didn't want to hear any more before telling the lawyers.

The judge informed O'Mara and Puente's lawyers that a juror had questions about the guilty verdicts, but he would take no action until after the penalty phase of the trial and after the final verdict was rendered.

In Sanchez, Puente had found, at the very end, another protector.

38

PUNCTUALLY ON SEPTEMBER 21, THE PENALTY PHASE BEGAN. There were impromptu reunions in the short corridor outside the courtroom as Puente's former neighbors, some of whom hadn't seen each other for years, clustered in groups, catching up on what they'd been doing. They were all waiting to testify for Puente.

In the courtroom, Vlautin got up and gave a forty-five-minute opening statement. He knew, he said, that the jury was overwhelmingly in favor of convicting Dorothea Puente of first degree murder. He told them they had "already decided that Dorothea Puente is going to die in state prison."

What they had to do next was an "awesome responsibili-ty." He appealed to "your hearts and your minds" in determining whether Puente lived or died.

Puente, contrary to what O'Mara had predicted, stayed on her best behavior. She may have whispered loudly once or twice to her lawyers, but otherwise she remained cool and apparently uninterested in the proceedings.

Vlautin and Clymo had taken steps to make sure the jurors wouldn't hear anything controversial. Puente had talked a number of times to psychiatrists brought in by her defense lawyers. O'Mara was to get copies of those interviews, according to California law. Puente's lawyers went before Judge Virga and sanitized the interviews, excising any incriminating or damaging material before O'Mara or the jury could hear it.

O'Mara looked at the jury. One person sitting there would never vote for the death penalty. But he had to make the argument anyway, at least for the other eleven jurors.

He had rested his part of the penalty phase when he had the Malcolm McKenzie preliminary hearing transcript read in court.

The defense led off with a grand opening, calling Puente's daughter, Linda Bloom. Like the other "good deed" witnesses, as O'Mara snidely referred to Puente's character defenders, Bloom said some extraordinary things.

She was well dressed, intelligent, a space planner and property manager with a master's degree. She looked middle-class and unremarkable, given that the defense knew the jury would instantly compare her to her infamous mother.

Puente didn't look at her daughter. They had met, said Bloom, in August 1988 after Bloom had spent years trying to find her real mother. Puente told her daughter that "she loved me very much, but knew she couldn't provide for me. She implied she had not had a very pleasant childhood, but didn't go into it very much."

Bloom, however, had traced some of Puente's childhood through other children of Jesse and Trudy Gray. "She has had a horrendous life," Bloom said sorrowfully, "neglected and let down every step of the way."

Bloom began crying, asking the jury to spare Puente's life.

O'Mara had decided not to ask any questions of the good

deed witnesses. So began a procession of people, men and women, who came into court, answered Vlautin's questions for fifteen or twenty minutes, and then left.

The jurors watched with growing boredom, several yawning as time wore on.

The witnesses tended to run together. The doctor who treated Puente's tenants at 2100 F Street said, "She did a lot of wrong. She did a lot of good. I would not impose the death penalty on her." He smiled at the jury and said what others would repeat. "She could still help people she came in contact with. I still believe this lady could be useful."

Puente gave no indication she thought the idea of spending her life as a secular nun in prison appealed to her.

A plump, pleasant young woman, who had been a neighbor at 1426 F Street in 1987, described how motherly Puente could be. They would sit on the porch and talk every day. Puente gave her toys for her newborn children and boxes of diapers "because she knew how expensive they were."

O'Mara knew, as the woman testified, that when Bert Montoya wandered by the porch or another future victim passed by, Puente was paying for her charity with their money and, later, their lives.

The woman sighed deeply. "I had the feeling she would do anything for you." She became, as she had for the Odoricas, "a grandmother to my kids."

Vlautin always ended his questioning by voicing the ultimate issue: What do you think should happen to Dorothea Puente?

The young woman swallowed and turned to the jury, then back to Vlautin. "Considering all the good things she's done for me, I think mercy should be let upon her."

Several Hispanic men and women, all of whom had been helped along by Puente, came into court and strongly urged leniency. One man had been taught English by her in 1986.

She had given him money and gifts for his family. Recounting her kindness, he cried. She should be spared, he said through an interpreter.

The problem for the defense was that everyone knew how Puente secured the means to be so helpful.

O'Mara waited, readying his hardest questions for the defense psychiatrists who would try to portray Puente as a helpless product of her upbringing.

But O'Mara, as much as anyone, got a genuine surprise.

Vlautin called his first psychologist on September 23. Dr. Mindy Rosenberg said, without sarcasm or irony that Dorothea Puente's crimes grew from "an overwhelming and desperate need for attention."

But, to O'Mara's amusement, Dr. Rosenberg wouldn't even mention the three murders Puente had been convicted of committing. The psychologist concentrated on Puente's lying, thievery, and general cheating. She had been turned into a "compulsive caretaker," said Dr. Rosenberg, at an early age by her neglectful parents.

A week later Vlautin astonished O'Mara by putting Dr. William Vicary on the stand. He was bluff, blunt, and disarming in his apparent honesty about Puente. Puente, he said, would never confess to her crimes. But she did commit all nine murders.

By insisting on her innocence, Dr. Vicary said breezily, "she can still act like the godmother, the aunt, the friend. So she's got some position in life," he added.

When he called her a very "sick lady," Puente began taking notes rapidly. She did not, O'Mara knew, like being called pathetic or dependent.

Vicary said he'd interviewed her, talked to family and friends, and reviewed all the old court records. She was in "one of the most sad, tragic, pathetic family situations any of us has ever had to deal with."

When her marriages soured, her businesses failed, or she went to prison, her rage and resentment grew, said the defense psychiatrist. The troublesome tenants at 1426 F

Street inflamed her. "It had to come out somewhere. It came out with all these missing people. That is the bridge between this traumatic past and these horrible crimes."

O'Mara, flipping through Vicary's sanitized report, wondered what Puente had told the psychiatrist.

Then, after he had blandly testified that Puente was guilty of nine murders, Dr. Vicary went on to declare that she knew right from wrong and had made a successful career out of "hoodwinking" mental health professionals into seeing false mental illnesses.

The jurors listened with folded arms and frozen faces. Eleven of them had spent twenty-four days trying to convince one man of exactly what the defense now openly conceded.

When O'Mara began a sharp, detailed cross-examination, he discovered he didn't have to work hard to get Dr. Vicary to say, "My assumption is she is responsible for murdering all these people. I attempted to get some kind of admission from her, but I didn't."

Then, a little later, Dr. Vicary sounded like Detective Cabrera. Puente, he said, actually wanted to be caught, and she's glad it's over. "I thought she would be indignant, outraged, and angry," he said when he saw her after the verdicts.

But, Puente was quite different. "She seemed very content, almost happy, like, 'Thank God, I've been stopped. It's over. I've been convicted.'"

As Dr. Vicary went on, Puente shook her head back and forth, wrote her notes more quickly.

O'Mara drew from the defense psychiatrist the lesson he hoped the holdout juror would learn. "It's not necessary," said Dr. Vicary, "for her to kill people and bury them in the yard in order to have enough money to survive, in order to have enough money to donate to people in the Hispanic community or to buy clothing and food for these little girls that she wants to help because they remind her of the pain that she had when she was a little girl."

The psychiatrist was rhetorical. "But this hate, where

is this hate going to come out?" The pent-up resentments against her parents, life, the desire for respect and love grew.

"That's the undercurrent that explains the killings. Why all these people wound up in the yard," Dr. Vicary said calmly.

O'Mara couldn't have said it better.

Dorothea Puente killed nine people, caused endless suffering to so many innocent people because she wanted to be loved.

And that, of course, excused none of it.

The final pleas to spare Dorothea Puente's life were made by both Clymo and Vlautin, which was unusual. Only Vlautin should have argued to the jury, but he and his co-counsel had been at odds over various aspects of the case and Clymo very much wanted to be heard at the end.

The courtroom was attentive, Judge Virga leaning forward, the clerk looking up every so often, the jurors alert. But there was obvious impatience. Everyone, now in early October 1993, was anxious for the trial to end. It was nearing the one-year mark.

Clymo, hands in his pockets, as bombastic as he had been at the start, said, "She will die in prison. Please don't take the next step. It's not necessary. You don't have to kill her."

The jurors watched him with empty politeness.

"We're not trying to excuse her conduct here," Clymo added, after having spent the entire penalty phase doing just that. "We're not trying to convince you you made the wrong decisions. There is no excusing the crimes of the magnitude for which she stands convicted."

Puente coughed slightly into her hand, as if to say, What crimes is he talking about?

Clymo tried tugging at a few heartstrings. He had gotten to know Dorothea Puente very well in the last year, he said to the jury. "There is still within Dorothea Puente a child of a tender age."

When he sat down in a silent courtroom and Vlautin came to the jury box, it was impossible to tell if one or ten of the jurors believed anything he had said.

Vlautin picked up the theme of a wayward child. The jury should recognize Puente's "humanity. There's life. There's hope. We are asking you not to give up hope on Dorothea Puente." She was "bent at a very early age and never overcame it." Vlautin spoke calmly. He showed the jurors again a picture of Puente in front of the orphanage she had been placed in, run by the Church of Christ. "That little girl," he said, "standing out in front of the orphanage is still in Dorothea Puente today."

Then he too sat down next to her, and they whispered together briefly.

O'Mara rose. He had spoken once to the jurors, and now, having the burden of proof, was entitled to the last word. O'Mara was as passionate as he had been during the guilt phase. He was tired and sick of the case, the months of immersion in the crimes of the woman who sat a few feet from him. He had lost his lease on the rented cottage and commuted daily from Sacramento. At least he saw his own family every day. The whole trial had become a terrific burden.

When he began speaking at the end, O'Mara had recently completed the melancholy duty of attending the funeral of a young deputy DA in Sacramento who had been shot and killed. The memory of that occasion may have touched his thoughts.

He said to the jurors, "How high does the body count have to get?" The jury had a "moral decision, a moral judgment" to make.

"Aren't the victims entitled to some measure of justice?" O'Mara demanded sharply of the jurors. "All they had were their lives and their little Social Security checks. She took their checks, and then she took their lives away from them.

"I want you to remember them as human beings. They had a right to live. Can we dismiss these three murders with the explanation she suffered from an abused child-hood?"

The trial, except for Judge Virga's instructions to the jury, ended soon afterward. When O'Mara left the court-room, the jury already in its room, deciding whether Puente should go to prison for life without parole or die in the gas chamber, he knew he didn't have twelve votes for death.

If the jurors, who'd had so much trouble working through her murders, couldn't decide on a penalty, the law decreed that Puente would automatically get life in prison without parole.

The jurors, themselves sick to death and angry after so many months of arguments, having nightmares about the sights they had been shown and the things witnesses had described, didn't stay out very long.

On October 13, 1993, they returned to a crowded court-room. Puente was brought in, looking pensive but anticipa-tory. She wore a plain dark blue dress, buttoned at the neck, almost like a cassock. She scratched her chin, chatted with her lawyers.

Esplin, when Judge Virga asked for the verdict, told the court the jury had been unable to decide on a penalty.

The judge asked how the jury was split.

Esplin said, "We're split at seven to five for life imprison-ment."

Vlautin patted Puente, and so did Clymo.

O'Mara, startled at how little sentiment there was, finally, among the jurors for the death penalty, waited until Judge Virga said, "I will declare a mistrial as to the penalty phase."

"The District Attorney will not retry the penalty phase, Your Honor," O'Mara announced. It was a decision White and he had made based on the problems of doing all the evidence again. For what purpose? they wondered. Puente, at sixty-four, would spend six or eight years at least on death row while her appeals were pursued. Would California, even if she lost everything, really gas an old woman? It was the same calculation she and her lawyers had made.

Judge Virga transferred the case back to Sacramento. He would sentence Dorothea Puente to prison for life, without possibility of parole, as he was bound by law to do, on December 10, 1993.

O'Mara was partly relieved as the jurors stood up, and court adjourned for the last time. The reporters and spectators hurried out; the whole legal stage broke up. He joked about overlooking the man who became the holdout on the jury, but like Detective Cabrera, he knew he and everyone else would second-guess and rethink that choice for years.

Clymo said, "For the first time in five years, I feel a sense of relief." He faced cameras outside the courthouse.

Vlautin, standing beside him, nodded slightly. "I'm ecstatic and looking forward to getting home to my wife and kids."

Everyone was going home.

In Sacramento, in Joe's Corner, the patrons watched the TV over the bar, saw Dorothea Puente's face fill the screen as the decision not to retry her was announced. There was a murmur among the bar's afternoon crowd, hard to hear over the music. A few people thought she should die. A few others thought she was old and would die in prison anyway, so why spend the money trying to gas her? A very few, the quietest, who had lived in Alkali Flat for years, still could not believe the sweet-faced old woman had done anything at all. But they all saw her expression when the judge formally saved her from the gas chamber.

Dorothea Puente sat at the counsel table, as stony as she had been in court for years. Her lawyers might appeal the convictions. They might raise Jesse Sanchez's apparent complaint of jury misconduct as a ground to overturn the verdicts. In a year of trial there were certainly other issues to raise on appeal, too.

When Judge Virga said he was declaring a mistrial, Puente knew those things and also that she might be going

332

back to Frontera, where there were old friends and new ones to make. She would be provided for, at public expense, whether she appealed the convictions or simply sat in her cell for the rest of her life.

She was unquestionably a celebrity.

The camera, full on her face, caught the smile that flickered and hung on.

The trial was over for Dorothea Puente.

Epilogue

GHASTLY FEATURES OF PUENTE'S CRIMES WOULD CONTINUE TO float to the surface. Everyone who had been around her would stumble over them, like the buried bones in her garden, horrors for the unwary.

The last horrors were deceptively preceded by parties. There was a brief high-schoolish cookie and lemonade party in Judge Virga's courtroom after the verdicts were announced and the bystanders, gawkers, and reporters were evicted. O'Mara mingled for a little while with some of the jurors, a general feeling of letdown hanging over them all after so much time. Jesse Sanchez had left the courthouse quickly, unwilling to talk to anyone.

A few days later O'Mara went to a more formal party at one juror's house. The clothes were casual, there were cocktails and hors d'oeuvres and agitated chatter about the dissension in the jury room.

O'Mara, in flannel shirt and pants, was philosophical. He knew Clymo and Vlautin would make obligatory motions for a new trial, file appeals about errors, real or imaginary, made during the trial. But one virtue of Puente going to prison rather than to death row was that her appeals would be handled much more quickly, the issues resolved more often in favor of the judge or the prosecutor than the defense.

He tried calming the upset, still churning former jurors. He fielded calls from the victims' families in recent days, trying to calm them, or just listening to them. Bill Clausen was persistent, angry, working to get a meeting with DA Steve White to persuade him Ruth Munroe's murder should be retried.

It wouldn't happen, O'Mara knew. It was finished.

He had resolved never to take another case like Puente. He wouldn't subject his wife again to being apart so long.

Drink in hand, O'Mara talked to the jurors at the party. Some were distraught. "I feel strongly that she murdered all nine of those people," one woman said. "I have a lot of pain, especially for the families of Vera Faye Martin and Ruth Munroe. I felt personally as though I let them down."

There was bitterness toward Jesse Sanchez.

"I'm heartbroken that we couldn't have come up with nine verdicts," Marjorie Simpson, the oldest juror, said. "I'm embarrassed."

Some of the former jurors had taken a victim almost as a friend. They argued vehemently for Bert Montoya or James Gallop or Betty Palmer.

Many were relieved when Dr. Vicary admitted that Puente had killed all the victims. They had been right about her.

O'Mara nodded, listened, and tried to smooth over their still turbulent feelings. "Look," he said, "let it go. It's over."

That was how he intended to handle the doubts and certainties about the Puente case.

But it was not possible for others.

One man who went on turning over the facts and puzzles of the case was John Cabrera. Each time he looked at some aspect of Puente's behavior and crimes, he found another tantalizing possibility. Cabrera's natural ebullience didn't dim as he looked at the reports or photos, but disturbing things were revealed to him.

Near the five-year anniversary of his trip to 1426 F Street in 1988, Cabrera was scheduled to present a discussion of the investigation to the annual conference of the California Coroners' Association at Lake Tahoe.

He made up 150 slides of the crime scene photos. With him came a coroner's assistant who had been present in November 1988 and the anthropologist from Berkeley who had examined the graves for clues.

As he studied the photos and thought about the graves, Cabrera noticed something for the first time. He had never thought of it or mentioned it to Frawley, Williamson, or O'Mara. It had never come out during any legal proceedings in Dorothea Puente's case.

Cabrera publicly voiced his opinion on the crime scene evidence at the Lake Tahoe conference before several hundred coroners from around the state. The anthropologist had never seen features like those in the photo Cabrera had revealed.

It was something horrible, which lent Puente's crimes a new and monstrous significance.

Body number six had been buried at about the midpoint in the backyard. Like most of the bodies, it was found in a shallow grave, only about twelve inches of dirt covering the blanket-wrapped, taped-up victim.

Cabrera told the coroners' conference that he and the anthropologist saw an unusual compaction of dirt on either side of the victim's wrapped legs, and a moundlike effect above the knees, as if the soil had been forced upward. A tunnel had been created between the victim's wrapped legs, caused by the packing of the dirt on either side.

What could this odd pattern mean? Cabrera wondered.

Body number six was Vera Martin, the woman I saw unearthed and resting on a board on November 14, 1988. She too, like Ruth Munroe, would color my thoughts, haunt me.

Cabrera's opinion was consistent with the open mouths of some of the other victims. He believed, and the anthropologist agreed it was possible, that Martin had awakened from her drugged stupor and begun jerking her wrapped legs, trying to kick to the sides or above her. But she succeeded only in mounding the dirt, packing it up on either side. She was too weak or restrained to do more.

It had always been the prosecution's belief that Dorothea Puente drugged her victims with Dalmane and alcohol and then smothered them or let them die when their breathing stopped.

Although she claimed to almost everyone for years that she was a doctor, Puente had no real medical knowledge at all. She wouldn't have known if someone was truly dead or merely unconscious, in a deep, drug-induced stupor.

So it looked, Cabrera told the shuddering audience, as if at least one victim had been buried alive.

ABOUT THE AUTHOR

WILLIAM P. WOOD was Deputy District Attorney in Sacramento County, California, and prosecuted Dorothea Montalvo Puente in 1982 on charges of drugging and robbing elderly people. He is the author of several books, including *Court of Honor*, *Quicksand*, *Fugitive City*, *Gangland*, and *Rampage*, a novel about the trial of a serial killer, which was made into a motion picture, directed by William Friedkin. Wood lives in Sacramento, California.